THE LIBERATION DEBATE

D0796645

Talking about rights invariably sparks controversy. As soon as the rights of a minority are at the centre of discussion, it becomes very difficult to distinguish polemics from rational argument, and moral from political concerns.

This collection of original commissions challenges the reader to examine and judge the arguments in six areas of contemporary unrest: women's liberation, black liberation, gay liberation, children's liberation, animal liberation and liberation in the Third World.

Designed both for students and a general audience, *The Liberation Debate* encourages readers to become active participants in fraught and topical debates.

Contributors: Bernard R. Boxill, Dan Cohn-Sherbok, Antony Flew, Jean Hampton, John Harris, Michael Leahy, Michael Levin, Andrew Linzey, Martha Nussbaum, Laura Purdy, Roger Scruton, John Wilson.

THE LIBERATION
DEBATE

Rights at issue

Edited by
Michael Leahy and
Dan Cohn-Sherbok

London and New York

First published 1996
by Routledge
11 New Fetter Lane, London EC4P 4EE

Simultaneously published in the USA and Canada
by Routledge
29 West 35th Street, New York, NY 10001

Routledge is an International Thomson Publishing Company

Selection and editorial matter © 1996 Michael Leahy and
Dan Cohn-Sherbok; individual chapters © 1996 the contributors

Typeset in Garamond by Florencetype Ltd, Stoodleigh, Devon

Printed and bound in Great Britain by
TJ Press (Padstow) Ltd, Padstow, Cornwall

British Library Cataloguing in Publication Data
A catalogue record for this book is available from the British Library

Library of Congress Cataloguing in Publication Data
A catalogue record for this book has been requested

ISBN 0–415–11693–7
0–415–11694–5 (pbk)

For Rosey and Lavinia

CONTENTS

CONTENTS

NOTES ON CONTRIBUTORS

Bernard R. Boxill is Professor of Philosophy at the University of North Carolina at Chapel Hill. He is widely respected in the field of international civil rights. He is the author of *Blacks and Social Justice* (1984). Boxill's articles on issues in moral and political philosophy have appeared in a variety of scholarly journals.

Dan Cohn-Sherbok has taught Jewish theology at the University of Kent at Canterbury since 1975. Educated in the USA, he received doctorates from Cambridge University and the Hebrew Union College – Jewish Institute of Religion and has served as a rabbi on four continents. He has been a Visiting Professor at the University of Essex and Fellow at Wolfson College, Cambridge. He is currently a Visiting Professor at the University of Wales, Lampeter, the University of St Andrews and the University of Middlesex. He is the author and editor of over forty books, including the *Atlas of Jewish History* (1994).

Antony Flew is Emeritus Professor of Philosophy at the University of Reading (UK). An expert on David Hume, he is a charter member of the Academic Board of the Adam Smith Institute and the Education Group of the Centre for Policy Studies. Notable among his dozen or so books are *Hume's Philosophy of Belief* (1961), *An Introduction to Western Philosophy: Ideas and Arguments from Plato to Popper* (1971 and still a bestseller), *Thinking about Social Thinking* (1985), *Equality in Liberty and Justice* (1989) and *Shephard's Warning: Putting Education back on Course* (1994).

Jean Hampton is Professor of Philosophy at the University of Arizona. She has authored *Hobbes and the Social Contract Tradition* (1986), *Forgiveness and Mercy* with Jeffrie Murphy (1988) and the forthcoming *Political Philosophy* (1996). She is presently working on a new book *For the Sake of Reason*, on metaethics and rational choice theory. She has published many articles in moral and political theory, rational choice theory, feminism and the philosophy of law. She has been the recipient of NEH, ACLS and recently, Pew Foundation fellowships.

John Harris is Professor of Bioethics and Applied Philosophy, and Research Director of the Centre for Social Ethics and Policy at the University of Manchester (UK). He frequently appears on radio and TV both in the UK and overseas to discuss biomedical ethics and related issues. He has published over sixty papers, is part-editor of three books and author of the following: *Violence and Responsibility* (1980), *The Value of Life* (1990) and *Wonderwoman and Superman: Ethics and Human Biotechnology* (1992). Three more are in preparation; one for Routledge, *Children's Liberation*.

Michael Leahy is currently a Senior Lecturer in Philosophy at the University of Kent at Canterbury (UK). He has previously taught at Penn State and Cornell, and been a Visiting Professor at Allegheny College and the University of New Hampshire (USA). He is the author of *Against Liberation: Putting Animals in Perspective* (1991, one of the only books to challenge the prevailing animal orthodoxy), and several articles and contributions to books on subjects such as the aesthetics of music, moral practices and the nature of seeing, as well as the psyche of animals.

Michael Levin is Professor of Philosophy at City College of the City University of New York. He is author of *Metaphysics and the Mind–Body Problem* (1979) and *Feminism and Freedom* (1987). In addition to issues in social philosophy, Levin's recent writings have dealt with the interpretation of second-order logic and philosophical analysis. His publications have also appeared in more popular periodicals such as *Fortune*, *Newsweek* and *The New York Times*.

Andrew Linzey holds the world's first post in theology and animal welfare – the IFAW Senior Research Fellowship at Mansfield College, Oxford. He is also Special Professor of Theology in the University of Nottingham. His first book *Animal Rights* (1976) heralded the modern animal rights movement. Among his books on theology and ethics are other pioneering works on animals: *Christianity and the Rights of Animals* (1987), *Political Theory and Animal Rights* (1990) and *Animal Theology* (1994). He is co-editor (with Paul

Clarke) of the *Dictionary of Ethics, Theology and Society* published by Routledge in 1995.

Martha Nussbaum is Professor of Law and Ethics at the University of Chicago, having previously been Professor of Philosophy at Brown University. She is an author of distinction: *Aristotle's De Motu Animalium* (1978), *The Fragility of Goodness* (1986), *Love's Knowledge* (1990), *The Therapy of Desire* (1994) and the forthcoming *Poetic Justice: The Literary Imagination and Public Life* (1996). With Amartya Sen, she edited *The Quality of Life* (1993), and with Jonathan Glover, *Women, Culture, and Development* (1995). She was an Advisor for the World Institute for Development Economics Research, Helsinki (1986–93).

Laura Purdy is Professor of Philosophy at Wells College, Aurora, in New York State. She received her doctorate from Stanford University; her main research interests are in applied ethics, especially family issues and bioethics. Her book *In Their Best Interest? The Case Against Equal Rights for Children* was a well-received and timely piece of iconoclasm (1992). A co-edited volume, with Helen Holmes, *Feminist Perspectives in Medical Ethics* appeared also in 1992. She is currently preparing a collection of her essays on feminism and bioethics.

Roger Scruton is Professor of Philosophy and University Professor at Boston University, where he works for part of the year. He is well-known in Britain as a writer, broadcaster and editor of *The Salisbury Review*. His recent books include *Francesca* (1991), *A Dove Descending and Other Stories* (1991), *Xanthippic Dialogues* (1992) and the magisterial *Modern Philosophy: An Introduction and Survey* (1994). His books and articles have been translated into most European languages. He is currently writing a book on the philosophy of music.

John Wilson is currently Senior Research Associate at the Oxford University Department of Educational Studies, and is a Fellow of Mansfield College. Previous posts were Professor of Religion at Trinity College, Toronto, and Lecturer in Philosophy and University Proctor at the University of Sussex (UK). He is a prolific author with more than thirty books, in philosophy, education and theology, to his credit. They include *Education in Religion and the Emotions* (1972) and *A New Introduction to Moral Education* (1990). His latest work is *Love Between Equals* (1995).

PREFACE

Dan Cohn-Sherbok

Around the world liberation movements of various kinds have exploded onto the contemporary scene. Convinced of the rightness of their cause, liberationists loudly proclaim their messages of freedom and emancipation from oppression. Yet in the face of competing convictions, it is not at all clear who legitimately occupies the moral high ground. The purpose of this volume is thus to untangle some of the key issues surrounding liberation and human rights in a number of central areas of debate.

Throughout this discussion the themes of liberation and rights intertwine – this is so because of their catalytic impact. In the wake of the fragmentation of recent tyrannies, the cry for liberation from poverty, disease and social unrest has fuelled both conflict and violence. More locally – particularly where there is sufficient affluence to allow individuals to dwell on inequalities – these conflicts have evolved into campaigns to ameliorate the financial and social situations of individuals and groups. Liberation has therefore given way to rhetoric about 'rights'.

Such rights language is invariably deployed by those who seek justice. Some regard these rights campaigns as justified and noble; others view with horror their impact on the major institutions of society: departments of government, the law, schools and universities, employment offices, the prison services, churches and the armed forces. Nothing, it appears, seems to be exempt from the influence of those who seek equality and liberty.

Critics of these rights campaigners are quick to castigate these developments. They argue, for example, that it is in fact the work-shy who demand a decent living with holidays in the sun as their right; it is the vicious prison inmates who claim it is their right to rise late and avoid physical exercise and work. Similarly, they argue that teenagers selfishly outrage and devastate their parents by leaving home to take up alternative lifestyles on the mistaken ground that it is their right to do so. Again, such critics react with hostility to animal rights campaigners who seek to impose their views on society as a whole. On the other side of the coin, defenders of the rights activists insist on the need for the modern world to undergo radical change. Such supporters frequently include social workers, teachers, liberal academics and clergy, poverty action groups and animal protection organizations. All of these bodies are convinced of the need to press their demands on the community.

This symposium, consisting of original contributions especially commissioned for the book, challenges the reader to examine and evaluate the polemics of six central areas of contemporary debate, each with aspects of liberation theory at its heart. All are minefields for the unwary dogmatist with ready conclusions – pro or con – about those who espouse liberation for women, gays, blacks, children, animals and the underprivileged of the First and Third World.

The book itself is divided into six major sections. In each a distinguished academic presents a defence of his or her position; this is followed by a counterargument by an equally experienced expert as well as a brief rejoinder. Attached to each of these sections is a list of further reading for those who wish to investigate the issues raised by this exchange. Finally, a concluding chapter provides an overview of the topics raised as well as a series of personal observations. It is our hope that this volume will give rise to further debate in these areas of liberation as well as in other related spheres. If so, it will have served its purposes, and our modest efforts will be amply rewarded.

Part I

WOMEN'S LIBERATION

1

THE CASE
FOR FEMINISM

Jean Hampton

Emerging as a kind of political movement in the 1960s, modern feminism owes its existence to ideas that were developed much earlier, not only in the suffragette movement but also in the work of writers (both men and women) from the eighteenth, nineteenth and early twentieth centuries. In the last thirty years, feminist concerns have spawned not only varieties of political activism but also new ethical and political theories, feminist critiques of science, advances in biological theories, medical research and medical theories, innovative approaches in the social sciences, particularly in sociology, psychology and anthropology, and new ways of doing, and thinking about, literature, drama and art. In this chapter, I hope to show that feminist theorizing has unleashed a host of new and creative ways of thinking about human beings, making it a catalyst for some of the most interesting theorizing in academia today. But more fundamentally, I shall argue that it has encouraged men and women to be committed to ending social systems and modes of thinking that, insofar as they promote oppression and various forms of violence against women, lead to the undermining of moral behaviour and moral regard that is bad for everyone – male and female alike.

THE REJECTION OF POLITICAL
SUBORDINATION

To begin we should define what feminism is, but that is no easy task because there are all sorts of feminists generating (sometimes opposing) theories in all sorts of areas. Before categorizing and evaluating them, it is a good idea to figure out what they all have in common, such that they are forms of *feminism*. I shall argue that the unifying theme in all forms of feminist theorizing is the

3

rejection of a normative thesis maintaining that women, by virtue of their nature, ought to be subordinated, either politically or socially, to men. In this section I shall concentrate on their rejection of the idea of political subordination; in the next section I shall discuss their rejection of the idea of social subordination.

The thesis of natural political subordination rests on the idea that some human beings' natures are such that they ought to be governed and controlled by other beings whose natures fit them for dominance, rulership and power. To be precise, it is the view that:

A person of type X has authority over a person of type Y if and only if a person of type Y has a nature fitted to take direction from a person of type X, and a person of type X has a nature fitted to give direction to those of type Y, so that we can say Xs are by nature fitted for rulership and dominance over Ys, and Ys are by nature fitted for governance and domination by Xs.

Such a theory has been used to explain and justify the political subordination of women to men, insofar as women have been taken to be 'fitted by nature' to be ruled by men, who are taken to be 'fitted by nature' for such rule.

There are many questions raised by this theory. First, is the biology of the human species as unequal as this theory assumes, such that each of us belongs to either a dominating or dominated type? If this assumption is wrong, the theory collapses. Moreover, what is a 'type' of human being, and why does being male or female make one a member of a type? It has been common throughout history for people to think of males and females as types, and even to believe that to be male or female is to have a certain kind of distinctive 'essence' that pervades behaviour, thought-processes, talents and interests; but such 'essentialism' is inconsistent with the assumptions of contemporary biology, which recognizes only genetically-based traits, and not some kind of spiritual essence pervading or supervening upon human personalities. Hence, this theory must develop an account of human 'types' that is consistent with modern biological theory, and that classifies males and females as two such types. (But are there more types? And if so, what political implications does that fact have?) Finally, this theory must explain why the male type is the superior or dominating type. For a biologist it is an empirical question whether there are any sex-linked traits that make females or males as groups likely to dominate or be dominated by each other.

The advocate of the political subordination thesis must adequately establish that the empirical evidence about sex-linked traits supports his claim.

However, this advocate must also defend the normative claim implicit in his position: i.e. that the superior or dominating type *ought* to rule the inferior type. We must understand the difference between a (mere) *descriptive* account of the origination of power relationships among human beings, which merely tells us what these relations are and where they come from; and a *normative* account of these relationships that establishes their legitimacy and tells us why these relationships 'ought to be'. To be a justification of the rule of some over others, the natural subordination theorist must develop a normative argument to the effect that the subordination of the inferior type by the superior type rule is somehow good or right.

There are two ways of developing such an account. The first way involves arguing that nature itself provides the entitlement. On this view, there is no more reason to object to the dominance of superior human beings over their inferiors than there is to object to the dominance of a queen bee over her worker bees, because there is a 'principle of governance' provided by nature itself. However, stating this principle of governance with respect to human beings is tricky, for it cannot be maintained that inferior humans are *unable* to dominate their betters, insofar as rebellion of people taken to be 'inferiors' against those taken to be their 'betters' happens all the time. Since this view cannot deny the reality of such events, it has to regard them as aberrant or abhorred by nature, given natural features predisposing the inferior group to behave in ways that are ultimately incompatible with dominion. So on this view, just as there are physical laws of nature, there are political laws of nature that invariably determine political hierarchies in human communities.

However, the idea that the world contains normative rules is antithetical to the view of reality taken by modern science. In particular, biologists today do not think that, within any species, nature provides its members with a 'right' way to behave, and if they claim that a particular gender of a species tends to be dominant, they do not purport to establish that such dominance is morally justifiable by virtue of some fundamental natural order.

Consistent with a more scientific view of nature, the natural subordination theorist can try a second way to justify the subordination of a class of inferiors by claiming that the community of which this

5

person is a part would, on the whole, be *better off* if his or her actions were subject to the control of the superior. This argument derives the justification for the superior type's rule from the good consequences that are taken to follow from such rule; hence I will call it a 'consequentialist' argument for natural political subordination.

Down through the ages, the supposedly bad consequences that would follow from allowing women to rule have often been cited as a reason for their political subordination. For example John Knox, in his (remarkably titled) 'The First Blast of the Trumpet Against the Monstrous Regiment of Women' (1558) argues that 'nature' (as ordained by God) has disabled women from having ruling authority by depriving them of virtues that are essential to good rule: 'Nature, I say, doth paynt them further to be weake, fraile, impacient, feble, and foolishe; and experience hath declared them to be unconstant, variable, cruell, and lacking the spirit of counsel and regiment' (Knox, 1966, p. 374).

Similar sentiments were expressed in the eighteenth century by the French philosopher Jean-Jacques Rousseau (1979, esp. pp. 357–63).

Yet many men suffer from the same sorts of vices that Knox accuses women of having, and we do not take such vices automatically to warrant their political subordination to more virtuous people. A more sophisticated justification of why women require ruling is made by Aristotle in *The Politics* (1981). Aristotle recognizes two forms of natural subordination: that of the (natural) master over the (natural) slave, and that of men over women, and he justifies both forms by claiming that slaves and women are unable to reason well, and so must be subordinated to the control of those (men) who can reason well, both for their own good and the good of the community. Unlike natural slaves, whose reasoning Aristotle says is quite radically deficient, women (who do not already qualify as natural slaves) have just as much rationality as (non-slavish) men. The problem is that their rationality is not 'effective' (1981, 1259a12, p. 95). Aristotle says little about what he means by this word, but scholars have generally interpreted him to mean that women's reasoning is often 'overruled' by passions or emotions. Assuming that only reason and not passion can direct people toward the good, Aristotle concludes that by virtue of being unable to rely consistently on their reason, women need (and are supposed to welcome) rule by those whose reason continually dominates.

In a sense, Aristotle's argument portrays women as 'permanent children'. It has been relatively uncontroversial in all times and places that parents have authority over children insofar as the latter are deficient in ruling themselves through reason, because they lack the experience necessary to draw rational inferences, or because they lack the intellectual development necessary to perform various sorts of reasoning or because they are easily swayed by emotions or passions. Aristotle is saying that female children never actually rid themselves of these immaturities, necessitating their subordination to free male adults who do achieve rational maturation.

Angry rejection of such ideas is surely one common characteristic of all feminists. To be told that one is a member of a group that is seriously deficient and, in virtue of that deficiency, in need of being governed by a kind of caretaker from a superior group, is deeply insulting, prompting anger against those who have delivered the insult. But aside from the fact that this is a view that feminists today hate, why is it wrong?

Such a theory can only succeed if its thesis of gender-based inequality in the capacity to reason effectively is true; but the claims of natural subordination theorists for women's inferiority are generally offered without a shred of empirical support: Aristotle, Knox and Rousseau give none. Moreover, natural subordination theorists frequently undermine their own empirical claims by inadvertently assigning to women tasks that require the capacity that these theorists have already claimed is deficient in them. For example, Aristotle has to rely upon women to rear the free male children in Athens so as to be capable of assuming a leadership role in the city, but this task requires (as any parent knows) enormous reasoning ability, maturity and rational effectiveness to be successfully carried out. This kind of inconsistency is remarkably common in the history of thought, as some feminists have documented. For example, natural subordination theorists (such as Rousseau) have often argued that women's emotionalism makes it virtually impossible to educate them to reason well; and throughout history women's education has lagged far behind men's. As a justification for keeping women out of secondary schools and colleges, nineteenth-century biologists and physicians claimed that women's ovaries and uteruses required much energy and rest to function properly – so their reproductive tasks precluded them from engaging in any hard intellectual labour. Yet these biologists and physicians failed to 'notice' that there were poor women doing backbreaking work in homes and factories, even while producing many children (see Hubbard, 1989, pp. 123ff.). Theorists who denigrate capacities in (what they call) 'inferiors' in order to justify their subordination to 'superiors' but who end up having to assume that the inferiors have these capacities after all in order for them to be of use to the superiors, are putting forward arguments designed (with, I suspect, a certain amount of bad faith) to keep the ruling group in power.

So what are the *facts* about our relative equality with respect to the one feature that is relevant to political subordination: i.e. the capacity for rational self-direction? Both observation and the experience of modern democracies show that despite all sorts of differences among human beings (of both genders) in physical abilities, mental abilities, temperament and so forth, from skiing to doing mathematics, from musical ability to carpentry, there is no group of human beings, outside of those who are small children, or severely mentally impaired, or seriously mentally ill, who are so deficient in reasoning skills, life experiences or the ability to control passions that they cannot direct their own lives and must be subject to the direction of others. So we find women and men of all races, classes and religions choosing how to lead their own lives and taking responsibility for doing so, voting successfully in democratic elections, raising children, earning money, etc. The failure of some to lead lives that others would regard as 'successful' (e.g. because they break laws, or become impoverished or experience misery) is not a failure distinctive to any particular group of human beings (certainly not a failure distinctive of women), and, if it is not taken to arise from social injustice or bad luck, is usually construed as arising not from inferiority with respect to the *capacity* for rational self-direction, but from the failure of that person to choose to live the right kind of life – a choice for which we hold him or her morally responsible (in a way that we would not, and should not, do of a genuinely mentally incompetent person).

So what unifies all feminists, no matter their differences in theoretical commitments, is the idea that there are no gender-based differences in the capacity for rational self-direction, so that there is no basis for the idea that women should be politically subordinated to men.

THE REJECTION OF SOCIAL SUBORDINATION

Because of widespread rejection of the political subordination thesis, women enjoy political equality with men in many western and non-western societies: they vote, serve in political offices and administrative positions, serve on court benches, etc. Yet despite that political equality, women are still, in many respects, socially unequal in these societies. Consider, for example, the extent to which women still suffer from violence directed at them both outside and inside the home; indeed, statistics grimly point to the fact that in the United States, violence of men against women, in the form of rape, battery and assault, is actually increasing, not decreasing.[1] Moreover, if one considers the way in which women's wages continue to lag behind those of men, in part because they are underrepresented in jobs that are high-paying and powerful, and combines this with statistics showing that in western societies women rather than men still assume the majority of childcare and housework, are by far the most likely to care for elderly relatives and are far more likely than men to give up full employment (dropping back to part-time work or giving up employment entirely) in order to care for small children,[2] then it becomes clear that even in those western societies strongly influenced by feminist ideals men and women still play roles (and experience problems associated with those roles) within the family and within society that are not as far from traditional gendered roles (and traditional problems with those roles) as some feminists might have hoped.

There are conflicting explanations of why change in these societies has not been more radical. One explanation, which is a kind of successor to Aristotelian-style natural political subordination theory, rejects the inevitability or legitimacy of *political* subordination of women to men, but instead accepts the inevitability or legitimacy of social structures in which men, rather than women, are the leaders or the ones in control. Hence I call this the social subordination thesis. On this view, the nature of men and women is biologically fixed to a much greater degree than many feminists like to admit. Males, on this view, naturally tend to engage in certain forms of behaviour (sometimes violent) and certain kinds of roles; in particular, leadership roles. Females, on this view, naturally tend to engage in other forms of behaviour (passivity, emotionalism, nurturing attitudes toward children), leading to victimization in certain situations and the inability to combat male violence, and a willingness to take on certain caring roles; e.g. the role of assuming primary care for children within the family. According to those who believe in these natural differences between males and females (e.g., Levin, 1987; Goldberg, 1973) the persistence of gendered social roles and male control in many areas of social life, despite feminist pressure to equalize the legal rights of males and females, reflects our biological nature. This explanation is quite old; but it has taken on new life with the popularity of sociobiology and evolutionary psychology, some of whose proponents purport to show, consistent with our best biological theories, the way in which behaviour of men and women expresses structures (e.g., in the brain, endocrine system, etc.) that have been evolutionarily successful, and which result in the social dominance of men over women.

Note, before we proceed, that the fact that anti-feminists now generally endorse the social rather than the political form of the subordination thesis represents a significant achievement of modern feminism: it is no longer plausible to people that women's natures are such that they should be politically dominated by men, and thus no longer plausible that they should be excluded from voting, or holding political office, because they are unable to govern themselves or others.

So the natural subordination theory is dead as a thesis of political subordination in western societies, but it survives as a thesis of social subordination. Is it any more successful in this form?

There are two ways feminists have attacked it. The first way, advocated by radical feminists, involves (perhaps surprisingly) accepting much of the factual basis that the social subordination theorists put forward for their views, but drawing completely different, pro-female normative conclusions on the basis of these purported facts. Recall my discussion above, distinguishing the descriptive and normative components of the political subordination thesis: the same two components exist in the social subordination thesis, and yet its anti-feminist proponents tend to believe naively that they can 'read off' from 'nature' the way human beings 'ought' to behave. The thesis of radical feminism ought to be a cure for that naivety, because while radical feminists are often happy to accept the idea that there are significant biological differences between men and women, and that men, in particular, are by nature more aggressive or violent or prone to dominate, they give it an anti-male normative spin by arguing that in virtue of their aggressive behaviour men ought to be spurned by women (both socially and sexually) and strictly controlled for the benefit of the community (in the same way that human beings control or isolate violent stallions or aggressive male Rotweilers so that they don't hurt anybody). If men, on this view, will not submit to being 'medicated into a humane state', their maleness, which leads to violence and aggression, will have to be strictly managed or even

10

eliminated, so that it no longer constitutes a menace to the society.[3] This is, in a way, an Aristotelian-style subordination argument for the subordination of men to women!

While I am intrigued by the way radical feminists have turned the normative tables on their anti-feminist opponents (who have yet to reply to these feminists, reflecting, I suspect, the failure of social subordination theorists to recognize or defend the normative claims in their own arguments), I have myself endorsed a second way of attacking social subordination theorists, which I will call social equality feminism. While recognizing the undeniable fact that there *are* differences between males and females (most obviously in their reproductive roles), this view claims that these differences do not inevitably result in women's social subordination to men, so that the explanation of this subordination, when it exists, must be cultural or political rather than biological. Such theorists therefore advocate reshaping our cultural and political practices and institutions so as to realize not only political but also social equality for women. The influence of this view on western societies cannot be underestimated: it has resulted in changes in the operation of the family, in child-care arrangements and particularly in employment practices. Up until recently, for example, there were almost no women in medicine, law, academia, veterinary science or construction work, because, it was said, being female meant one couldn't do these things. (Prior to the creation of self-serve gasoline stations, I was told by a man, in complete seriousness, that women could not pump fuel into a car.) The fact that women do all these things now makes such claims appear, in hindsight, ridiculous (although, as I noted before, ridiculous claims are often made by those who are less interested in the truth than in preserving their power), and supports the social equality feminists' claim that the skills and talents of males and females are relatively equal.

Proponents of social equality feminism also attack the science that undergirds the anti-feminist position. The biologist Ruth Hubbard, for example, ridicules sociobiological studies of non-human species that are often used by those who argue that women are by nature socially subordinate to men. She cites, among other things, a study of algae by Wolfgang Wickler, an ethologist at the University of Munich, who writes:

> Even among very simple organisms such as algae, which have threadlike rows of cells one behind the other, one can observe

that during copulation the cells of one thread act as males with regard to the cells of the second thread, but as females with regard to the third thread. The mark of male behavior is that the cell actively crawls or swims over to the other; the female cell remains passive.[4]

(Hubbard, 1983, p. 57)

Says Hubbard sarcastically:

The circle is simple to construct: one starts with the Victorian stereotype of the active male and the passive female, then looks at animals, algae, bacteria, people, and calls all passive behavior feminine, active or goal-oriented behavior masculine. And it works! The Victorian stereotype is biologically determined: even algae behave this way.

(Hubbard, 1983, p. 57)

However, the practice of assuming conclusions in order to prove them is not sound science! Hubbard calls on feminists to persist in exposing the mythologies inherent in science. In my view, some of the most interesting work in the sciences today is generated by women attempting to 'see' the world undistorted by the biases and stereotypes that serve the interests of those who are in power (e.g., see Hardy, 1981).

Apart from discrediting the biology of the social subordination theorists, social equality feminists tend to generate theories explaining the persistence of social roles and practices favouring men and oppressing women by blaming certain cultural and social traditions for creating and perpetuating them. The reasons behind the social construction of these practices cry out for analysis and have been the subject of much feminist debate. There are, for example, psychoanalytic explanations of the development of these practices, developed by Firestone, Chodorow and Dinnerstein (discussed by Tong, 1989, ch. 5). Explanations that explore the influence of both psychoanalytic and philosophical modes of thought have been proposed by postmodernist feminists such as Luce Irigary (1985), who attempt to 'deconstruct' popular conceptions of the world that they take to animate patriarchal views. And there have even been game-theoretic explanations: for example, the legal theorist Carol Rose (1992) has argued that if many women happen to be, by nature, just slightly more disposed to co-operate with their fellows than men, this seemingly desirable trait can nonetheless put them at a disadvantage in

12

certain kinds of game-theoretic situations, resulting in social practices that institutionalize this disadvantage.

Such theorizing has, in my view, greatly enriched our thinking
about human interactions. And yet Ruth Hubbard's caution that it
is hard to know 'the facts' makes me question whether such theories are right to assume the database they seek to explain. Are social
equality feminists who reject the social subordination theorists' view
of female and male biology still influenced by a male-biased perception of the world to the extent that they accept the reality of
considerable female powerlessness? Might not the reality of social
relations be considerably more complicated and more equal than
traditional theories allow, so that explanations of women's subordination are misguided in what they seek to explain? We should, I
think, heed Hubbard's worry about the difficulties of 'seeing' the
biological and social world as it 'really' is: perhaps the best contribution feminist theory has made to the study of human beings is to
point out how little we actually *know* about who we (male and
female) human beings are, and how much our scientific theories in
human biology, psychology and social relations are still subject to
mythologies as profound as those which influenced Aristotle or Knox.

FEMINIST MORAL THEORY

Moral theory has been particularly influenced by feminist theorizing.
One of the most influential books in this area is Carol Gilligan's *In
A Different Voice* (1982). On the basis of interviews with people of
a variety of ages and backgrounds that address real or hypothetical
moral problems, Gilligan argues that in our society there are currently
two different 'moral voices', which she calls the 'ethic of justice' and
the 'ethic of care', and she finds some evidence, which she takes her
subsequent work to have only partially confirmed (see Gilligan, Ward,
McLean and Bandige, 1988), associating the first with men and the
second with women. Gilligan originally initiated these interviews in
order to test Lawrence Kohlberg's theory of moral development,
which Gilligan believed did not adequately describe the moral development of many females. Indeed, Kohlberg's analysis suggested that
the 'highest' stage of moral development, involving abstract reasoning
and a commitment to abstract principle, was reached more often by
men than by women; yet Gilligan argues that this stage is merely
one way of morally responding to the world, and that many women
have an equally good and equally 'high' perspective, that encourages

care, particularized concern and active involvement. Some feminists go even further, and regard the male response as lower, insofar as it represents morality as mere 'traffic rules for self-asserters' (Baier, 1985, p. 62), reflecting the mistaken assumption that each of us is self-sufficient, able and desirous of 'going it alone'. These feminists commend as genuinely mature a perspective on morality that emphasizes care and 'relational' rather than 'atomistic' thinking, more responsive to the value of community than to the value of disconnected autonomy.

Those who are attracted to the idea that women tend to manifest a different moral voice accept the idea that there are differences between males and females (although they tend not to speculate on the source of their differences in moral perspective); yet such feminists vigorously deny that these differences justify (or even explain) the social or political subordination of women. After all, why should justice-thinkers control care-thinkers, especially when the society needs and relies upon the latter in order to function? Why shouldn't the society be prepared to honour and support women's development, welcome its integrity, welcome its entry into fields in which women have traditionally been excluded? On this view, no lessons of political or social domination follow from any differences in reasoning and development – of either a moral or a non-moral sort – because those differences aren't markers for women's social or political inferiority (any more than differences in how people learn to read, or learn physical skills, are markers for the inferiority of some to others).

Other feminists, myself included, have been suspicious of Gilligan's claims of difference. These critics have challenged Gilligan's evidence for the two moral voices, offering alternative interpretations of her data. For example, I have interpreted many of Gilligan's interviews as uncovering the extent to which men and women, boys and girls, in our society manifest either of two forms of moral immaturity (see Hampton, 1993). One form, commonly but not exclusively experienced by men, involves the failure to appreciate the extent to which we have positive duties to other people; another form, commonly but not exclusively experienced by women, involves the failure to appreciate the extent to which we have positive duties to *ourselves*. Indeed, in a society that encourages males to believe they are dominant and females to believe they are subordinate, wouldn't you expect to see the immaturities of each group take these forms? Under pressure to regard themselves as 'higher', men may have trouble respecting others, where this manifests itself not only in a failure to care, but also in acts of crime, violence, domestic abuse and so forth. Under pressure to regard themselves as 'lower', women may well have trouble respecting themselves, and society's interest in using them may result in their being socialized to care unduly for others. Whatever differences in moral development may exist between men and women may therefore be more a function of the extent to which they have been affected by a sexist social and political system, and not by anything 'natural'.

Whether or not this is true is a subject for psychological research. But if we are to think philosophically rather than psychologically about Gilligan's two voices, we can, I believe, learn that each of Gilligan's voices has something right to say about morality: the voice of justice correctly captures the fact that each of us has needs, aspirations and interests that genuinely matter, and that self-abnegation is both morally wrong and personally destructive. The voice of care correctly captures the fact that each of us exists not as a disconnected soul, but within relationships that are necessary to both our survival and our flourishing. If women's tendency to give care has been exaggerated and abused by a sexist society, nonetheless it is surely right that caring is fundamental to the moral life.

In this regard, many feminists have become interested in examining mothering, a highly important and complex example of a caring practice. While some feminists (e.g., see Dworkin, 1983) have worried about the extent to which women's role in reproduction and parenting has contributed to their oppression, others have commended it and sought to understand it better. For example, Sara Ruddick has explored the way in which mothering involves both a kind of complicated reasoning and a kind of faith, of the sort exemplified in the story of a mother and her family who waited in a shelter in Texas while a tornado destroyed their home: as they waited, the mother sat and worked on a quilt, recalling later, 'I made my quilt to keep my family warm. I made it beautiful so my heart would not break' (Ruddick, 1986, p. 344). This mother's care for her family that day came from enormous strength and self-confidence, as she looked disaster in the eye, and insisted that her family believe, despite the destruction, that something good would nonetheless prevail. The service of such a mother can be extraordinarily important to those who receive it, and an understanding of the nature of that service is surely relevant to an understanding of what a fully mature moral life involves.

15

In my view the entry of women into moral philosophy – an entry that is itself the product of both social and political activism on the part of feminists in this century – has broadened and changed the way in which moral theorizing is done, both because of the way women have taken seriously the importance of positive duties to the moral life, and because (perhaps surprisingly) some of us have been highly sensitive to the moral importance of self-regard, in the face of living in a society that has attempted to deny many of us this regard.

POLITICAL FORMS OF FEMINISM

Feminist political theorizing comes in many forms, depending upon the overarching political theory in which a feminist chooses to embed her feminist ideas. For example, there are liberal feminists of both the left and right, starting as early as the nineteenth century, with J.S. Mill and Harriet Taylor and exemplified in contemporary political groups such as the National Organization for Women and popular writers such as Betty Friedan and Gloria Steinem. There are also socialist feminists, Marxist feminists and communitarian feminists (see a discussion in Jagger, 1983). In part, these feminists disagree about the best theory of distributive justice to link with feminist concerns (although they all reject the political and social forms of the subordination thesis discussed earlier). However, I believe feminism is in the process of generating its own quite distinctive approach to political theory, with links to both liberal and Marxist traditions. This theory, which I shall call (for lack of a better name) 'post-liberal' feminism, arises from a dissatisfaction with the achievements of liberal, socialist and Marxist political movements in western societies.

It is worthwhile noting, at the start, how considerable these political achievements have been. They have resulted in statutes that give women the right to vote, require equal access to political offices, prohibit discrimination in hiring, educational admission and so forth. Indeed, I wouldn't be in a position to write this chapter, and many of you readers wouldn't be in a position to understand it, had not this approach enjoyed success in winning women access to higher education and university positions. However, advocates of such legislation have had some trouble getting the form of it right. Initially, feminists advocating such legislation insisted that insofar as there were no *politically* relevant differences between the sexes, therefore,

16

there could be no justification for different legal treatment of men and women. On this basis, they attacked laws and practices prohibiting women from employment, educational access and so on. However, this 'no difference' thesis generated results that no one, including the feminists, liked: for example, in the mid-1970s in the United States, this thesis resulted in cases (e.g., *Geduldi v. Aiello* and *Gilbert v. General Electric Company*) in which the US Supreme Court ruled that excluding pregnancy from insurance coverage was not a violation of the Civil Rights Act insofar as 'there is no risk from which men are protected and women are not'. Recoiling from this implausible result (doesn't it imply that insurance need not cover prostate surgery for the same reason?), the United States Congress passed legislation that required such coverage, recognizing that sexual equality does not need to deny relevant differences between the sexes. This 'difference thesis' (as Catherine MacKinnon calls it; see MacKinnon, 1987, pp. 32–45) has been attached to the pursuit of formal equality; it requires that there are differences between the sexes that can legitimately be taken into account by laws that nonetheless recognize sexual equality (so that both pregnancy and prostate surgery can be covered by insurance, and bathrooms and certain sports activities segregated by sex). But where sexual differences are irrelevant in employment, access to educational institutions, access to political office, etc., this doctrine insists that the law allow no differential treatment according to gender, and instead enforce equal opportunities for men and women. Note how the difference thesis is both consistent with and generated by what I have called social equality feminism: it recognizes differences between the sexes, even while insisting that these differences are consistent with, and in no way undermine, both the social and political equality of men and women.

Yet as I discussed above, after many years of such battles, the status of women in liberal societies still reflects subordination in some social, albeit not political, contexts. Apart from speculating about various biological and sociological explanations for the persistence of subordinating social roles and practices, many feminists have insisted that a review of the history of western legal societies shows that oppressive and liberty-limiting social practices (such as rape or persistent spousal abuse or unequal allocations of childcare and household duties) have actually received the *support* of the law in liberal societies, making them particularly robust (where otherwise they might have collapsed), and difficult for those who are victimized by them to combat.

Consider the legal history of domestic abuse cases. In the early modern period, courts (and famous legal scholars such as Blackstone) actually *approved* of wife-beating – if done in moderation. US cases such as *State v. A.B. Rhodes* (61 N.C. 453 [1868]), *Bradley v. State* (Mississippi, 1824) and *State v. Oliver* (North Carolina, 1874) cite what they call the 'old law' that a husband has the right to whip his wife provided that he use a switch 'no thicker than his thumb'. One explanation of these legal practices is the persistence of the idea that women are naturally subordinate to men even in liberal societies supposedly committed to human equality. The Supreme Court of Georgia, in *Warren v. State* (255, GA 151; 336 S.E. 2d 221 [1985]), reviews the way in which three traditional views of the subordinate status of women contributed to the reluctance of liberal courts to recognize the concept of spousal rape. This implies that by virtue of marriage a woman implicitly consents to having intercourse with her husband under any circumstances; the view that a woman is the property, or chattel of her husband; and the view that by marriage the woman's person is subsumed by that of the man, so that in a marriage there is only one legal person – the husband, meaning that the wife has no legal standing to object to an act of abuse against her. All three views are expressions of the idea that women are naturally subordinate, not only socially but also politically, to men, and articulate the slave-like terms of that subordination in the context of a marriage that the law is prepared to uphold.

However, liberalism itself denies any doctrine of natural political subordination, and liberal rhetoric celebrates human equality. So why haven't we seen more hostility to subordinating practices in liberal states? The answer, I believe, is that the effect of liberal reasoning and liberal reluctance to involve the state in personal relations has played an important role in allowing practices subordinating women to men not only to continue, but even to flourish. Consider a nineteenth-century American court's decision in *State v. A.B. Rhodes* (61 N.C. 453 [1868]), in which it refused to allow a woman to file a claim against her husband, who had beaten her. The court reasoned that to allow such a claim would mean involving the state in the private affairs of its citizens:

> Our conclusion is that family government is recognized by law as being as complete in itself as the State government is in itself, and yet subordinate to it; and that we will not interfere with or attempt to control it, in favor of either husband or

wife, unless in cases where permanent or malicious injury is inflicted or threatened, or the condition of the party is intolerable. For, however great are the evils of ill temper, quarrels, and even personal conflicts inflicting only temporary pain, they are not comparable with the evils which would result from raising the curtain, and exposing to public curiosity, the nursery and the bed chamber. Every household has and must have, a government of its own, modelled to suit the temper, disposition and condition of its inmates.

(p. 108)

The problem with this argument, however, is that when the whipping is virtually always of the wife by the husband, in a culture that implicitly approves, or at least does not disapprove, of the husband doing so by virtue of the fact that he is the rightful 'king' of the family 'kingdom', then a legal system that refuses to stop those whippings is essentially licensing women's subordination, abuse and loss of liberty within the family. Hence, in the name of autonomy, the liberal court in *State v. A.B. Rhodes* denied women the possibility of freedom, and confirmed their mastered status. The residual effects of this way of thinking persist up to the present day, where, for example, in many states in the US spousal rape is considered a less severe felony than stranger rape (and is also a crime that is very difficult to prosecute successfully).

Compare these social facts to the facts of racial discrimination in a highly racist liberal society: just as the racists who hold power in such societies used liberal rhetoric to justify legal policies that permitted or supported their racist practices ('It's my house, so I can sell it only to whites if I like', or 'It's my business, so I can hire whom I like, and I don't like hiring blacks'), so too have those enamoured of patriarchal family structures used liberal rhetoric to justify (and even formulate) legal policies that permitted or supported those structures even when they resulted in violence ('Family life is private, and government should stay out of the private affairs of people, so as a husband I can do what I like with my wife, because she's mine').

By the mid-twentieth century, reformers began to succeed in getting laws regulating certain forms of behaviour *within* the family, such as those against spousal battery and spousal rape. Such laws were meant to change family practices that had disadvantaged women (in just the way that laws proscribing employment discrimination were meant to change social practices that had disadvantaged people of certain races). However, note that liberalism has not only failed to encourage such legislation, but also generated rhetoric that (as I noted above) has actually been used to block it.

An example of the failure of liberalism to respond to social denials of these values has occurred in the area of employment. There was a legal case in the United States (*Sears Roebuck and Company v. Equal Employment Opportunities Commission*),[5] in which Sears successfully argued that it had not discriminated against women even though few of them were represented in its relatively high-paying sales commission jobs. According to Sears, women's greater devotion to their families, and in particular their greater interest in caring for their children (which Carol Gilligan's research was taken to prove) made them less interested in these sales positions, and less likely to remain in them. There is good reason to question Sears' evidence purporting to establish that fact (see Williams, 1993, pp. 538–42). But even leaving aside the issue of the genuineness of their evidence, there is the issue of whether social practices in this society are such that women are *forced* to be less interested in these jobs, for if women live in a society that is structured around the assumption that they will be the primary childcare providers, it is hardly surprising that such women will find it difficult to seek or maintain jobs that make that role difficult. As one British feminist puts it,

> If a group is kept out of something for long enough, it is over-whelmingly likely that activities of that sort will develop in a way unsuited to the excluded group. We know for certain that women have been kept out of many kinds of work, and this means that the work is quite likely to be unsuited to them. The most obvious example of this is the incompatibility of most work with the bearing and raising of children; I am firmly convinced that if women had been fully involved in the running of society from the start they would have *found* a way of arranging work and children to fit each other. Men have had no such motivation, and we can see the results.
>
> (Radcliffe Richards, 1980, pp. 113–14)

There are many other examples I could use to make the same point; the opposition of feminists such as Catherine MacKinnon and Andrea Dworkin to pornography and the liberal use of the idea of freedom of speech laws to oppose them, is another example of the clash between, on the one hand, liberal theory attempting to combat threats to the liberty and equality of the individual coming from government by restricting governmental power and, on the other hand, feminists attempting to combat threats to individual liberty and equality that come, not from government, but from cultures or social forms.

Whether feminists are right to rely so heavily on the state to combat these threats is controversial: for example, feminist opponents of MacKinnon's and Dworkin's proposed laws prohibiting pornography have argued that such laws are ones that the reformers themselves might come to regret, insofar as they may license the government to restrict speech in a way that could hamper the feminists' cause. Hence even though post-liberal feminist reformers may long to use the state to aid them in their fight against unjust social structures, the liberal argument against doing so is that such laws are too dangerous not only to the society but also to the feminists to make it the right course of action. (For a discussion of the pornography debate, see R. Dworkin, 1985.) Moreover, liberals might counsel reformers to have faith in the power of their reform movements to change the structure of society to their liking without the help of government.

The reformers can reply, however, that the law in liberal societies has been (and continues to be) at least indirectly supportive of the social practices they wish to change. So how can these practices be changed unless the law 'changes sides'? In the view of the reformers, the abstract quality of liberal reasoning blinds liberals to the way in which existing legal structures in liberal societies have worked to advantage those who hold cultural power in virtue of the racist or sexist social traditions in that culture. Thus, MacKinnon recites the variety of ways in which the sexist culture in western societies has encouraged social practices advantaging men over women that have been not only permitted but also supported by law:

> Men's physiology defines most sports, their needs define auto and health insurance coverage, their socially-designed biographies define workplace expectations and successful career patterns, their perspectives and concerns define quality in scholarship, their experiences and obsessions define merit, their objectification of life defines art, their military service defines citizenship, their presence defines family, their inability to get along with each other – their wars and rulerships – define history, their image defines god, and their genitals define sex.

For each of these differences from women, what amounts to an affirmative action plan is in effect.

(MacKinnon, 1987, p. 36)

As I have discussed, the liberal state has helped to reinforce the 'affirmative action' favouring men, because its conception of the state has given men a powerful conceptual tool to prevent the state from interfering with these advantageous practices, namely, the idea that the state should stay out of the private affairs of individuals (e.g. in families, clubs or businesses) so as not to compromise autonomy. So at the deepest level, feminists are challenging liberals to rethink what is 'political' and what is 'private', where the jurisdiction of government ends, and where the private and personal decisions of each autonomous individual begin, in order to secure a genuinely free and equal society.

CONCLUSION: THE LIBERATION OF FEMINISM

Despite their criticism of liberalism, feminists tend to be highly supportive of, and inspired by, the liberal values of freedom and equality. Consider the following remarks by Andrea Dworkin:

> [T]he refusal to demand . . . one absolute standard of human dignity is the greatest triumph of antifeminism over the will to liberation . . . A universal standard of human dignity is the only principle that completely repudiates sex-class exploitation and also propels us into a future where the fundamental political question is the quality of life for all human beings.[6]

In this passage Dworkin accepts liberal values and the universalism that goes along with a commitment to these values (that is, a commitment to the idea that no matter the culture, the place, the time, these values should be endorsed and implemented by a well-operating political community) by advocating the idea that there is an aspect of each human being – namely, his or her dignity – that is conceptually prior to socialization, so that no matter what form that socialization might take, it cannot remove, destroy or lessen that dignity. Moreover, that dignity is taken to provide the foundations for assessing the morality of any social, political or legal practice.

For my money, the ultimate pay-off of feminism, aside from the creative theorizing it has engendered in all sorts of areas, is the way it has encouraged commitment to the equal dignity of both men and women, in the face of a history that has tried to deny women that dignity. It cannot be morally good for men to mistake themselves for masters; and it certainly has been highly damaging to women to have been regarded as subordinates. No decent society should think that gender determines worth. But to take seriously the worth of every person has ramifications in every area of human life: it means ending social and political practices denying freedom, equality and opportunity, and giving every human being the chance to experience the moral respect that is a necessary condition for human flourishing. If feminism can accomplish this, it will be a victory for all of us.[7]

NOTES

1　In statistics compiled for a congressional hearing on violence against women, it was found that the most serious crimes against women are rising at a significantly higher rate than total crime. For example, rape rates have risen nearly four times as fast as the total crime rate. A woman is ten times more likely to be raped in the United States than to die in a car crash. See *Statistical Record of Women Worldwide*, compiled and ed. Linda Schmittroth, 1st edn (Detroit: Gale Research, Inc., 1991), p. 75; and see pp. 76–87.

2　For statistical details, see *ibid.*: for household income, see pp. 314–30; for care-giving statistics, see pp. 88–95. Note that in 1991 women employed full-time in the United States earned 70 cents for every dollar earned by men, and women with four years of college education earned less on average than men who had not completed high school (reported in *The New York Times*, 6, 18 and 19 October 1992).

3　Atkinson, 1974, p. 54; extracts in Pearsall, 1986. Other radical feminist writers include Andrea Dworkin, Charlotte Bunch, Marilyn Frye and Jeffner Allen.

4　Quoted by Hubbard, 1983, p. 57; she cites Wickler's *The Sexual Code: The Social Behavior of Animals and Men* (Garden City: Doubleday/Anchor Books, 1973), p. 23.

5　628 F. Supp. 126 (N.D. Ill, 1986); affirmed 839 F. 2d 302 (7th Cir. 1988).

6　From Dworkin, 1983; cited by MacKinnon, in 'Crimes of War, Crimes of Peace', in Mehuron and Percesepe, 1995, p. 388.

7　I would like to thank Lynne Baker, Linda Hirshman and Ken O'Day for their help in the writing of this chapter. I am also in the debt of those women before me who paved the way for the entry of women into philosophy. This chapter is, in a way, an attempt to honour them, and to promote what they started. While working on this chapter 1 was supported by a fellowship from the Pew Foundation's Evangelical Scholars Program. I am extremely grateful for their support. My thanks also to Mary Becker, David Estlund, David Halperin, Michael McConnell, Rachel Nussbaum, Richard Posner and Cass Sunstein for comments on a previous draft.

2

A RESPONSE TO
JEAN HAMPTON'S
FEMINISM

Antony Flew

Jean Hampton begins by distinguishing two radically different forms of feminism, but without presenting them as such. The first form, to which she devotes nearly a third of her chapter, may conveniently be described as traditional, or classical or even classically liberal feminism. Today in the USA, the UK and most other democratic countries this form of feminism is scarcely controversial. In that understanding, but only in that understanding, we are all feminists now.

It is a second form of feminism, which might be dubbed neo-feminism or New Wave Feminism, which is, I consider, a menace; and which would surely have been seen as such by those writers (both men and women) from the eighteenth, nineteenth and early twentieth centuries who developed the ideas to which 'modern feminism owes its existence' (p. 3). The nearest that Jean Hampton comes to indicating what and how much this New Wave Feminism actually involves is in her claims about some of its supposed achievements:

> In the last thirty years, feminist concerns have spawned not only varieties of political activism but also new ethical and political theories, feminist critiques of science, advances in biological theories, medical research and medical theories, innovative approaches in the social sciences, particularly in soci-ology, psychology and anthropology, and new ways of doing, and thinking about, literature, drama and art.
>
> (p. 3)

But we are never told to what any of these feminist critiques of science in fact amounted or how they enabled subsequent scientists, whether male or female, either to put right something which they had previously got wrong or to discover anything which they could not perfectly well have discovered without the benefit of any feminist critiques. Again, we are never told either what any of these alleged advances in biology and medicine actually were or to what fresh discoveries in the social sciences these innovative approaches actually led. Even if we were to be given an impressive or even *any* list of scientific discoveries made by feminist women, then it would still be very much to the point to ask what reason there is for believing that these discoveries were made thanks to either the feminism or the femininity of the discoverers.

Not only are we not given any indication of what the cognitive achievements are which supposedly we owe to New Wave Feminism, but neither are we told of any of the really remarkable achievements of a quite different kind which we actually do owe to its very effective 'varieties of political activism'. No one, for instance, could ever guess from reading Jean Hampton that whereas in 1954 when I first visited an American university, and for several years thereafter, no one had ever heard of courses in Women's Studies, by 1987 between '15,000 and 20,000' such courses were 'being offered on almost 500 American campuses' (Levin, 1987, p. 175).

Again, no one would ever guess from reading only this chapter on 'The Case for Feminism' that, just as legislation to outlaw all *racist* discrimination has – thanks to a combination of misguided judicial decisions, bureaucratic imperialism and political pressures – eventually resulted in an explosion of racist discrimination in favour of the radical set[1] previously discriminated against,[2] so the drive to outlaw sexist discrimination has – thanks to a similar combination in which the largest part has been and is being played by the political pressure of New Wave Feminists – resulted in a similarly widespread extension of legally enforced sexist discrimination in favour of women.

In the US the Equal Employment Opportunities Commission (EEOC) has since its creation under the Civil Rights Act of 1964 been misguided by the principle that if workforces are not proportionately representative of the populations from which they are recruited, then this can be for no other reason than that employers have in their hirings discriminated against members of sets which are proportionately underrepresented. Although that Act was originally intended to benefit only blacks, an afterthought amendment was added to also outlaw sexist discrimination (Epstein, 1992,

p. 278). Since the misguiding assumption of the EEOC and so many others is in fact false, insistence upon its truth has misled all concerned into promoting an enormous extension of racist and sexist discrimination; but discrimination in favour of precisely and only those sets against which the original legislation was intended to outlaw discrimination.

The terms 'racism' and 'sexism', by the way, are here always employed strictly, to refer only to the advantaging or disadvantaging of individuals for no other or better reason than that those individuals happen to be members of one particular racial or sexual set and not another. For it is in these senses, and surely in these senses only, that the terms refer to obviously unfair and unjust forms of behaviour; as opposed, for instance, to what are too many scandalously heretical beliefs about matters of fact.

Eleanor Holmes Norton was certainly taking a staunchly racist, sexist and New Wave Feminist line when, as EEOC Commissioner during the Carter administration, she responded to a questioner in a TV programme who challenged the legal enforcement of quotas for the employment of women and of blacks by firmly insisting: 'White males will just have to bite the bullet' (Levin, 1987, p. 110).

THE REJECTION OF POLITICAL SUBORDINATION

Under the above heading, and while concentrating for the moment on the rejection by feminists of the idea only of 'political subordination', Jean Hampton argues 'that the unifying theme in all forms of feminist theorizing is the rejection of a normative thesis maintaining that women, by virtue of their nature, ought to be subordinated, either politically or socially, to men' (pp. 3–4).

A definition on these lines certainly captures what in 1776 Abigail Adams had in mind when in a famous letter she urged her husband John to try to ensure that the Continental Congress took steps 'to relieve her sex from the tyranny of his' (Pole, 1978, p. 300).[3] Elizabeth Cody Stanton expressed the same demand in addressing the New York State Legislature in 1854: 'We ask no better laws than those you have made for yourselves. We need no other protection than that which your present laws secure to you' (Dubois, 1992, p. 51). And of course that and only that was what the suffragette movement was all about.

Jean Hampton has thus provided an unexceptionable account of what and all that professing feminists have in common. But who is there of substance in either of our two countries who today seriously propounds the normative thesis which those traditional feminists rejected? Lacking any convenient contemporary opposition, Jean Hampton resorts in the first instance to John Knox. Since – although it was provoked by the behaviour of one particular ruler, Mary Queen of Scots – his thesis was universal, alleging the political unsuitability of all women, it can be decisively and rather elegantly falsified (shown to be false) by pointing out that Queen Elizabeth I of England came to the throne in the very same year that Knox published 'The First Blast of the Trumpet Against the Monstrous Regiment of Women'. And no one, surely, would want to accuse *her* of political incompetence? If, however, anyone prefers a contemporary falsifying counterexample then they could – at the cost of infuriating all left-thinking people – cite Margaret Thatcher.

Jean Hampton's second choice of opponent is an even longer-dead white male, Aristotle. With reference to his contention about the political incapacity of women she notes that 'Angry rejection of such ideas is surely one common characteristic of all feminists' (p. 7). Indeed it is. But that is all the more reason to go carefully in determining the range of ideas to be embraced by this employment of the word 'such'. For several different sorts of assertion can be and are made about human sets. All or some or none of some sets' members may be said to possess some characteristic. Or something can be said only about the average across all members of that set, with no implications about any particular individual members. Jean Hampton herself immediately goes on to say:

> To be told that one is a member of a group that is seriously deficient and, in virtue of that deficiency, in need of being governed by a kind of caretaker from a superior group, is deeply insulting, prompting anger against those who have delivered the insult.
>
> (p. 7)

Certainly it would be upsetting to be told that one was a member of some human set all members of which were in some respect seriously deficient, especially if and when that was manifestly not true. But most of the interesting, non-tautological claims about human sets which attain some substantial degree of scientific plausibility are not of this universal form, in principle falsifiable by the

28

presentation of even a single correct counterexample. They are, rather, assertions not about all but about *most*, or about the average across the whole set. Especially this appears to be the case with assertions about characteristics which are wholly or in part genetically determined; and hence to be conceived as wholly or in part features of our nature.

From the proposition that, for instance, the average height or the average IQ across all members of such-and-such a set is whatever it may be, it is impossible validly to draw any direct inference about the height or the IQ of any particular member of that set. It therefore follows that to say that someone is a member of some set which on average is in some respect seriously deficient is precisely not to say that he individually or she individually is in that respect either seriously or even slightly deficient. And, since by saying something about the average across some set nothing is said about any particular individual member of that set, *a fortiori* nothing insulting is said. Hence no legitimate ground of offence has actually been given.

Elementary points about what certain forms of assertion do and do not logically imply have to be made and emphasized because, especially in controversies about such hot topics as racism or sexism, an assertion of one form is so often misunderstood or misrepresented either as being, or as carrying the true implications of, an assertion of another form.

For instance: suppose that someone asserts that the measured IQ of US blacks averages one standard deviation below that of US whites. Then he or she is sure to be denounced for having implied, if not for having actually said, that (all) blacks are stupider than (any) whites. Again, suppose that people claim that the research evidence shows, as indeed it does,[4] that the children of father-absent one-parent families are much more likely than the children of traditional two-parent families to underachieve educationally and/or to become delinquent, then they will certainly have to face down attempts to falsify this finding by pointing to cases in which the children of father-absent one-parent families have done extremely well.

The relevance of all this insistence upon what does and does not follow from propositions about the averages of measured characteristics across particular human sets, and about the differences between different human sets in respect of those averages, becomes clear just as soon as we begin to take account of the remarkable phrasing of Jean Hampton's remark that 'According to those who believe in these natural differences between males and females . . . the persistence of

gendered social roles and male control in many areas of social life
... reflects our biological nature' (pp. 9–10).

Scientists might well be surprised if they discovered natural,
genetically determined differences even on average between the dispositions and abilities of members of different racial sets. For all the
defining characteristics of racially defined sets appear to be superficial. So if scientists were to discover such natural differences between
them, then they would have to seek an explanation in terms of differences between the environments in which the different races
supposedly evolved (Rushton, 1995).

The defining differences between the two sexes or, if we must,
genders are, however, the reverse of superficial. For they relate to
their radically different biological functions and, so far from being
merely superficial, involve what – with apologies to Noam Chomsky
– might be called 'the deep structure' of the organism. So to speak
of those who believe in 'natural differences between males and
females' which explain 'the persistence of gendered social roles and
male control in many areas of social life' as if, among those best
qualified to speak, this was some sort of eccentric and slightly perverse
minority view is itself a remarkable eccentricity and perversion. What
should we expect of any evolutionary biologist, or indeed of any lay
person with any knowledge of that subject; and how else could 'the
persistence of gendered social roles and male control in many areas
of social life' be explained?[5]

To say that some or all of our dispositions and our capacities are
natural, in the sense of being genetically determined, is not to say
either that we are necessitated to behave in the ways in which we
are thus disposed to behave or that we are necessitated to exercise
those capacities and to exercise them in any particular way. For
perhaps the most peculiar characteristic of our species, and certainly
the one which does most to distinguish the subject matter of the
human from that of the other sciences, is that we are members of a
kind of creatures which can, and therefore cannot but, make choices
(Flew, 1991).

We cannot, therefore, validly infer from statements about such
natural yet inhibitable dispositions that those thus disposed must
necessarily behave in the ways in which they are disposed to behave.
So Jean Hampton is right to rebuke the naivety of those unnamed
'anti-feminist proponents' who believe 'that they can "read off" from
"nature" the way human beings "ought" to behave' (p. 10). But,
having said this of unnamed opponents of feminism, it would have

been gracious to point out that neither of her two named opponents – Michael Levin and Steven Goldberg – ever make this elementary mistake. The latter, for example, writes in the work to which Jean Hampton refers,

> I shall also be criticized as having suggested that society *should* emphasize sex differences in its socialization. What society *should* do is a question that cannot be answered on scientific grounds and it is one that I do not concern myself with here.
>
> (Goldberg, 1993, p. 107, original emphasis)

THE REJECTION OF SOCIAL SUBORDINATION

Under the above heading Jean Hampton begins by conceding that 'women enjoy political equality with men in many western and non-western societies'. But she then proceeds to complain that 'despite that political equality, women are still, in many respects, socially unequal in these societies' (p. 9). It is unfortunate that she apparently sees no need to provide us with either a definition of 'social equality' or any reason for accepting whatever is to be meant by that expression as an ideal. Instead she offers a series of examples of what she identifies as social inequalities. Apparently they are as such unacceptable to her. The first is:

> the extent to which women still suffer from violence directed at them both outside and inside the home; indeed statistics grimly point to the fact that in the United States, violence of men against women, in the form of rape, battery and assault, is actually increasing, not decreasing.
>
> (p. 9)

Suppose that we dismiss here any doubts which we might have about the reliability of these statistics.[6] Then the question to press is why we are asked to deplore inequalities, which are essentially relative, rather than the actual numbers of the victims and the seriousness of the injuries suffered. No one, surely, would judge that all would be well or even substantially better if the amount and the seriousness of violence by women against men had increased to equal that of men against women? Or again, given that 'For the last several decades, the suicide rate among American males has been more than three times that for American females' (Levin, 1987, p. 7), do we have here another social inequality which is as such unacceptable; if not, why not, or, if so, why?

What, however, would be unacceptable inequalities would be either for the law to treat offenders of one sex more gently or more harshly than offenders of the other; or for there to be similar discrimination in the amounts of effort devoted to the apprehension and prosecution of offenders. But these would be not social inequalities but inequalities before the law.

The second example of a supposedly scandalous social inequality is 'the way in which women's wages continue to lag behind those of men, in part because they are underrepresented in jobs which are high-paying and powerful' (p. 9). Now what exactly is the perceived scandal here? Is it that some women are being paid less than men for devoting the same amount of their time to exactly the same jobs? Or is it that some well-qualified women candidates for jobs 'which are high-paying and powerful' are being turned down for no other or better reason than that they are women – for, that is to say, sexist reasons?

Cases of either of these two kinds are admittedly scandalous. But those of the first kind are now in fact very difficult if not entirely impossible to find in countries which have rejected 'the political subordination thesis'. As for those of the second kind, at least in the USA the pressures to appoint more women to jobs of this sort, and indeed to jobs of all other sorts in which they have been proportionately underrepresented, are so strong and so pervasive that the number of suitably qualified women candidates rejected for no other or better reason than that they are women must be very much smaller than that of the men rejected for the correspondingly sexist and, to opponents of sexism as such, equally unacceptable reason.

Or again, is the perceived scandal that some women are being paid less than men for devoting the same amount of their time to jobs which, though not strictly the same as those done by those men, are nevertheless judged – by some standard other than their price as freely determined in the labour market – to be of comparable worth?

There are many powerful objections to attempts to establish standards of comparable worth and to impose them on an economy (Paul, 1989). But what makes the concept of comparable worth an unsuitable instrument for generating feminist grievances is the fact that men too can be found among those being paid less for devoting the same amount of their time to work supposedly of comparable worth with that done by others.

The perceived scandal in the second example of social inequality therefore has to be that the sum total of all the wages actually paid to women – presumably after adjustment to allow for the difference in the numbers of those participating in the labour force – is less than the sum total of all the wages paid to men. This perceived scandal is in part explained as consequent upon another; namely that women are (proportionately) 'underrepresented in jobs that are high-paying and powerful'. But, again, no reasons have been offered for taking these inequalities – or, indeed, any other inequalities – to be as such, and not for any more absolute reason, scandalous.

Without decisively identifying herself with 'those people'[7] Jean Hampton suggests, although without actually stating, the reasons which presumably motivate New Wave Feminists. If, she says, one considers the aforementioned grievances with respect to wages:

and combines this with statistics showing that in western societies women rather than men still assume the majority of childcare and housework, are by far the most likely to care for elderly relatives and are far more likely than men to give up full employment (dropping back to part-time work or giving up employment entirely) in order to care for small children, then it becomes clear that even in those western societies strongly influenced by feminist ideals men and women still play roles (and experience problems associated with those roles) within the family and within society that are not as far from traditional gendered roles ... as some feminists might have hoped.

(p. 9)

True enough; and what all this suggests is that as essential elements in the realization of their curious ideal of social equality New Wave Feminists desire: first, that men and women living together should do equal shares of the housework and of any necessary childcare; second, that men and women should become equally likely to care for their elderly relatives; and, third, that men and women should become equally likely 'to give up full employment ... in order to care for small children'. This last is presumably desired by those who do desire it either because they do not want men and women to play traditional gendered roles or because they do not want them to play any kind of gendered roles at all. But whyever should individuals not play traditional or indeed any other kind of gendered roles if that is what they want to do and if their so doing does no harm to others?

33

Certainly if a man and woman are living together, if both are in full-time employment, and if both find both housework and childcare equally distasteful or equally congenial, then we have to presume that both tasks ought to be shared equally. As for the care of elderly relatives, the first thing which anyone with a long memory is bound to say is that no one, whether man or woman, should be required to sacrifice their whole lives to the care of elderly relatives, as so many women once were expected to do, and did. But, this said, the unfeasible presumption must again be that all the obligations actually arising fall upon men and women equally. Whether they are, in view of their different natures, equally likely actually to fulfil these or any other obligations is another matter altogether.

It is the third of the three demands which is both the most controversial and the most revealing of the distinctive character of New Wave Feminism. It amounts to the demand either that (roughly) equal numbers of men and women should give up full-time employment 'in order to care for small children' or that no one should. The first and to any classical liberal the decisive objection to the adoption of either of these two alternative objectives is that – in the name, apparently, of social equality and New Wave Feminism – it has no respect for individual preferences.

If a couple of parents want their small child, or small children, to enjoy for a few crucial years the full-time or nearly full-time care of one of its own, or their own, parents, as most such couples in fact do, and if – in the light both of any differences between the opportunity costs of giving up the jobs of the mother or of the father and of any differences between the preferences and capacities of the mother and of the father – they decide that the full-time carer is to be the mother, as in fact they nearly always do decide,[8] then why is their decision not one to be respected? The two parents making this decision surely constitute a paradigm case of people co-operating as equals? So should then the statistical sum of all the decisions of so many couples co-operating as equals be put down as an unacceptable social inequality?

If, on the other hand, no one is to abandon full-time employment in order to care for their own small children, then everyone's small children will have to be cared for, at least in the main, by full-time professionals. This is a solution of the sort proposed by Plato's Socrates in Book V of *The Republic*. But he proposed it only for the raising of the children in the ruling Guardian class. So far as I know no one even among the most radical of New Wave Feminists is currently advocating the universalization of such arrangements.

This mention of proposals for the raising of children other than those of the traditional two-parent family provides a welcome opportunity to reiterate that those traditional procedures, though very far from uniformly successful, nevertheless do appear to be very much more successful in taming and socializing the potentially violent and predatory male than the female-headed one-parent family.[9]

This is a finding which ought to be considered by, among others, the radical feminist who, Jean Hampton tells us, is 'happy to accept the idea that there are significant biological differences between men and women',[10] and even the idea that men are 'by nature more aggressive or violent or prone to dominate'; and who goes on to contend that, 'If men . . . will not submit to being "medicated into a humane state", their maleness will have to be strictly managed or even eliminated, so that it no longer constitutes a menace to . . . society' (pp. 10–11).

THE REDIRECTION OF SEXIST DISCRIMINATION

In reviewing what she rightly characterizes as 'considerable . . . political achievements' Jean Hampton mentions statutes to 'prohibit discrimination in hiring, educational admission, and so forth' (p. 16). But she nowhere finds it necessary to mention that, certainly in the USA and – although to a much lesser extent – in some other countries too, statutes which were originally intended to outlaw sexist discrimination, like statutes which were originally intended to outlaw racist discrimination, have in the long run had the effect of giving legal backing to both kinds of discrimination provided only that the beneficiaries are members of the previously victimized sets (Epstein, 1992). This development was apparently promoted and continues to be sustained by feminists of every tendency.

Its intellectual foundation lies in what was earlier described as the misguiding principle of the EEOC; namely, that, 'if workforces are not proportionately representative of the populations from which they are recruited then this can be for no other reason than that employers have in their hirings discriminated'. It was right to describe it as *mis*guiding since what the EEOC insists on assuming is demonstrably false. For there is abundant evidence to show that those human subsets which anyone could have any interest in defining as such all differ, on average, from other such subsets in respect of numerous employment-relevant characteristics, including the desires for employment and for employment of particular kinds.[11]

In defence of this dubious assumption it is sometimes argued that any admitted and employment-relevant average differences between different human sets can properly be discounted, either because they are differences in desires which are for some reason disfavoured and/or because they are relatively small. Thus Jean Hampton suggests that women 'are *forced* to be less interested' than men in certain jobs because they have been raised 'in a society that is structured around the assumption that they will be the primary childcare providers' (p. 20: original emphasis). But the only reason offered for saying that their desires are desires which they have been illiberally *forced* to have precisely is that these are desires of which feminists disapprove.

Again, a study by the US Department of Labor entitled *Women in Traditionally Male Jobs: The Experience of Ten Public Utility Companies* cites 'the lack of female interest in many blue-collar jobs' as the 'ubiquitous problem' in achieving 'equal opportunity goals'.[12] But this is, characteristically, to collapse the fundamental distinction between equality of opportunity and equality of outcome (Flew, 1981). For, given the known falsity of the misguiding assumption of the EEOC, equality of opportunity can be taken as a good predictor not of equality but of inequality of outcome while equality of outcome provides a similarly if not perfectly reliable index of inequality of opportunity.

A difference may be in some way relatively small but nevertheless relevantly crucial; or, if you like, 'a big difference is what makes a big difference' (Levin, 1987, p. 86). For instance: two sets of people may on average differ by as little as one standard deviation in respect of some sort of ability which is normally distributed. But this produces very visible differences between the numbers at the top and at the bottom ends: the superior set has many more at the top and far fewer at the bottom; while the reverse is true of the inferior. There are many spheres of activity in which the difference between making the grade and failing, between winning and losing, is relatively small. Yet, as the coach said: 'Winning isn't everything. But losing isn't anything.'

By insisting upon the soundness of their misguiding assumption the EEOC and its judicial allies have been misled into compelling employers not only to introduce proportionate quotas for the hiring of women but also to establish different and lower standards for their acceptability as employees. A memorably flagrant illustration of both aberrations is drawn from the experience of the New York City Fire Department. Because the eighty-eight women who took its entrance examination in 1977 all failed its physical strength component they took their case to court. In *Berkman v. City of New York* the court ruled that this test was not job-related and therefore was in violation of the Civil Rights Act. It consequently:

> ordered the city to hire forty-five female firefighters and to construct a special, less demanding physical examination for female candidates, with males still held to the extant, more difficult – and ostensibly inappropriate – standard.
>
> (Levin, 1987, p. 1)[13]

Even that was by no means all. But, for anyone whose rejection of sexist discrimination is not a merely one-way militant feminist rejection, it is surely sufficient to stimulate sympathy for that traditional 'liberal reluctance' to involve the state in the private affairs of its citizens of which Jean Hampton is inclined to complain (p. 18).[14]

NEW WAVE FEMINISM SUBVERTS THE ACADEMY

What will in the long term probably prove to have been the most important of the changes being brought about by New Wave Feminism is its subversion of the academy. Outside North America this process is only just beginning. Its nature and enormous extent is well displayed in Sommers (1994).[15] But since Jean Hampton has said almost nothing on this subject it is not appropriate to attempt much discussion of it here.

As was remarked at the beginning, she makes big claims about discoveries arising out of 'feminist concerns'. Such discoveries have allegedly been made in biology, medicine and the social sciences. But the only example she offers is the work of Carol Gilligan. Whether or not Gilligan is right in her contentions there seems to be nothing about her findings as presented here which would surprise even an antifeminist male. It is Jean Hampton's claims about moral philosophy which are not only surprising but also embarrassing. For she writes:

> In my view the entry of women into moral philosophy – an entry that is itself the product of both social and political

activism on the part of feminists in this century – has broadened and changed the way in which moral theorizing is done,
both because of the way women have taken seriously the importance of positive duties to the moral life, and because . . . some
of us have been highly sensitive to the moral importance of
self-regard.

(p. 16)

Why I am so embarrassed by this view is that I can remember philosophizing in Oxford during the second half of the 1940s. Among my
many contemporaries there at that time were Mary Wilson (later
Warnock), Mary Scruton (later Midgley) and, slightly senior, Iris
Murdoch, Philippa Foot and Elizabeth Anscombe. None of their
male colleagues needed to go to them to be instructed in the moral
importance either of positive duties or of self-regard; nor, so far as
I recall, did any of them ever indicate that they believed we needed
any such egregiously elementary instruction. And they themselves
would, of course, have been as baffled if not as outraged by talk of
feminist epistemology or feminist moral philosophy as we all had
been by National Socialist talk of Jewish physics.

The objection is not, of course, to studies of women or by
women. It is to dragooning various studies which properly belong
in traditional departments of biology, psychology, literature, law, and
so on into Departments of Women's Studies. What, we ought to ask,
are the distinguishing features of female biology, female psychology,
female literary achievement and female everything else which are
supposed to justify such separate and divisive scrutiny? If there was
any satisfactory answer to this question – and none, it seems is ever
actually offered – then it would require either the renaming of the
other existing departments to indicate that their investigations should
henceforward be limited to male biology, male psychology, male
literary achievement and male everything else; or else that the whole
academy should in future be brigaded into two monster faculties,
one of Women's Studies and the other of Men's Studies.

But the truth, of course, is that Departments of Women's Studies
have not been and are not being established and maintained for any
such academic reasons, however mistaken. Instead, like Departments
of Black Studies, they are all consequences and expressions of the
transformation of a campaign against hostile, negative discrimination into policies of positive discrimination in favour of members
of what was originally the victim set; transformations altogether

repugnant to those of us whose opposition to racism and sexism is universal and principled rather than parochial and partisan. These pretendedly academic institutions have been and are established and maintained in order to preserve and even to increase the resentments which those policies were intended to appease. Thus:

> Many of the programs now called 'Women's Studies' began as 'Feminist Studies'. Florence Howe, a founder of the discipline, writes: 'Feminism and women's studies ... for me the two terms are interchangeable.' A Report for the Department of Education prepared under Howe's supervision recognizes 'the necessity that all who teach women's studies be not only singularly prepared in the relevant academic area but also *in feminism*', and it stresses that Brooklyn College requires its women's studies courses to incorporate 'feminist analysis'.
>
> (Levin, 1987, p. 176, original emphasis)

But feminist analysis, unlike logical or economic analysis, is not a species of detached, impartial, truth-directed enquiry. Rather it is an exercise in what is called consciousness-raising – leading women to feel an exclusive solidarity with their fellow women and a corresponding resentful hostility against men. Departments devoted to indoctrination and agitation ought never to have been established, and should now be disbanded with all possible speed; allowing any of their teaching members capable of winning such appointments on merit and without reference to their race or gender to transfer to the appropriate traditional departments.

NOTES

1 By Cantor's Axiom for Sets, the sole essential feature of a set is that its members have at least one common characteristic, any kind of characteristic.
2 See, for instance, Belz, 1991 and Epstein, 1992.
3 For Mrs Adams in 1776 to have written 'gender' rather than 'sex' would have been to have committed the solecism of confounding a grammatical with a biological term; and thus shown her to be, what she emphatically was not, uneducated.
4 See, for instance, Dennis, 1993, Dennis and Erdos, 1993, Davies, 1993 and Morgan, 1995.
5 The stock reply to this question, that these are results of social conditioning, provoke the caustic comment that 'Environmentalism shares many of the intellectually stultifying traits of classical theology. It posits a society which itself has no cause, for instance' (Levin, 1987, p. 67).

6 Compare and contrast, for instance, the chapter 'Rape Research' in Sommers, 1994.

7 This, I am told, was the expression regularly employed by General Lee to refer to the Union armies.

8 But not always. Our younger daughter and her husband recently decided, because her earning power is presently so much greater than his, that she would have, however reluctantly, to return to her job full-time immediately after the end of her maternity leave, leaving the care of our granddaughter to her devoted and very competent father.

9 See again the references given in note 4, above; and compare Levin, 1987, pp. 283–5.

10 Why should I resist quoting the response made by Thomas Carlisle to Margaret Fuller on her announcement: 'I accept the Universe.' It was: 'Gad! she'd better!'

11 See above all the works of Thomas Sowell, especially his 1981, 1990 and 1994.

12 Research and Development Monograph 65 (Washington, DC: US Government Printing Office, 1978), p. 117.

13 For numerous examples of such small but nevertheless properly crucial difference see, for instance, Levin, 1987, ch. 4 and *passim*.

14 Compare, again, Epstein, 1992.

15 Usefully supplemented by Levin, 1987, chs 7–9.

3

HAMPTON'S REPLY

Anthony Flew criticizes me for quoting John Knox's 'First Blast of the Trumpet Against the Monstrous Regiment of Women', but his emotional condemnation of 'New Wave Feminism' is a reaction to an imagined new 'monstrous regiment' of feminists, intent on depriving men of their rights and powers. It turns out, according to Flew, that it is men, not women, who are the real victims in our times.

One problem with Flew's argument is that there is no such thing as 'New Wave Feminism'. In my review of feminist literature, I tried to give the reader a sense of the wide variety of views that feminists have held in a wide variety of areas, and there is nothing to correspond to Flew's vision of 'Medeas Rising'. Despite their many differences, all feminists working in the academy today reject the subordination of men, and instead strive for justice and dignity for women in societies that have traditionally operated so as to deny them social, political and economic equality.

So in describing the rise of 'New Wave Feminism' Flew is seeing ghosts. Why?

Flew's inability to perceive the reality of contemporary feminism has precedents. The suffragettes, whom he regards as reasonable, were hated and condemned in their time. Indeed, in Flew's own Britain, those suffragettes who were arrested for their protests, and who responded by going on hunger strikes while in prison, were forcibly fed by prison doctors – a form of torture that indicates the extent to which they, and their message, were hated. Women's call for a place of equality has continually been misrepresented, feared and reviled – both in the time of the suffragettes and in our own time. Why?

There is, I think, a straightforward answer: to the extent that women succeed in changing political practices, social roles and

41

economic institutions, men will lose privilege and power. When the world is unequal and your kind is on top, it can be hard to welcome attempts to construct a new and more equal world. If you like the world the way it is, it will not seem like a good idea to change it. And it will be easy to see those who advocate change as enemies of (what you regard as) a good order, rather than as proponents of justice.

Thus take Flew's discussion of EEOC regulations and certain court decisions in the United States designed to secure justice in employment for women and minorities. Flew represents the civil rights concerns of these institutions as attacks on the civil rights of (white) men. But the reality is interestingly and importantly different. Consider his discussion of *Berkman v. City of New York* (US Court of Appeals, 812 F. 2d 52 (2nd Cir. 1987)). The district court that initially heard the case required the City of New York to, among other things, hire females as firefighters, agreeing with those who brought the suit that the City's exams for applicants for firefighting jobs unfairly privileged men. Flew takes this decision as paradigmatic of the man-hating, anti-liberal political response pushed by 'New Wave Feminism'. Yet the truth is different – and more complicated. The district court was concerned that the primary purpose of the exams used by the City to select its firefighters was to keep out women, and not to select the best firefighters. The City had used two tests: a written exam and a physical exam. Both men and women tended to do extremely well on the written exam. However, men did much better on the physical exam, which stressed anaerobic abilities. Had the test included more emphasis on aerobic abilities, women would have done better, because females have been shown to do well on aerobic tests. So why did the City require a test that stressed anaerobic abilities? The City had no answer, and admitted that aerobic abilities were just as important to firefighters as anaerobic abilities. Concluding that the City had 'failed lamentably to establish a basis for the emphasis placed on maximal strength and speed' rather than aerobic abilities, the court suspected the City of arranging a test designed to keep women out of these jobs, and ordered a series of remedies, among other things, involving the hiring of women as firefighters. Confirming the court's suspicions is the fact that historically police and firefighters were not hired on the basis of test results or even height or weight requirements (in most US cities, police and firefighters received their jobs through the patronage system); indeed tests or physical requirements (like those used by New York City) came into being only when cities began to be pressured to hire women.[1] Perhaps most men would do better than most women on a physical exam that adequately tested for the best kind of firefighter; but *Berkman* is not about such an ideal test. It is about whether the City of New York designed a test in order to keep women out, under the guise of 'trying to find the best person for the job', thereby attempting to sustain a sexist practice by masquerading under a meritocratic guise.[2]

To pretend to go along with such a masquerade and to fail to listen to the arguments of those who are challenging it, is to acquiesce in the injustice that masquerade is attempting to hide. Can Flew be so naive as not to know about that injustice? Perhaps. And yet his anger against feminists is instructive. That anger correctly records the fact that feminists have been effective in changing all sorts of social and economic institutions in our time. If some of us are worried that the change has not been great enough, it has still been significant, something to which legions of women now in the workforce, doing work that they would never have been able to get twenty-five years ago, can testify. It is interesting that even while agreeing with those who claim that male dominance in social institutions is inevitable, Flew worries about this sea-change in our social institutions, fretting that it has been accomplished by 'New Wave Feminists' who have used political power against men. Such worries, and the anger it generates, show that patriarchy, to those who would defend it, doesn't seem so 'inevitable' after all. Hence, his worries confirm the success reformers (both male and female) have had in changing societies that have traditionally operated along patriarchal lines so that they are now better able to ensure equal opportunity for all, sometimes using policies mandating the hiring of a kind of human being that prejudiced institutions or firms have hitherto been hell-bent not to employ. Is it any wonder that people, such as Flew, who like the world the way it was, are highly uncomfortable with this new reality, and lash out at the midwives of a society that no longer automatically privileges men?

By the way, Flew complains about my remarks concerning contemporary moral philosophizing by women such as myself. But he seems not to have read any of it – assuming it to be 'egregiously elementary'. Yet these new moral theories, of which he is ignorant, are very much unlike the traditional philosophizing about self and others that his generation knew. I commend this work to him and to interested readers,[3] as well as the work of such contemporary feminist moral philosophers as Annette Baier, Barbara Herman and Martha Nussbaum. All of us have learned from the philosophers – both male and female – of Flew's day, but all of us have new things to say, which I would suggest people of his generation would enjoy reflecting upon. So read our work, Mr Flew: you may decide that we feminist philosophers aren't so monstrous after all.

NOTES

1 For a history of employment practices in police and fire departments in US cities, see Erie, 1988, esp. pp. 7, 59 and 127, and Colker, 1986.

2 It should be noted that the district court's ruling was reversed on appeal, after the City of New York generated an argument defending the anaerobic emphasis of its exam. However, it provided no evidence that the exam selected out the best potential firefighters; as far as I can determine from looking at the legal literature, no study on this matter has ever been done, raising in and of itself, the question of what these exams are *really* for.

3 Susan Wolf's most prominent piece in this area is 'Moral Saints', *Journal of Philosophy*, 79(8) (1981), 419–39. Other works in moral philosophy by contemporary women in the field appear in the bibliography.

BIBLIOGRAPHY

Aristotle (1981) *The Politics*, trans. T.A. Sinclair, rev. T.J. Saunders, London: Penguin.

Atkinson, Ti-Grace (1974) *Amazon Odyssey*, New York: Links Books.

Baier, A. (1985) 'What do Women Want in a Moral Theory?', *Nous*, 19(1), 53–64.

Belz, H. (1991) *Equality Transformed: A Quarter-century of Affirmative Action*, New Brunswick, NJ and London: Transaction Books.

Colker, Ruth (1988) 'Rank-order Physical Abilities Selection Devices for Traditionally Male Occupations as Gender-based Employment Discrimination', *University of California Davis Law Review*, 19.

Davies, J. (ed.) (1993) *The Family: Is it Just Another Lifestyle Choice?*, London: IEA Health and Welfare Unit.

Dennis, N. (1993) *Rising Crime and the Dismembered Family: How Conformist Intellectuals Have Campaigned Against Common Sense*, London: IEA Health and Welfare Unit.

Dennis, N. and Erdos, G. (1993) *Families without Fatherhood*, 2nd edn, London: IEA Health and Welfare Unit.

Dubois, E. (ed.) (1992) *The Elizabeth Cody Stanton–Susan B. Anthony Reader*, Boston: Northeastern University Press.

Dworkin, A. (1983) *Right-wing Women: The Politics of Domesticated Females*, New York: Coward-McCann.

Dworkin, R. (1985) 'Do We Have a Right to Pornography?', in *A Matter of Principle*, Cambridge, Mass.: Harvard University Press.

Epstein, R.A. (1992) *Forbidden Grounds: The Case Against Employment Discrimination Laws*, Cambridge, Mass.: Harvard University Press.

Erie, Steven, P. (1988) *Rainbow's End: Irish-Americans and the Dilemmas of Urban Machine Politics, 1840–1945*, Berkeley: University of California Press.

Flew, A. (1981) *The Politics of Procrustes: Contradictions of Enforced Equality*, London: Temple Smith and Buffalo, NY: Prometheus.

—— (1991) *Thinking about Social Thinking*, 2nd edn, London: Harper-Collins.

Gilligan, C. (1982) *In A Different Voice*, Cambridge, Mass.: Harvard University Press.

Gilligan, C., Ward, V. and MacLean, J. (eds) with Bandige, B. (1988) *Mapping the Moral Domain*, Cambridge, Mass.: Center for the Study of Gender, Education and Human Development.

Goldberg, S. (1973) *The Inevitability of Patriarchy*, New York: William Morrow.

—— (1993) *Why Men Rule: A Theory of Male Dominance*, Chicago and La Salle, Ill.: Open Court.

Hampton, J. (1993) 'Feminist Contractarianism', in L. Antony and C. Witt (eds), *A Mind of her Own*, Boulder, Col.: Westview.

Hardy, S. (1981) *The Woman That Never Evolved*, Cambridge, Mass.: Harvard University Press.

Hubbard, R. (1983) 'Have Only Men Evolved?', in S. Harding and M. Hintikka (eds), *Discovering Reality*, Dordrecht: D. Reidel.

—— (1989) 'Science, Facts and Feminism', in N. Tuana (ed.), *Feminism and Science*, Bloomington: Indiana University Press.

Irigary, L. (1985) *This Sex Which is not One*, trans. C. Porter, Ithaca, NY: Cornell University Press.

Jagger, A. (1983) *Feminist Politics and Human Nature*, Totowa; NJ: Rowman & Allenfeld.

Knox, J. (1966) 'The First Blast of the Trumpet Against the Monstrous Regiment of Women' (1558), in D. Laing (ed.), *The Works of John Knox*, vol. 4, Edinburgh: AMS Press.

Levin, M. (1987) *Feminism and Freedom*, New Brunswick, NJ: Transaction Books.

MacKinnon, C. (1987) *Feminism Unmodified*, Cambridge, Mass.: Harvard University Press.

Mehuron, K. and Percesepe, G. (eds) (1995) *Free Spirits: Feminist Philosophers on Culture*, Englewood Cliffs, NJ: Prentice Hall.

Mill, J.S. and Taylor, H. (1970) *Essays on Sex Equality*, ed. A. Rossi, Chicago: University of Chicago Press.

Morgan, P. (1995) *Farewell to the Family: Public Policy and Family Breakdown in Britain and the USA*, London: IEA Health and Welfare Unit.

Paul, E.F. (1989) *Equity and Gender: The Comparable Worth Debate*, New Brunswick, NJ and London: Transaction Books.

Pearsall, M. (1986) *Woman and Values*, Belmont, CA: Wadsworth.

Pole, J.R. (1978) *The Pursuit of Equality in American History*, Berkeley and London: California University Press.

Quest, C. (ed.) (1992) *Equal Opportunities: A Feminist Fallacy*, London: IEA Health and Welfare Unit.

—— (1994) *Liberating Women . . . From Modern Feminism*, London: IEA Health and Welfare Unit.

Radcliffe Richards, J. (1980) *The Sceptical Feminist: A Philosophical Enquiry*, London: Routledge & Kegan Paul.

Rose, C. (1992) 'Women and Property: Gaining and Losing Ground', *Virginia Law Review*, 78 (2) (March), 421–59.

Rousseau, J–J. (1979) *Emile*, trans. A. Bloom, New York: Basic Books.

Ruddick, S. (1986) 'Maternal Thinking', in M. Pearsall (ed.), *Women and Values: Readings in Recent Feminist Philosophy*, Belmont, CA: Wadsworth.

Rushton, J.P. (1995) *Race, Evolution and Behaviour*, New Brunswick, NJ and London: Transaction Books.

Sommers, C.H. (1994) *Who Stole Feminism? How Women Have Betrayed Women*, New York and London: Simon & Schuster.

Sowell, T. (1981) *Ethnic America: A History*, New York: Basic Books.

Sowell, T. (1990) *Preferential Policies: An International Perspective*, New York: William Morrow.

Sowell, T. (1994) *Race and Culture: A World View*, New York: Basic Books.

Tong, R. (1989) *Feminist Thought*, Boulder, Col.: Westview Press.

Williams, J. (1993) 'Deconstructing Gender', in P. Smith (ed.), *Feminist Jurisprudence*, New York: Oxford University Press.

Part II

BLACK LIBERATION

4

BLACK LIBERATION – YES!

Bernard R. Boxill

The demand for black liberation may seem empty. Countries that once permitted black slavery have long abolished it, and their laws now accord black citizens the same political and civil rights as other citizens. Further, no one today suggests that black slavery should be revived, or that blacks should not have the right to vote or to hold political office, and in the US, no respectable challenges have been raised against the repeal of *de jure* racial segregation the *Brown* decision of 1954 set in motion.

NATIONAL LIBERATION

The above discussion assumes that liberation applies to individuals; individuals are liberated when they enjoy the political and civil rights inscribed in the constitutions of liberal democracies. But liberation is usually understood as national liberation. National liberation is achieved when a nation is freed from foreign domination, and becomes self-governing, that is, when it becomes a state. In this sense of liberation the call for black liberation is not a call to emancipate black slaves and accord them the rights enshrined in liberal democracies, but a call to free black nations from foreign domination, and enable them to become self-governing.

But taken in this way the call for black liberation may also seem empty. Some groups of black people, the former colonies of Europe in Africa and the Caribbean, for example, may be nations, and when they were in their former condition, calling for their liberation might have been appropriate. But they are now independent self-governing states, with black legislators, prime ministers and presidents. What more can black liberation demand?

A good answer is that black liberation demands that these states

51

be fully liberated from the foreign powers and multinational companies that continue to dominate them. But a more radical response
suggests that such an answer is superficial, because all black people
taken together are one nation, and what black liberation really
demands is the liberation of that nation. Of course, even the most
visionary black nationalists who made this kind of claim did not
seriously think that there was anywhere on earth to establish their
black nation as a state, though Africa was usually mentioned. But
this is a tangential difficulty. There is nothing absurd about a nation
not having a place to be a state. And it may even be theoretically
possible for a state not to be established in any particular place.
Finally, even if a nation cannot establish itself as a state, and so
cannot be liberated in the usual way, it may be able to find some
alternative or lesser way to liberate itself. It is necessary therefore to
demonstrate that there is no such thing as a nation of all the black
people in the world.

I do not mean that the very idea of such a nation is objectionable. If black people all willed to be governed together that would
be the end of the matter. Any number of adult human beings in
possession of their faculties who are otherwise free may will to be
governed together. But in the absence of a roll-call that records that
they do, there is only one way we can be justified in calling them a
nation: we must show that they think that they have good reasons
to will to be governed together. I am not aware of any argument
that shows that all black people think that they have good reasons
to will to be governed together.

Let us review the possibilities. The argument that races are nations
is beneath serious consideration, at least if race is understood in its
current sense as referring to a group of people with physical characteristics, like a particular skin colour, that they do not share with
other people. But race can be understood in its older sense as referring to a cultural group, and in this sense the argument is not
necessarily objectionable. Indeed it is persuasive if the group is a
cultural group because it has a history of successful self-government.
In that case the group's members probably share a political culture,
that is, they probably agree on how they should be governed and
have the customs and skills necessary to be governed in that way;
given that their experience of being governed together was positive,
they will probably want to continue being governed together.

But since the argument is usually used to show that a cultural
group has claims to be a state, but is not one already, it usually does

not assume that the group has a history of successful self-government. Instead its usual assumption is that the group's members share
a basic philosophical outlook, religious and aesthetic ideas, and
perhaps a language and morality. It that form it is deeply flawed,
despite its popularity. People may not want to be governed together
even if they share a political culture; two politically identical states
on opposite sides of the globe may see no reason to have a common
government. The difficulty is even clearer if the people of the group
share only the similarities cited. Admittedly, such people are likely
to find learning how to live together under one government relatively easy, but if they do not already share a government, they may
not have any reason to try to. Consider a culturally similar people
who are scattered in different countries, and who have absorbed the
political culture of these countries. That they are culturally similar
and could learn to live and be governed together, if they had to,
gives them no reason to uproot themselves from their homelands to
experiment with a common government. And the argument cannot
even begin to show that blacks are a nation. The spiritual and
aesthetic ideas blacks are alleged to share – and even this allegation
is highly controversial – cannot outweigh their enormously varied
political experiences and give them any reason to want a common
government.

The argument that cultural groups are nations becomes more
persuasive if it is supplemented with an argument that the cultural
group faces difficulties it can only solve if it has a common government. This takes us to the argument that blacks are a nation because
anti-black racism threatens and endangers all of them. If blacks shared
a culture, and could easily learn to share a government if they had
good reason to, having a common enemy like racism may give them
such a reason; sharing a government may make them strong enough
to defend themselves against it. Further, in stressing that blacks are
threatened and endangered by racism the argument seems to imply
that they have memories of a common history of suffering, which
is an important source of the sympathy that the members of a nation
typically feel for each other. Still, the argument is not persuasive.
Racism has affected most blacks, but probably in such disparate ways
that it would be misleading to say that they have memories of a
common history of suffering. They probably feel a special sympathy
for each other, but hardly of the sort that binds the members of a
nation. Further, although black co-operation to oppose racism would
be useful and reasonable, it may not require that blacks share a

government, and given their political differences, may even be less
effective if they do.

BLACK NATIONAL LIBERATION

If the above discussion is sound there can be no reasonable talk of
the national liberation of the nation of all black people. But there
may be another way in which the call for black liberation is a call
for national liberation. Earlier I allowed that the independent black
states of Africa and the Caribbean may be nations. Why suppose
that they exhaust the list of black nations? Black Nationalists in the
US have long maintained that the black population there is a nation.
Martin Delany, for example, claimed in the nineteenth century that
this population was 'a nation within a nation'.[1] If he was right, the
call for black liberation may be a call for the national liberation of
that nation within a nation.

I am inclined to believe that Delany's claim was true when he
made it. Of course all African Americans in the nineteenth century
did not share a political culture. Their political experiences were too
different. Some were free with several generations of free ancestors,
while others were slaves just off the slave ships from Africa. Still, the
dangers of being black in the US, especially after the passage of the
1850 Fugitive Slave Law, were definite and threatening enough to
forge strong bonds of sympathy among them, and give them ample
reason to want the protection of a common government. Against
this conjecture it may be argued that most African Americans did
not respond positively when Delany offered them a homeland in
Africa; it may seem that a nation would seize any opportunity for a
homeland. But Delany did not offer a homeland to the nation within
a nation he had identified. He wanted only the best African
Americans to emigrate to Africa, and was therefore calling on that
nation to sunder itself, and abandon its aspirations to be a state.
Now Delany's strategy was not necessarily mistaken. As I have noted,
sometimes a nation cannot liberate itself in the usual way, and must
find another path to liberation. Perhaps Delany was pointing to such
a path. In any case, since self-division is the last thing a nation wants
it is no wonder that he never had a large following.

But nations sometimes die, and I think that Delany's nation within
a nation has expired. The most popular argument for its continued
existence drew an analogy between the colonies set up by Europe in
Africa and elsewhere and the black population in the US describing

that population as a 'black colony', or an 'internal colony'.[2] Now the colonies Europe set up in Africa did not start off as nations. They usually started off as conglomerations of independent tribal groups with no common history of suffering, no particular sympathy for each other, and certainly no will to be governed together. If these conglomerations of tribes became nations – and they do not always do so as recent events remind us painfully – it was because the experience of being colonized gave them a common history of suffering, sympathy for each other, and a desire to be governed together. So when the black population in the US is described as a colony, the suggestion is that the forces that operated to turn European colonies in Africa into nations are also at work in the US turning its black population into a nation.

The colonial analogy limps. Prior to gaining independence, the typical colony often developed extensive institutions of internal self-government, as well as institutions dedicated to education, culture and public service. These institutions played an important role in changing the various peoples of the colony into one nation. The experience of suffering the same indignities may have helped them identify and sympathize with each other, and may have motivated them to combine to force their common oppressor out, but it need not have given them a will for a common government. Given their differences the tribes may not have believed that this was possible. But if they worked together in institutions of internal self-government, education and public service, they could come to believe that their differences were not insuperable, and that a common government would be to their advantage. If they did come to such a belief, they could acquire a will for self-government and could thus become a nation.

Similar nation-building forces were at work in the US when the races were legally separated. Since blacks were generally not permitted to work together with whites in institutions dedicated to religion, education, culture and public service, such institutions tended to develop in black communities. They were not as effective as the institutions performing similar functions in white communities, but they offered blacks opportunities to learn how to run organizations, to discover common problems and to negotiate and settle disagreements, and in thus giving them experience in something approaching self-government, may have given them a will for a common government. However, with the end of *de jure* segregation of the races, and the expectation that blacks and whites would share the same institutions, these nation-generating institutions were abolished, or allowed to decay, and with their end the will for self-government probably ended too.

BLACK INDIVIDUALS

The above discussion does not imply that there are no black nations struggling for liberation in various parts of the world; there may be. The discussion only implies that the black population in the US is not a nation, and consequently that there can be no reasonable talk of its liberation as a nation. However, we must return to the possibility that black liberation is a call for the liberation of blacks as individuals. The conclusion that it was an empty call was premature.

While the constitutions and laws of liberal democracies no longer require segregation of the races, or say that blacks may not vote, or hold political office or enjoy their civil rights just because they are black, many black citizens of these democracies are prevented from enjoying the rights they are legally entitled to because they are too poor or ignorant to defend themselves when their rights are threatened by the carelessness or malice of others. The call for black liberation may be a call to educate such blacks and help them to get good jobs so that they can enjoy their political and civil rights.

These advances will require broad-based colour-blind policies that benefit the poor and uneducated of all races.[3] For example, economic policies to stimulate the economy and create more jobs may be necessary. But such policies must be properly designed. Someone must always make sure that colour-blind policies ostensibly designed to help all the poor, for example, do not slight, overlook or otherwise injure the black poor. This would be advisable in any country, but it is essential in a country with a history of black slavery, legalized racial segregation, and continuing racial bigotry. And to justify it one need not assume malice; it is enough to remember that policymakers all have blind spots, and may have more blind spots when it comes to black people. This may seem an extreme. Racism is not the only problem blacks face in the US; as I have allowed, blacks are also often plagued by poverty and a lack of education. The further question, however, is whether racism is among the causes of these problems. Arguments that it is not are never fully satisfying. For example, the argument that blacks are unemployed because the economy is not producing enough jobs does not explain why the burden so inevitably falls disproportionately on blacks. And if the explanation is that blacks are disproportionately unemployed because they are less well educated than other races, this does not explain why they are less educated than other races.

I maintain therefore that colour-blind policies ostensibly designed to help the poor and uneducated of all races should always be carefully examined to ensure that they do not contain unrecognized – or carefully concealed – problems for the black poor and uneducated. I also maintain that normally only black people can be relied on to conduct such examinations. This does not appeal to any absurd epistemological theory that there are some things only black people can see. It appeals to the commonsense fact that the people most likely to recognize a problem are those most interested in recognizing it and most sensitized to its nuances, taking it for granted that blacks are generally more interested in recognizing the problems in question than whites, and more sensitized to their nuances. Finally, it seems that the black people most capable of conducting these examinations would be those with the education necessary to understand the policies in question.

It may be objected that the last claim suggests that educated affluent blacks have special obligations to help poor blacks that educated affluent whites do not have. Where could such special obligations come from?

Some may be satisfied with the answer that affluent educated blacks have special obligations to help the black poor because they are in a unique position to help, and can do so without excessive costs. But since some others may not be satisfied with this answer it is worth noting that there are two reason why affluent educated blacks may be expected to help the black poor even if they have no special obligations to do so. The first is that they have self-interested reasons for helping. All blacks, including affluent blacks, are threatened and endangered by racism. But racism would be at least contained if black poverty and ignorance were checked, for it feeds on those evils. Someone may wonder why affluent blacks are threatened and endangered by racism since they seem to be in a position to defend their rights against it. But affluent blacks incur costs in defending their rights against racism that their white fellow citizens do not incur, never think of and often cannot even imagine; also they are unduly and unfairly distracted by the rumours of their inferiority and depravity that racists continually give voice to. Surely they would be liberated by its elimination or containment.

The second reason why affluent educated blacks may be expected to help the black poor, and it is admittedly much weaker than the first, is that they may still be bound by special ties of sympathy to the black poor. Indeed the suggestion may seem incredible given that 'black on black' crime decimates the black ghettos, and affluent blacks flee to the suburbs. But it is not altogether implausible. Sympathy is only a feeling. People need to work together in suitable institutions to give direction and effect to the sympathy they feel for each other. Without such institutions sympathy is reduced to individual acts of help, or to handwringing. Further, even people with ties of sympathy may have serious disagreements, and need to have suitable institutions in which to meet and work out ways to settle their differences. Without such institutions, they will come to blows, however great the sympathy they may feel for each other. But as I have noted, black institutions performing these functions collapsed when legalized segregation was repealed. Consequently it is hardly surprising that systematic evidence of sympathy among the black population has dramatically declined, and violence has taken its place.

It may be objected that since the fear that violence arouses is among the best-known destroyers of sympathy my argument actually suggests that sympathy has declined among blacks. But this objection relies on a false assumption. When people fear being maimed or killed they usually try to save themselves, sometimes at others' expense; it does not follow, however, that their sympathy evaporates. It may remain and assert itself when the claims of self-interest become less pressing. A deeper objection is that affluent blacks fleeing black neighbourhoods must lose sympathy for those they leave behind. The assumption behind this objection seems to be that when people put large distances between themselves and others, and thus reduce their liability to the same dangers, they also correspondingly lose their disposition to identify with and feel sympathy for each other. This assumption seems true for many kinds of dangers, but it is false for the danger of racism because there is no running away from it in the US. And as a matter of fact racism seems to continue to dispose African Americans of all classes to identify and sympathize with each other. When a highly-paid black executive is passed up for a promotion, and suspects racism, he is likely to claim a kind of kinship with the black poor.[4] And if they hear of his disappointment, they too are likely to feel that on some absolute level he is no more secure than they are.

I agree that these claims of sympathy are paltry compared to the sympathy that must have existed among blacks in the nineteenth century when those who were free risked life and freedom to help their brethren in chains escape. Still, the sympathy that may still exist among the black population may combine with the claims of self-interest to make the kind of co-operation I have described possible. This co-operation does not rest on the grandiose and dismal claim that racism is a permanent feature of American society. Hopefully racism will pass. But it exists now, and black co-operation to fight it seems necessary. Strangely, however, one still sometimes hears the objection that this co-operation is itself based on racism. This is silly. Racism commonly takes the view that important psychological qualities are correlated with the gross physical differences, like skin colour, that divide human beings into races. If black unity were based on such a view it would be racist. But it is not racist if it is simply based on the view that blacks need to unite to protect themselves from racism.

A more scholastic objection is that black unity makes no sense because there is not, and cannot be, an adequate definition of who is black. It seems to be vaguely based on the view of some geneticists that race cannot be adequately defined, and it has gained a big boost from the fact that the various US censuses have defined race so inconsistently that many people cannot tell how to classify themselves when the censuses are conducted.[5] Despite its pretension of getting to the root of things this objection is more than a little silly. If no one could tell who was black we would not have to worry about racists. In fact, how the biologists, or the US censuses define or try to define who is black is irrelevant here. Since black unity is supposed to defend black people against racists, what is relevant is how the racist defines who is black. It is these people who had better unite if they want to be safe from racists. Certainly the individuals their definition picks out share nothing important that they do not share with others; and certainly racists may not always be able easily to identify every individual their definition says is black; still the definition is tolerably coherent and picks out millions of people with no trouble or ambiguity at all. People are black if their skins are black, and their hair and facial and other features are like those typical of the people of sub-Saharan Africa, or if people fitting this description are among their ancestors.

A third and more serious objection argues that the call for black unity is divisive, counterproductive and self-defeating because the best allies of the black poor are not affluent blacks, who are traitors bent on securing their class interests, but the poor of all races, including the white poor. This objection does not simply argue that black organizations should join forces with others when this is mutually advantageous. The position I endorse insists on such co-operation. The objection says that there should be no special black co-operation at all. Such co-operation should be totally submerged in co-operation with the other groups. The objection comes in three versions. The Marxist version urges black and white proletariat to unite and overthrow capitalism for socialism. A less ambitious version argues that poor blacks should unite with the poor of other races, including the white poor, to exact concessions from the richer classes. The most cautious version argues that poor blacks should unite with the other poor non-white victims of racism for the same end.

Consider, first, the Marxist version of the objection. There are enormous difficulties in the claim that the white proletariat will unite to overthrow capitalism. If the poorest workers feel they have nothing to lose but their chains, they may feel that they have reason to unite to try to overthrow capitalism for socialism. But if the better-paid workers are self-interested, as we must suppose they are, they are not likely to feel that they have any reason to unite with the poorest workers to do this. Capitalism treats them well; why should they help destroy it, and risk everything on an untested system? These obstacles to white working-class unity combine with racism to make unity of the black and white proletariat a far-fetched hope indeed. If self-interest cautions the better-paid workers against uniting with the poorest workers to overthrow capitalism, combined with racism it will determine them not to. A disproportionate number of the poorest workers are black. To better-paid white workers socialism will not only seem a risky project economically, but one that may put them on equal terms with people they despise.

The likelihood that black and white poor will unite to exact concessions from the rich white classes is even more remote. If the rich white classes are induced to offer concessions four considerations suggest that they will offer the lion's share to the white poor: (1) such a strategy will hold concessions to a minimum; (2) it will divide and weaken the opposition; (3) the ruling classes are racist and prefer that any concessions they have to make go to the white poor; (4) the ruling classes know that, being racists, the white poor will not mind at all if the black poor get little or nothing. The white poor, for their part, will probably go along with the strategy because the ruling classes have correctly read their racist attitudes. Finally with a cynicism born from being betrayed so often in the past the black poor will instantly intuit this dirty little game, and participate only halfheartedly, if at all, in any joint effort with the white poor to exact concessions from the rich classes.

The third and most cautious version of the objection was that blacks should unite with other non-white victims of white racism. Let us now consider it. It seems to envisage all non-white racial groups as equally the victims of white racism. If that view were the whole truth, black unity would probably not be the best way to secure black rights. White racists would find it easier to take advantage of united blacks than a combination of blacks, Asians and Latinos, for example. But the view is a double half-truth.

First, though blacks and the various non-white racial groups may all be victims of white racism they are not equally victims of this racism. Of course, certain white extremists hate all non-white people equally, and usually Jews and Catholics as well. But the pervasive white racism in the US, what I shall call discriminating racism, is prepared to make distinctions. Discriminating racism feels distrust and contempt for blacks, but its feelings about other non-white races are less harsh and more varied, in some cases even being moderated with a grudging respect. It is a greater obstacle to black advance than the racism of the extremists, despite the latter's frightening rhetoric and costume. Blacks have reliable allies against the extremists – all the groups the extremists hate as much as they hate blacks. Blacks do not have reliable allies in dealing with discriminating racism. Suppose, for example, that its various victims – in general, the non-white races – join forces to fight it; and suppose that it begins to feel hard-pressed, and must make some concessions to avoid losing everything, or to avoid a fight in which it will lose more than it is prepared to lose. In that case the rational thing for it to do is to make concessions to, or accept as near equals, the non-white race it views with least distaste. This is not only its immediately least unpalatable option, seeing that it has to give up something, but also has the good consequence of simultaneously weakening the opposition, and as an added bonus, strengthening its hand with an especially zealous ally. This takes us to a second half-truth in the view that all non-white races are equally victims of racism. These races are not only victims of racism. They are often racists themselves, victimizing each other, and usually reserving a special animus for blacks. Most of them would jump at the opportunity to join the exploiters, especially as this gives them a chance to express their distaste for their former black allies.

I doubt that anyone will challenge my claim that most non-white races have racist attitudes, often with a special contempt for blacks. But my claim that the pervasive white racism in the US is discriminating racism is likely to be challenged. It is now almost a cliché that Europe, and this is meant to include white America, put all the races it subjugated into the same bag. The reasonable hope behind this cliché is that it would motivate all these races to combine forces without fear of being betrayed. But the cliché is false. It is not proved by the fact that Europe subjugated different non-white races, since this is perfectly consistent with Europe viewing these races with different contempt. Nor is it made plausible because white racists have been heard referring to different non-white people as 'niggers' as if words are not often used in an extended sense in contexts where distinctions are not called for. And in fact the judicious sophisticated men who most helped to develop and give expression to the discriminating racism that is pervasive today did consistently rate blacks below all the other races.

Consider, for example, how Thomas Jefferson rated Indians and blacks. The evidence, he claimed, was such as to 'prove' the 'existence of a germ' in the minds of Indians that 'only wants cultivation'; for, he continued, Indians 'astonish you with strokes of the most sublime oratory; such as prove their reason and sentiment strong, their imagination glowing and elevated'. But Jefferson claimed that blacks, 'never uttered a thought above the level of plain narration', had 'no poetry' and were not capable of understanding the 'investigations of Euclid', arguing further that this was a result of their 'nature' rather than of their 'condition'.[6]

Or consider David Hume. In a footnote added to his essay 'Of National Characters' in 1753 Hume wrote, 'I am apt to suspect the negroes and in general all other species of men (for there are four or five different kinds) to be naturally inferior to the whites'. The history of this footnote displays the special contempt Hume reserved for blacks. Under criticism challenging his general claim that all non-white races – including blacks – were inferior to whites, he dropped the general claim but continued to insist on the specific claim that negroes were inferior. The revised footnote read, 'I am apt to suspect the negroes to be naturally inferior to the whites'.[7]

CONCLUSION

The only really troubling aspect of the call for black unity is that it may seem to delay realization of the great ideal of a society where a person's skin colour is no more noticed or significant than his eye colour is in present society.[8] This kind of society, the colour-blind society, is a worthy ideal. Only racists spewing nonsense about racial contamination could object to it. The problem with the colour-blind society is how to achieve it. Colour-blind policies that take no notice of racial difference between individuals would probably be ineffective because they are likely to leave inequalities between blacks and whites that would make race seem significant. To eliminate such inequalities many who favour the colour-blind society have therefore urged colour-conscious policies that require that racially different people be treated differently.[9] One of the most controversial of these policies requires that the qualifications of black people be considered more carefully and sympathetically than those of white people, or that blacks be given preference when they apply for jobs and positions. Many people have objected that such policies are unjust, and that they are self-defeating if their object is the colour-blind society. I cannot take up these objections here.[10] But whether or not they are sound, and the second may have weight, the historical record suggests that colour-conscious policies inevitably begin to be interpreted so that the white majority and the favoured non-white races replace blacks as their primary beneficiaries.[11]

If this is the case the policies allegedly most likely to achieve the colour-blind society can only be kept doing their job if black organizations and institutions – acting independently of white and other non-white organizations – see to it that they do. This may delay arrival of the colour-blind society, exacerbate racism and even conceivably recreate the nation within a nation that I allowed has expired. This would be a pity, but it would be a fair price to pay for black liberation.

NOTES

1 Martin Delany, *The Condition, Elevation, Emigration, and Destiny of the Colored People of the United States Politically Considered* (Salem: Ayer Company, 1988), p. 209, first published in 1852.
2 See, for example, Eldridge Cleaver, 'The Land Question', in Herbert J. Storing (ed.), *What Country Have I? Political Writings by Black Americans*

(New York: St Martins Press, 1970), p. 184. This essay originally appeared in *Ramparts* (May 1968).

3 William Julius Wilson, *The Truly Disadvantaged* (Chicago: University of Chicago Press, 1987).

4 See, for example, Ellis Cose, *The Rage of Privileged Class* (New York: Harper Collins Publishers, 1993).

5 See, for example, Lawrence Wright, 'Annals of Politics, One Drop of Blood', *The New Yorker*, 70(22) (25 July 1994).

6 Thomas Jefferson, 'Notes on the State of Virginia', in *Jefferson*, ed. Merrill D. Peterson (New York: The Library of America, 1984), pp. 266, 267.

7 The point is discussed in John Immerwahr, 'Hume's Revised Racism', *Journal of the History of Ideas*, 53(3) (Fall 1992). The views of Immanuel Kant on this are also revealing. See his *Observations on the Feeling of the Beautiful and Sublime* (Berkeley: University of California Press, 1960), p. 110.

8 This way of understanding a colour-blind society is due to Richard Wasserstrom's account in 'On Racism and Sexism', in Richard Wasserstrom (ed.), *Today's Moral Problems* (New York: Macmillan, 1979).

9 See, for example, ibid.

10 See, for example, Howard McGary, 'Reparations, Self-Respect, and Public Policy', in David T. Goldberg, *Ethical Theory and Social Issues* (Fort Worth: Holt, Rinehart and Winston, 1989).

11 See Derrick Bell, *Faces at the Bottom of the Well* (New York: Basic Books, 1992).

5

BLACKS DON'T NEED LIBERATING

Michael Levin

It is difficult to comment on Bernard Boxill's chapter, as it hardly addresses the question posed, namely whether blacks are in fact oppressed. Boxill speculates desultorily about the nationhood of blacks and discusses liberation tactics in rather dated Marxist jargon. At the end he introduces the important issue of race-consciousness without developing his remarks. As the basic issue is never directly joined, I will have to impose my own structure on the debate.

The first section presents evidence, far from exhaustive but in my view sufficient, that 'white racism' is no longer a factor in American society. The second and third sections consider alternative explanations of black 'ignorance' and 'poverty,' the conditions from which Boxill says blacks need liberating. The fourth section takes up race-consciousness.

BLACK PRIVILEGES

Boxill certainly writes as if the prevalence of racism is an incontestable fact. 'All blacks, including affluent blacks, are threatened and endangered by racism,' he says (p. 57), citing no evidence. 'Hopefully racism will pass. But it exists now' (p. 59). He speaks of the racism of the 'ruling classes' and the 'cynicism' of poor blacks 'betrayed so often' by the alliance of poor and rich white racists (p. 61).

None of this is so. Far from being endangered, blacks currently enjoy privileges the white majority denies to itself.

Slavery ended one hundred and thirty years ago; *de jure* school segregation ended in 1954; the 1964 Civil Rights Act banned private discrimination. Affirmative action for blacks was introduced by Lyndon Johnson in 1965, and turned into numerical quotas by the Nixon Labor Department in 1970. Since that time, blacks have

received set-asides, special programmes and the sympathetic attention of academics, the media and business. There are literally
thousands of training programmes, internships and awards for blacks
alone (or blacks, women and non-European Hispanics). The National
Science Foundation and the National Institute of Health, just two
of many bodies concerned to increase black participation in science,
have spent $2.5 billion on programmes reserved for blacks since 1972
(Culotta, 1992). If Ellis Cose believes he was denied a promotion
because of his race, he can sue with a far greater prospect of success
than a similarly situated white.

A double standard favouring blacks is carried to extreme lengths
in the academic world. Blacks at Pennsylvania State University – but
not whites – receive $550 for maintaining a C grade point average,
$1,100 for a B average (Taylor, 1992, p. 175). The mean SAT score
of blacks admitted to American colleges is one hundred and eighty
points below the white SAT mean (Herrnstein and Murray, 1994,
p. 452); the mean Law School Aptitude Test score of first-year
black law students is 1.5 standard deviations below the mean LSAT
score for first-year whites (Herrnstein and Murray, 1994, p. 455).
A ten-minute tour of the bulletin board of my own college turned
up fellowships reserved for blacks offered by Wayne State University,
Williams College, Indiana University, the University of Michigan,
New York University, the University of North Carolina, the Univer-
sity of Rochester, the University of Southern California, the
University of Texas, Washington University, the University of
Wisconsin, The American Society for Microbiology, the Ford
Foundation and General Motors.

Financially, whites have been remarkably generous to blacks in
other ways. To take a typical recent year, in 1990 the outlay for
'welfare' i.e. Aid for Families with Dependent Children, food stamps,
housing and other subsidies for the poor, totalled $215 billion. In
that year, blacks received over forty-one per cent of this outlay, or
about $88 billion (Rector, 1992). A more recent data-set assembled
by Herrnstein and Murray indicates that in 1991 black women
constituted forty-nine per cent of all women receiving AFDC
(Herrnstein and Murray, 1994, p. 331). As per capita black earnings
have been stable at roughly sixty per cent of per capita white earnings since the early 1970s (Jaynes and Williams, 1989, p. 287), and
income taxes are progressive, the annual tax bill for the average black
is no more than half that for the average white. So blacks, at twelve
per cent of the population, collectively pay perhaps six per cent of

the cost of welfare, or $13 billion. There is thus – using the 1990 figures – an annual transfer of about $75 billion from whites to blacks. By way of comparison, the American Marshal Plan, which rebuilt Europe after World War II, amounted to a total outlay of $12 billion between 1948 and 1952, or $204 billion in 1990 dollars. In other words, blacks in the US are given a Marshal Plan every three years. In yet other terms, the black population, containing forty-one per cent of the beneficiaries of public assistance and paying in six per cent of its cost, receives $6.80 in benefits for every dollar paid, while the remaining population pays ninety-four per cent of the cost and receives fifty-nine per cent of the benefits, or $0.63 on each dollar. Thus, the black rate of return on its spending for welfare is more than ten times that for whites (a ratio which increases when non-European Hispanics are not counted as white). As for education, integration has given black children access to a public school system *funded almost entirely by whites* and incomparably superior to any educational institution ever developed in a black society. (Contrary to the complaints of many writers, such as Jonathan Kozol (Kozol, 1992), mean per capita spending on black and white children is about equal in the US.) Indeed, the black schools of the segregated South, also funded by whites, were superior to anything ever created in an all-black country.

It is insufficiently appreciated that many institutions thought of as 'black' were created by whites and continue to be sustained largely by whites. The National Association for the Advancement of Colored People was founded in 1909 by Mary Ovington, William Walling and Dr Henry Moskowitz, three whites, and was given crucial early support by the white New York newspaperman Oswald Garrison Villard. Most of the budget of Howard University, the best-known black college, is supplied by the Federal Government. The legal staff of the National Association for the Advancement of Colored People Legal Defense Fund (an organization not affiliated with the NAACP) is primarily white, and was for years headed by Jack Greenberg.

White attitudes seem equally generous. The laws forbidding discrimination against and mandating preferences for blacks were, after all, enacted by a white majority in a democracy. The election in recent decades of black mayors in New York, Los Angeles, Trenton, Philadelphia, Chicago, Cleveland and Denver surely indicates white willingness to give blacks a chance. A black has achieved Chairmanship of the Joint Chiefs of Staff. Public utterances in any way unflattering to blacks bring instant censure and sanctions, as

Al Campanis, Jimmy 'The Greek' Snyder and Dale Lick discovered. Campanis, an employee of the Los Angeles Dodger baseball team for forty-three years, was fired within hours of remarking during a television interview that there were few black managers in baseball because blacks lack the mental 'necessaries' for management. Snyder was fired from his post as a television sports commentator when he speculated that blacks might be better athletes than whites because they have stronger thigh muscles. Lick, about to be appointed the president of a major university, was forced to resign when it came to light that, some years previously, he had said: 'A black athlete can actually outjump a white athlete, so they're better at the game. All you need to do is turn to the NCAA playoffs in basketball to see that the bulk of the players on those outstanding teams are black' (cited in the *New York Times*, 29 July 1993, p. A21). Not only do white elites censor statements in any way construable as unflattering to blacks, they strive to put blacks in a favourable light: producers of movies and television programmes go out of their way to cast blacks as high-status characters, even in defiance of the source material; advertisers scrupulously include blacks in group photos; stories on education in *USA Today*, a 'sort of' national newspaper, characteristically focus on a black child.

So far as I know, the sole concrete evidence of ongoing racism still cited in the grievance literature is white mistrust of blacks. (Statistical discrepancies *per se* are not concrete evidence, since the question is whether they remain when race-neutral factors are controlled for. Thus, discrepancies in rates of mortgage approval, often cited as proof of discrimination, vanish when creditworthiness is controlled for (Brimelow and Spencer, 1993).) Tales are told and retold of white women clutching their handbags when black men walk by, of taxis passing up blacks and of clerks watching blacks in stores. But such precautions are neither racist nor oppressive. They are not racist, because 'racism' denotes an *irrationally* negative view of a racial group, and the high rate of black crime warrants white suspicions. Blacks commit sixty-three per cent of all robberies in the US and fifty-five per cent of all murders (Hacker, 1992, p.181).[1] At twelve per cent of the population, they are thus overrepresented in both categories by a factor of roughly five. This number actually understates black criminality, since whites are *under*represented – among robbers, for instance, by a factor of $37/88 = 0.4$. Comparing the two rates, the average black is twelve times more likely than a white to be a robber and ten times more likely to be a murderer.

Aside from the reasonableness of white mistrust, the burden it imposes on blacks is hardly heavy enough to be called oppressive. Let us grant that it is irritating to an honest black to be ignored by unoccupied taxis, and let us not ask him to reflect that the ultimate cause of his irritation is the criminal behaviour of other blacks. Still, is that *IT*? Is this white racism at its most venomous? That is a matter of judgement, but it seems to me unworthy of the fuss, and trivial when compared to the advantages of affirmative action.

The acid test of what someone thinks of a situation is what he does about it, and blacks plainly prefer to be in the United States rather than elsewhere, especially non-white elsewheres. Thousands of Haitians risk the trip from Hispaniola to Florida in rickety boats, and the immigration quotas of black African countries are filled every year. At the same time, the Back-to-Africa movement has had few takers, American blacks showing no interest whatever in emigrating to Haiti, Zaire, Ghana, Liberia, Senegal or Rwanda. This is not what one would expect were blacks in America threatened, endangered and constantly betrayed.

BLACK IQ AND PHENOTYPE

Why then do blacks lag behind academically and economically? I agree with Boxill that 'poor education' is no explanation, begging as it does the question of why blacks remain poorly educated. Unlike Boxill, I recognize possibilities other than racism. In particular, it is also possible that blacks are less mentally able than whites, and possible in turn that a black deficit in ability is due to adventitious environmental factors, or genetic factors or a combination thereof, rather than obstacles imposed by whites. Motivational factors may play a role as well; Boxill elsewhere cites 'chronic tardiness' as a contributor to black poverty (Boxill, 1985, p.158). Such motivational differences too may be due to genes and non-invidious environmental factors.

Emotions so cloud this issue that many widely-held positions on it are, on a moment's reflection, incoherent. For instance, black children are said to be just as intelligent as white and to do badly in school because racism stunts their intellectual growth – even though 'stunted intellectual growth' amounts to lower intelligence. A large part of the problem is confusion between intelligence as an overt trait, what in behavioural genetics is called 'phenotypic' intelligence, and the genetic basis of intelligence, with people in effect reasoning that if the race difference in intelligence is due to environmental factors, not genes, blacks are 'really' as intelligent as whites. Reinforcing this mistake is a widespread tendency to treat wrongfully caused differences as if they were unreal. So some clarifications are urgently in order.

As noted, a phenotype is any trait of an organism. Birth weight, height at eighteen and eye colour are all phenotypes. So too is an organism's ability to learn, or what in ordinary discourse is called intelligence. Every phenotype is the result of the organism's genes, or 'genotype', expressing itself in the organism's home environment. The same genotype may express itself differently in different environments, and the range of variation of different genotypes may differ. This makes the relative importance of genotype and environment to a particular phenotype difficult to prise apart. Eye colour depends wholly on genes, in the sense that the same genotype will express itself as the same eye colour in all environments, while one's native language depends on where one is raised (although the capacity to acquire some language is gene-based). The relation of genotype to environment in other cases, such as mental illness, is less clear. However, *it is perfectly possible to verify the presence of a phenotype without having any idea of its cause.* Smith at twelve stone outweighs Jones at ten stone, whether they have different 'metabolism genes' or the same 'metabolism gene', and Smith is kept from getting as much exercise as Jones because of a game leg. If Smith and Jones are genotypically identical, Smith would have weighed ten stone had he had Jones' diet and exercise regimen from birth. But we do not need to know whether this is so to be quite sure that Smith does weigh twelve stone. So too an individual's 'phenotypic' intelligence, his actual ability to learn and manipulate data, can be determined quite apart from its causes, and one can determine individual and mean group differences in the intelligence phenotype without needing to find out what causes them. Smith with an IQ of ninety is really less intelligent than Jones with an IQ of one hundred and twenty, whether this difference is due to a difference in their genes, or to a difference in their childhood experiences or to differences in both.

Assume for a moment it is true that 'blacks are really as intelligent as whites, and only do less well in school because racism stunts the intellectual development of black children'. Far from reconciling black academic performance with parity of black and white intelligence, this popular remark implies that blacks are less intelligent than whites, when 'intelligence' is used in its phenotypic sense. After all, what can 'stunted intellectual development' mean but that black intellectual ability is less than it could and should have been? What is being said is that the *genetic potential* of blacks and whites is the same, but that, because of racism, blacks do not develop the same level of intelligence that whites do. But this is just the situation of two individuals with the same 'metabolism gene' who develop different physiques because of environmental contingencies. The difference in their physiques, although environmentally induced, is nonetheless real. Bertrand Russell once defined a metaphysician as a man who says that something does not exist, and then defines evil as the counterexample. Many people are by this definition metaphysicians of intelligence, reasoning that, since blacks should have developed levels of intelligence equal to whites, the differences that exist are unreal, or, conversely, that since blacks are as intelligent as whites, their difference in intelligence is a result of white wickedness.

There is little doubt that blacks are on average phenotypically less intelligent than whites. Blacks are not observed in everyday experience to perform cognitive tasks as well as whites, and blacks regularly score about one standard deviation below whites on IQ tests (Shuey, 1966; Garner and Wigdor, 1982, vol. 1, pp. 71–2; vol. 2, p. 365; Hartigan and Wigdor, 1989, p. 27; Scarr, 1981). It is said with ritual regularity that these tests are biased against blacks, but this is simply not so. The evidence of test fairness is of two sorts: definitive but somewhat abstract, and less conclusive but intuitively more compelling.

Speaking abstractly, a biased IQ test assigns a lower score to blacks than to whites of equal intelligence, or, equivalently, blacks are *more* intelligent than whites with the same measured IQ, if IQ measurements are biased against blacks. Hence – if IQ tests are biased – blacks should *outperform* whites with the same IQ at other tasks requiring intelligence, such as getting good grades in school and performing well at jobs that make significant cognitive demands. In statistical jargon, biased IQ tests will underpredict black performance on criterion tasks. In point of empirical fact, however, blacks regularly do *worse* than whites on criteria when IQ is held constant (Garner and Wigdor, 1982). This surprising result may be due to race differences in motivation, or a statistical artifact known as 'regression to the mean'. Roughly put, the latter hypothesis holds that, since the mean black score is lower than the white, a high black score on any given IQ test is more likely to be due to lucky guessing than the same score achieved by a white. Therefore, a high IQ is more likely to overestimate black ability as subsequently revealed on criterion tasks. Whatever the correct explanation of the over-prediction of black performance, IQ tests do not *under*predict it, and therefore are not biased.

It might be replied that IQ tests and their validators both assume a knowledge of white culture and training in white standards denied to blacks. At this point the bias hypothesis threatens to become *ad hoc* in the extreme, but it is still capable of empirical test. It predicts that black and white performance should converge on more culture-free questions, such as those testing mathematical reasoning. In fact, blacks do *worse* on tests of numerical reasoning than on more culture-loaded material such as vocabulary (Jensen, 1980, pp. 552ff.). The race gap on culture-fair tests is as great as on conventional IQ tests (Jensen, 1980). Also, if poor black performance is due to unfamiliarity with standards and information available to whites, the questions blacks find difficult should not be the same as those found difficult by whites. (Suppose your German were spotty and you took an IQ test that for some reason used a sprinkling of German words. You would find all the questions incorporating German words equally baffling, while the questions found hard by testees fluent in German would be just those making heavy demands on thinking ability.) Yet empirically, the very questions whites find hardest are those that blacks find hardest, and the questions whites find easiest are those blacks find easiest (Jensen, 1980), a finding difficult to explain if white culture is an opaque curtain obscuring all test items.

Finally, the white-culture hypothesis cannot explain why the Japanese and Chinese, certainly less familiar with white norms than American blacks, outperform whites on IQ as they do.

A popular variant of the cultural-norms hypothesis is that IQ is a proxy for social status. Since blacks tend to be of lower status, they naturally fare ill on IQ tests. This hypothesis can be tested by seeing if the race difference in IQ persists among blacks and whites of the same socioeconomic status, and, to the surprise of many people, it does. Depending on what study is consulted, sixty to eighty per cent of the black/white difference remains when social status is controlled for (Jensen, 1980, p. 43). In fact, children of low socio-economic status white and Asian families outperform children of high-status black families on the Scholastic Achievement Test (formerly the Scholastic Aptitude Test) (Hacker, 1992, p. 143).

It seems clear that the race difference in (phenotypic) intelligence contributes heavily to the attainment gap. There is a close correlation between IQ and on-the-job success, a correlation which tightens as the minimum IQ for a job rises (Hunter, 1986). The prestige associated with a job increases in lockstep with the IQ required for it. Differences in IQ account for almost all the variation in academic success in the lower grades, and at least half the variation in success in college and graduate school. Black income is ninety-eight per cent that of white when IQ is controlled for (Hernnstein and Murray, 1994, pp. 323–4). Linda Gottfredson has shown that IQ *completely* explains race differences in representation in various professions (Gottfredson, 1986), a finding extended by Herrnstein and Murray (Herrnstein and Murray, 1994, pp. 321–6). For instance, although blacks make up twelve per cent of the population, fewer than three per cent of doctors are black, which certainly looks like evidence of discrimination. However, doctors are drawn from an IQ range in which, holding population constant, there are about twenty whites for every black. Hence insofar as a medical career depends on IQ only about one twentieth of twelve per cent, or 0.06 per cent, of doctors in the US should be black. Taking IQ into account suggests bias in favour of blacks in medicine. Overall, then, inferior black performance at work and in school is just what one would expect from the IQ difference if racism did not exist.

BLACK IQ AND CRIME

At the other end of the attainment scale there is a strong correlation between IQ and law-abidingness: the mean IQ of violent offenders in prison is about ninety (Herrnstein and Wilson, 1985). This correlation is important because a key exhibit in the case for the existence of white oppression is the high rate of black incarceration and the overrepresentation of blacks on death row. A second exhibit, that killers of whites are more apt to receive the death sentence than are killers of blacks, leads to race differences in non-cognitive variables.

About half the US prison population is black. This means that the rate of incarceration for blacks is almost five times their proportion of population, or – since there are seven times as many whites as blacks in the US – that the average black is more than eight times likelier to be incarcerated than the average white (Jaynes and Williams, 1989, pp. 458–61, Figures 9.1 and 9.2, Table 9.1). This in itself is no evidence at all of discrimination, since, as noted earlier, blacks commit proportionately more violent crime than whites. Many people maintain that blacks are driven to crime by racism, and Hacker suggests that black crime is 'retribution' for injustice,[2] but a simpler explanation is the race difference in intelligence. As the mean IQ of blacks is closer than that of whites to the mean IQ of violent offenders, there are bound to be proportionally more blacks in the intelligence range typical of violent offenders. For instance, holding population constant, more than twice as many blacks as whites have IQs below roughly the range from which murderers are drawn.[3] In a random sample of more than 12,000 individuals, two per cent of all whites and thirteen per cent of all blacks were incarcerated, however, only five per cent of the blacks with IQ of one hundred, a reduction of the black/white ratio from 6.5 to 2.5 were incarcerated (Herrnstein and Murray, 1994, p. 338). Robert Gordon (Gordon, 1975) has found that the race difference in juvenile crime rates disappears if it is assumed that all juvenile criminals are recruited from the IQ range of eight-five and below. Other statistical techniques for controlling for IQ achieve further reductions.

Controlling for IQ eliminates or inverts race differences in occupational representation and income, but, as incarceration data indicate, it leaves a significant gap in criminality. It would appear that in this case race differences in temperament play a role. A recent study by J.P. Rushton (Rushton, 1994, ch. 7) assembles evidence that blacks tend to be more excitable, aggressive and impulsive, traits associated with criminality across races. Blacks achieve higher average scores than whites on the psychopathy, schizophrenia and hyperactivity scales of the Minnesota Multiphasic Personality Inventory, indicative of 'estrangement and impulse-ridden fantasies . . . unusual thought patterns and aspiration-reality conflict [and] tendencies to act impulsively and with poor judgment' (see Dahlstrom, Lachar and Dahlstrom, 1986, pp. 29–31, 34, 36, 39, 41, 47, 95, 135; Gynther, 1972). The US prison population as a whole differs from the general population in having elevated scores on precisely these scales, and the MMPI is as predictive for blacks as whites.

Race differences in response to certain MMPI items are so robust that they can reliably distinguish blacks from whites. Among the statements blacks agree with more frequently are: 'It wouldn't make me nervous if any members of my family got into trouble with the law,' 'A person shouldn't be punished for breaking a law that he thinks is unreasonable', 'It would be better if almost all the laws were thrown away', 'Most people are honest chiefly through fear of being caught', and 'I am an important person' (Dahlstrom, Lachar and Dahlstrom, 1986, pp. 229–31). These responses are interpreted by the designers of the MMPI to indicate cynicism, conflict with authority, and externalization of blame for one's problems. Further evidence of a quite different sort of race difference in temperament is the higher level of serum testosterone in the blood of black males, reported in two studies (Ross *et al.*, 1986; Ellis and Nyborg, 1992). Testosterone is a known facilitator of aggression. One might argue that the strain of racism raises the serum testosterone levels in blacks, but the usual finding among humans and primates is that, to the contrary, humiliation and defeat *lowers* testosterone levels in males.

As blacks commit more murders than whites, seemingly as a result of greater impulsivity, the disproportionate number of blacks on death row is not surprising. (Given the number of murders committed by blacks, too *few* blacks may be under sentence of death.) But black impulsivity may also explain why killers of blacks are less likely to receive capital sentences. The death penalty is usually reserved for premeditated murder or murder committed in the course of a felony, not murders committed in personal disputes. If blacks are more prone than whites to react violently to frustration, more blacks will be victims of non-capital homicides in personal disputes, which tend to occur between members of the same race. The non-capital killing of friends and relatives is less frequent among whites. But black-on-white killings are more frequent than white-on-black, and tend to be committed in the course of robberies, making them capital offences. The race difference in temperament thus explains both alleged biases in capital sentencing.

THE GENETIC FACTOR

I have so far ignored the extent to which intelligence and motivation is controlled by genes. And many people who might agree that the immediate cause of black failure has to do with intelligence (and motivation) will insist that low black intelligence (and persistence) is caused by the racist environment in which blacks are forced to function. Is this so?

At the *individual* level, differences in IQ are now thought to be due largely to genetic variation. When identical twins – individuals with the same genes – are reared apart, in unrelated environments, their IQs as adults tend to be very similar (Bouchard *et al.*, 1990).

On the other hand, genetically diverse adopted and natural children reared together – and thus exposed to similar environments – end up diverging in IQ by almost as much as randomly paired individuals. In statistical language, genetic variation is now thought to explain about seventy per cent of the variance in individual IQ (Bouchard *et al.*, 1990), where the *variance* of a variable is the square of its standard deviation. In yet other terms, the heritability of intelligence, or h^2, is 0.7. Letting SD^2 be the variance in IQ over the human population, G^2 the variance in genes and E^2 the variance in environments – which by definition explains all of SD^2 not explained by G^2 – it follows that $SD^2 = h^2 G^2 + (1 - h^2)E^2$.[4]

That genes explain most of the intellectual differences between individuals does not mean that they explain *group* differences. After all, genetically identical batches of corn seed may yield corn of very different heights in different soils. So it remains possible that the mean IQ of blacks is lower than that of whites because of differences (imposed by racism) between black and white environments. Yet, while a group difference always *may* be environmental in origin, this becomes implausible if the groups' environments are too similar. Africa is unlike Alaska, but that is not why Masai are so much taller than Eskimos. A Masai baby raised by Eskimos in Alaska will not grow into a short, stocky adult. So the question is: do the typical environments of blacks and whites differ enough to yield the observed race difference in ability?

Roughly speaking, the more 'heritable' a trait is the more the environments of two groups must diverge to produce a given group difference, if environment is assumed to be doing all the work.[5] Look again at the equation connecting variation in IQ to genetic and non-genetic variation. If we are dealing with identical twins, *all* of whose variation in IQ is explained environmentally, we can set G^2 equal to 0. Furthermore, if we 'normalize' so that 1 SD becomes our unit of measurement, we have $1^2 = (1 - h^2)E^2$, and $\sqrt{1^2} = 1 = \sqrt{(1 - h^2)}E$. Hence, if two identical twins differ in IQ by 1 SD, the environments in which they were raised must have differed by $1/\sqrt{(1 - 0.7)}$ = 1.85 standard deviations, a large gap. And when we assume blacks and whites to be indistinguishable with respect to the genes controlling intelligence, we are in effect treating the average black and the average white as if they were identical twins. Hence, if environment completely explains race differences in intelligence, the typical black environment must be assumed to be 1.85 standard deviations below the typical white environment, on some scale of environments.

It seems unlikely that the black and white environments differ by that much. Intuitively, blacks and whites see the same movies and television shows, speak the same language and are exposed to the same curricula in school. Insofar as social scientists have been able to measure environment, blacks and whites typically differ on environmental variables by about 0.75 to 1 SD. Furthermore, the non-genetic variables that appear to have the most influence on IQ concern the micro-environment within families, such as birth order, rather than variables on which whole families differ from each other – the ones on which blacks and whites characteristically differ. It must also be borne in mind that most of the environmental factors standardly cited as causes of black behaviour are in part its *effects*, leading the explanation in a circle. For instance, the New York press recently covered a Harlem high school in which all the lockers were smashed and the halls covered with graffiti. The sense of disorder caused by these conditions no doubt encourages further misbehaviour, but since it was misbehaving black students who created these conditions in the first place, they can hardly be why black students act as they do.

Further evidence that the race difference in intelligence is not due to environment, racist or otherwise, has been the failure of black adoptees raised in white families to reach intellectual parity with whites. The mean IQ of transracial adoptees is somewhat above the national mean for blacks, but it is as far below the mean IQ of the birth children of the adopting families, and of white children adopted by these same white families, as the national black mean is below the white (the mean IQ of the birth children was considerably above the national white average) (Weinberg, Scarr and Waldman, 1992; Levin, 1994). It may be suggested that the black adoptees were somehow affected by ubiquitous American racism, but black African children score even lower than American blacks on the most culture-free ability tests (Owen, 1992). This difference may be related to the partial white ancestry of American blacks.

Accusations against whites die hard, and the performance of contemporary black Africans may be blamed on colonialism. However, this attribution does not account for the failure of sub-Saharan cultures to develop mathematics, a written language, the calendar or mechanical devices prior to contact with Caucasians (Baker, 1974). The inference that this failure is intrinsic is strengthened by the inability of Africans to sustain the technology that has been left them by departing Europeans (see Darnton, 1994a, 1994b;

Noble, 1994; Kaplan, 1992). Ironically, the sole First World sub-Saharan nation is the Union of South Africa. If genes matter, the transfer of power to blacks in that country together with black seizure of industries will be followed by a steep drop in the standard of living, which will doubtless be blamed on whites.

Everyday perceptions of groups crystallize as 'stereotypes'. These generalizations tend to be accurate, their current ill-repute notwithstanding. Boxill cites negative comparative assessments of black ability from Jefferson, Hume and Kant (and could also have cited Galen, Ibn Khaldun, Voltaire, Hegel and Russell to the same effect) to show how blacks have had to contend against the prejudices of even the greatest white thinkers. Reformulated in neutral language, however, these assessments have turned out to be essentially correct.

RACE-BLINDNESS

Boxill is ambivalent toward race-blindness. As an 'ideal' he considers it 'great' and 'worthy', one to which 'only racists spewing nonsense about racial contamination could object (p. 63)'. He sees virtue in 'broad-based colour-blind policies that benefit the poor and uneducated of all race (p. 56)'. Yet he fears, for reasons not made quite clear, that colour-blind approaches will leave conspicuously racial inequalities. At the same time, he fears that colour-*conscious* policies will be self-defeating and (he offers no examples) warped to the advantage of whites. On the whole, he thinks that black racial awareness may be a necessary, and is certainly an acceptable, price to pay for black liberation.

While disagreeing *in toto* about the need for liberation, I commend Boxill's view as more nuanced than those of most proponents of race-consciousness-to-achieve-race-blindness, who see no tensions whatever in their position. But I think the truth may lie elsewhere.

I certainly endorse race-blindness in many contexts. Whenever there is a task to be done, recruitment should be based on evidence of ability, period, the chip of racial proportionality being allowed to fall where it may. This is the most efficient way of doing things, and the way most people will sooner or later choose if given the chance. One forgets that *Plessy v. Ferguson*, in which the Supreme Court enunciated the 'separate but equal' doctrine, upheld a Louisiana statute *requiring* trains to provide separate accommodations for the races, a law the railroads considered burdensome. (See Epstein, 1992, pp. 99–108, for a fascinating account of *Plessy*.) Free-market liberals object to laws of this sort as strongly as they do to laws *against* white (or black) cars for customers who want them.

But why would anyone want them? Boxill writes as if the only possible grounds for this or other forms of race-consciousness is a lunatic fear of 'contamination'[6] but he is attacking a straw man. There are other grounds.

(1) The high black crime rate justifies whites in seeking to avoid blacks, and keeping their neighbourhoods white.[7] This preference is especially reasonable in light of the apparent preference of blacks for white victims. Take rape. If rapists chose victims randomly, twelve per cent of the victims of both white and black rapists would be black, and eighty-eight per cent would be white. However, between 1979 and 1986 only three per cent of the victims of white rapists were black while fifty per cent of the victims of black rapists were white (Whittaker, 1990, Tables 1 and 16). Using the white victimizer/black victim ratio of $0.03/0.12 = 0.25$ as a baseline for cross-racial victim choice – an ideal baseline would reflect the demographic distribution of the races – the black/white ratio of $0.50/0.88$ is 2.2 times greater. Also between 1979 and 1986, fifty-nine per cent of the simple assaults committed by blacks were directed against whites, while three per cent of the assaults committed by whites were directed against blacks (Whittaker, 1990), yielding a relative black preference for white victims of 2.6.[8] Someone faced with the split-second decision of whether to remain on an otherwise empty subway car when three teenage boys step aboard is justified in attending to their race. He is right to think he is in more danger if they are black rather than white or Asian, and in greater danger still if he himself is white.

(2) Parents are presumably entitled to want quiet, stimulating classrooms for their children. Given the lower mean intelligence and greater restlessness[9] of black children, along with the increased probability of violence as black pupils become more numerous, it is reasonable for white parents to use racial composition in judging schools. It is also natural, for the same reasons, for *black* parents to prefer predominantly white schools – a dilemma that can be resolved equitably only by respecting freedom of association. Parents and children should be able to associate with whomever wishes to associate with them. Restoring this right by repeal of the Fair Housing Act would probably result in segregation, but I cannot see what is wrong with this if it is voluntary.

(3) Preferences about personal deportment also justify race-consciousness. In deciding whether to take a walk through the park it is legitimate and reasonable to wonder whom one is going to meet. Suppose two outdoor events are scheduled for a certain day, a performance of Mozart's *Magic Flute* and a rap concert. The first will attract a white crowd, the second a black crowd likely to be far rowdier. Very few people are indifferent between which one they would like to find themselves surrounded by. I would expect every reader of this chapter to avoid the rappers and seek out the Mozart devotees.

One might say that I'm talking about 'crime-consciousness' or 'safety-consciousness' rather than *race*-consciousness. But why define 'race-consciousness' to require the belief that race is important in and of itself? Most of the things people pay attention to, like bank accounts and biopsy reports, are important only because of their correlates. To observe that race matters because of its correlates is to explain *why* people are aware of it, not to *deny* that they are. The man on the subway notices the boys' race out of fear of being mugged, not contamination, but it is still race he notices, not shoe size. Verbal issues aside, the substantial point is that nobody would care about race if the blacks and whites were alike in all ways but physical appearance. But they aren't, and that is why people are aware of race.

Ironically, use of racial information is now largely illegal in the US. By mandating civil rights and affirmative action, whites have denied themselves the freedom to think or act on the basis of race, except when discriminating against other whites to favour blacks. Whites need liberation, from misplaced guilt feelings.

NOTES

1 Hacker himself views black crime as 'retribution' (Hacker, 1992, p. 187).
2 Hacker makes the particularly objectionable assertion that the preference of black rapists for white victims – controlling for population size, black-on-white rape is more frequent than black-on-black or white-on-black rape – is a, displaced, venting of frustration against 'the real centers of power' (Hacker, 1992, p. 186).
3 Normalizing to standard deviation units, or z, an IQ of 95 is $-0.33z$ for whites and $+0.66z$ for blacks. Seventy-five per cent of a population lies below $0.66z$ and 37 per cent lies below $-0.33z$ for a normally distributed variable (see for instance the z table in Lindgren, 1962, pp. 392–3).
4 A good explanation of these basic statistical ideas is Armore, 1966 pp. 136–70, 403–53.

5 So Gould is simply in error when he writes '. . . group heredity [is] not tied by rising degrees of probability as heritability increases within groups and differences enlarge between them. The two phenomena are simply separate' (Gould, 1981, p. 157).

6 Many opponents of 'racism' treat negative attitudes toward blacks as a form of insanity. Rosenfeld, an admirer of quotas for blacks, can only think of one reason why anyone might want to discriminate against them: 'the claim of a religious fanatic who believes it to be his divine mission to establish a racially segregated society to preserve racial purity, to force others to convert to his religion and to give up the right to make moral decisions for themselves' (Rosenfeld, 1991, p. 254).

7 I ignore here the inability of blacks to maintain housing stock, about which I have no reliable statistics, but which is apparent in any black neighbourhood originally occupied by whites.

8 Jared Taylor has observed that FBI statistics include a category for Hispanic victims but not for Hispanic victimizers. Hence many 'white' crimes against blacks are committed by Puerto Ricans and Mexicans, non-European Hispanics who are supposed to be further victims of white racism.

9 Janet Benson, a professor of education, claims that 'black pupils need more chances for expressive talking rather than writing. Black children also require more freedom to move around the classroom without being rebuked' (cited in Berger, 1988, p. B8).

6

BOXILL'S REPLY

Michael Levin has hardly replied to my essay; predictably he has let fly his usual barrage of claims that blacks are mainly stupid and criminal, and that white discrimination against blacks is therefore rational and justifiable. These claims are familiar, false and offensive, and the shoddy fallacies and equivocations that feed them have long been exposed. Nevertheless it seems that I must deal with them, though I do so with distaste.

Levin claims to present evidence 'sufficient' to show that ' "white racism" is no longer a factor in American society' (p. 65). Indeed he claims that 'blacks currently enjoy privileges the white majority denies to itself' (p. 65). His list of 'privileges' is revealing. The first two are that 'Slavery ended one hundred and thirty years ago'; and *'de jure* school segregation ended in 1954' (p. 65). Evidently Levin thinks it is a privilege for blacks not to be enslaved and for their children not to be quarantined. The reader may protest that Levin does not mean this. He does. He insists that whites rationally and justifiably segregate themselves from blacks because blacks are mostly stupid and criminal. On that account blacks are privileged not to be enslaved or quarantined for they deserve to be. Levin's longer list of the privileges blacks enjoy include affirmative action and welfare. He begs the question. Affirmative action and welfare would be privileges only if they are not deserved. But they are. You do not grant a person a privilege when you throw him a crumb after you starve him half to death.

Levin points out that whites have created and supported 'black' institutions like the NAACP. What on earth does he think he is proving? Did anyone – except the foolish black racist – ever deny that many whites have been just, fair and even heroic in defence of their fellow human beings who happened to be black? But Levin claims that the white majority is 'generous' because it enacted laws forbidding discrimination against blacks. His use of 'generous' is curious, and again revealing. To be generous you must do more than justice demands. Since Levin thinks the white majority was generous to forbid discrimination I can only conclude that he thinks that it would not be unjust to discriminate against blacks. And given his claims about black stupidity and criminality it is clear that this is exactly what he thinks.

As further evidence of the irrelevance of racism Levin cites the well-publicized cases of a few prominent whites who were censured for making thoughtless remarks about blacks. The fact that these remarks were censured is an improvement over the recent past in which far more serious comments were standard and approved. But the fact that things have changed, and may even in some respects have improved, does not mean that they are not bad. Indeed, in the case under consideration the extravagant publicity cases received were a smokescreen to cover up the unglamorous but still serious racial discrimination that continues to thrive and to wreck aspirations. As several recent studies indicate, race continues to be an important factor in hiring decisions.[1] Levin will, of course, respond that racial discrimination in hiring is rational and therefore justified. He means that since very many blacks are incompetent or dishonest, the employer saves money by eliminating all blacks from consideration for jobs. This is a frightening argument, even if we give him the premise that very many blacks are incompetent or dishonest. It implies that any practice that is rational, in the sense that it saves or makes money, is also justified. On that account theft and murder can be justified.

I pass next to Levin's discussion of black intelligence. As Levin makes clear his claim is not simply that blacks usually score lower on IQ tests than whites; his claim is that the difference between black and white IQs is caused by genetic differences rather than by environmental differences. Given the importance of such a claim it should be taken seriously if it is made by an acknowledged expert in the science of genetics. As far as I know Levin is not such an expert. At least he does not refer us to experiments he has conducted, or to books and articles he has written, that have been taken seriously by geneticists. It may be that he cites geneticists who support his claim. But it would be easy to cite geneticists who reject it. Since Levin's philosophical arguments show how disposed he is to be biased against blacks, I think it safe to dismiss his chatter on the subject of genetics and black intelligence as mere bluff.

But suppose – only for the sake of argument – that we give Levin his claims about most blacks being unintelligent. And let us throw in as well the rubbish about blacks being impulsive and having high testosterone levels. Levin argues that these 'facts' explain the high crime rate among blacks. His argument is arrant nonsense. Levin must know that the correlations he cites do not establish causation. But this is the blunder his argument rests on. Everyone knows impulsive and unintelligent people who are not criminals. Whether such people become criminals or respectable citizens depends on their experiences, the institutions of their society and how these institutions are arranged. But Levin's argument here is not simply nonsense. It is evil nonsense. It is an essential part of a philosophy that has justified theft, murder, slavery and genocide.

NOTE

1   See, for example, Joleen Kirschenman and Kathryn M. Neckerman, 'We'd Love to Hire Them, but . . .', in Christopher Jencks and Paul E. Peterson (eds), *The Urban Underclass* (Washington, DC: The Brookings Institution, 1991).

BIBLIOGRAPHY

Armore, S. (1966) *Introduction to Statistical Analysis and Inference for Psychology and Education*, New York: John Wiley.

Baker, R. (1974) *Race*, Oxford: Oxford University Press.

Berger, J. (1988) 'What Do They Mean by "Black Learning Style?"', *The New York Times* (6 July), B8.

Bouchard, T., Lykken, D., McGue, M., Segal, N. and Tellegen, A. (1990) 'Sources of Human Psychological Differences: The Minnesota Study of Twins Reared Apart', *Science*, 250, 223–8.

Boxill, B. (1984) *Blacks and Social Justice*, New York: Rowman & Littlefield.

—— (1985) 'The Morality of Preferential Hiring', in Wasserstrom, R. (ed.), *Today's Moral Problems*, 3rd edn, New York: Macmillan.

Brimelow, P. and Spencer, L. (1993) 'The Hidden Clue', *Forbes* (4 January), 48.

Culotta, E. (1992) 'Two Generations of Struggle: A Special Report on Minorities in Science', *Science*, 258, 1176–237.

Dahlstrom, W., Lachar, D. and Dahlstrom, L. (1986) *MMPI Patterns of American Minorities*, Minneapolis: University of Minnesota Press.

Darnton, J. (1994a) ' "Lost Decade" Drains Africa's Vitality', *The New York Times* (19 June), A1–10.

—— (1994b) 'In Poor, Decolonized Africa, Bankers are New Overlords', *The New York Times* (20 June), A1–9.

Ellis, L. and Nyborg, H. (1992) 'Racial/Ethnic Variations in Male Testosterone Levels: A Probable Contributor to Group Difference in Health', *Steroids*, 57, 72–5.

Epstein, R. (1992) *Forbidden Grounds*, Cambridge, Mass.: Harvard University Press.

Garner, W. and Wigdor, A. (1982) *Ability Testing*, Washington, DC: National Academy Press.

Gordon, R. (1975) 'Crime and Cognition: An Evolutionary Perspective', in *Proceedings of the 11th International Symposium on Criminology*, São Paolo. International Centre for Biological and Medico-Forensic Criminology, 7–55.

Gottfredson, L. (1986) 'Societal Consequences of the g-Factor in Employment', *Journal of Vocational Behavior*, 29, 379–410.

Gould, S. (1981) *The Mismeasure of Man*, New York: Norton.

Gynther, M. (1972) 'White Norms and Black MMPIs: A Prescription for Discrimination?', *Psychological Bulletin*, 78, 386–402.

Hacker, A. (1992) *Two Nations*, New York: Scribner's.

Hartigan, J. and Wigdor, A. (1989) *Fairness in Employment Testing*, Washington, DC: National Academy Press.

Herrnstein, R. and Murray, C. (1994) *The Bell Curve*, New York: The Free Press.

Herrnstein, R. and Wilson, J. (1985) *Crime and Human Nature*, New York: Simon & Schuster.

Hunter, J. (1986) 'Cognitive Ability, Cognitive Aptitudes, Job Knowledge, and Job Performance', *Journal of Vocational Behavior*, 29, 340–62.

Jaynes, G. and Williams, R. (eds) (1989) *A Common Destiny: Blacks in American Society*, Washington, DC: National Academy Press.

Jensen, A. (1980) *Bias in Mental Testing*, New York: The Free Press.

Kaplan, R. (1992) 'Continental Drift', *The New Republic* (28 December), 15–20.

Kozol, J. (1992) *Savage Inequalities*, New York: Harper Collins.

Levin, M. (1994) 'Comment on the Minnesota Transracial Adoption Study', *Intelligence*, 19, 13–20.

Lindgren, B. (1962) *Statistical Theory*, New York: Macmillan.

New York Times (1993) 'Racial Remark Ends a Job Candidacy' (July 29), A21.

Noble, K. (1994) 'Zaire's Rich Mines are Abandoned to Scavengers', *The New York Times* (21 February), A3.

Owen, K. (1992) 'The Suitability of Raven's Standard Progressive Matrices for Various Groups in South Africa', *Personality and Individual Differences*, 13, 149–59.

Rector, R. (1992) *How the Poor Really Live*, Washington, DC: The Heritage Foundation.

Rosenfeld, M. (1991) *Affirmative Action and Justice*, New Haven: Yale University Press.

Ross, R., Bernstein, L., Judd, H., Hanisch, R., Pike, M. and Henderson, B. (1986) 'Serum Testosterone Levels in Healthy, Young Black and White Men', *Journal of the National Cancer Institute*, 76, 45–8.

Rushton, J. (1994) *Race, Evolution and Behaviour*, New Brunswick, NJ: Transaction Books.

Scarr, S. (1981) *Race, Social Class, and Individual Differences in IQ*, Hillside, NJ: Erlbaum.

Shuey, A. (1966) *The Testing of Negro Intelligence*, 2nd edn, New York: Social Science Press.

Taylor, J. (1992) *The Cost of Good Intentions*, New York: Carroll & Graff.

Weinberg, R., Scarr, S. and Waldman, I. (1992) 'The Minnesota Transracial Adoption Study: A Follow-up of IQ Test Performance at Adolescence', *Intelligence*, 16, 117–35.

Whittaker, K. (1990) *Black Victims*, Washington, DC: Bureau of Justice Statistics, Office of Justice Programs, US Department of Justice.

Part III

GAY LIBERATION

7

LESBIAN AND GAY RIGHTS: PRO

Martha Nussbaum

Now in my own cases when I catch a guy like that I just pick him up and take him into the woods and beat him until he can't crawl. I have had seventeen cases like that in the last couple of years. I tell that guy if I catch him doing that again I will take him out to the woods and I will shoot him. I tell him that I carry a second gun on me just in case I find guys like him and that I will plant it in his hand and say that he tried to kill me and that no jury will convict me.

> (Police officer in a large industrial city in the US,
> being interviewed about his treatment of homosexuals;
> Westley, 'Violence and the Police', quoted in
> Comstock, 1991, pp. 90–5)

Whose rights are we talking about when we talk about 'gay rights', and what are the rights in question? I shall take on, first, the surprisingly difficult task of identifying the people. Next, I shall discuss a number of the most important rights that are at issue, including: (1) the right to be protected against violence and, in general, the right to the equal protection of the law; (2) the right to have consensual adult sexual relations without criminal penalty; (3) the right to non-discrimination in housing, employment and education; (4) the right to military service; (5) the right to marriage and/or its legal benefits; (6) the right to retain custody of children and/or to adopt.

WHOSE RIGHTS?

This is no easy question. Legal and political disputes sometimes speak of 'gays and lesbians', sometimes of 'gays' only, sometimes of 'gays, lesbians and bisexuals'. Moreover, there are two different ways of defining these groups, each of which contains an internal plurality of frequently conflicting definitions. One broad class focuses on *conduct*, another on *orientation*.

Conduct first. Frequently, at least in American law, gay and lesbian people are taken to be all and only those people who commit 'sodomy'. Sodomy is usually defined today as a sex act in which the genital organs of one partner make contact with the mouth or anus of the other. (Earlier this was not the case: fellatio is a relatively late addition to US sodomy law and has never been counted 'sodomy' in England: an 1885 statute criminalizing 'gross indecency' between men was added to cover it. Female–female sex acts have never been illegal in Britain.) Obviously, however, this definition is both over-inclusive and underinclusive: underinclusive because many gay males and lesbians have sex but do not commit these acts, especially in the age of AIDS; overinclusive because these acts are extremely common in male–female relations as well. The famous US case *Bowers v. Hardwick*, in which the Supreme Court upheld the constitutionality of a Georgia sodomy law, originally included a heterosexual couple as plaintiffs alongside Hardwick, since the Georgia law as written plainly covered them. (Their case was dismissed for lack of standing, since they were said to be in no danger of prosecution.) At one point, too, Hardwick's lawyers moved to disqualify any member of the Georgia attorney general's office who had ever committed sodomy. Had the motion succeeded, we could have expected a large number of heterosexual disqualifications. (More than seventy per cent of Americans, both male and female, have engaged in heterosexual oral sex during their lifetime; approximately one quarter have engaged in heterosexual anal sex (Laumann *et al.*, 1994).)

More promising, then, would be a definition in terms of the biological sex of the actors: gays and lesbians are all and only those people who commit sex acts with partners of the same biological sex. Once again, however, there are problems: (1) what acts? and (2) how many such acts? Some accounts limit the acts to acts actually terminating in orgasm for one or both parties; some instead include all acts *intended* to induce orgasm in one or both parties (an elusive concept). But given the frequent lack of access to evidence about orgasmic reality or intent, the zeal of the American prosecutorial mind has found other more sweeping categorizations. Thus, the old US Army regulation under which Sgt Perry Watkins, described by his commanding officer as 'one of our most respected and trusted soldiers', was ejected from the military, referred to 'bodily conduct between persons of the same sex, actively undertaken or passively permitted, with the intent to obtain or give sexual gratification'. The act alleged in Watkins' discharge proceedings was described as 'squeezing the knee of another male soldier'. (All through his army career, as well as before it, Watkins publicly declared his sexual identity and practices; but his own evidence was considered insufficient, since he was suspected of trying to avoid military service.) The new US military policy goes still further, defining 'homosexual conduct' as 'a homosexual act, a statement that the member is homosexual or bisexual, or a marriage or attempted marriage to someone of the same gender'; hand-holding and kissing 'in most circumstances' are explicitly mentioned as examples of 'homosexual acts' – though it was determined that a person may visit a gay bar, march in a gay pride rally in civilian clothes or list a person of the same sex as an insurance beneficiary, without thereby committing a homosexual act (*Symposium*, 1993, p. 1802).

Frequently the law has considered the definition in terms of acts unsatisfactory – both because of the evident problem of vagueness and, more significantly, because many people who commit the prohibited acts are not the people against whom policy is really being directed. The US Army, for example, is well aware that many soldiers engage in same-sex sexual acts. (Watkins points out that he never had to approach any one for sex: once his reputation was established, all kinds of men who would never have called themselves 'gay' came to him for oral sex – Humphrey, 1993, p. 370.) So the old policy, while specifying 'homosexual act' in the loose way I have described, actually made the basis for discharge 'homosexual orientation' rather than homosexual acts, used acts only as evidence of orientation and defined 'orientation' in terms of the 'desire' for any of the large menu of acts. (A still larger menu of evidentiary acts is used by the US Department of Defense: in a recent case membership of a gay organization was sufficient to brand one a 'homosexual': cited in Rubenstein, 1993, *High Tech Gays*.)

Since such an account might prove overinclusive – presumably the men who repeatedly asked Watkins for sex desired what they got – Army policy allows that a soldier who has committed a homosexual act may escape discharge if he can show that the conduct was 'a departure from the soldier's usual and customary behavior', that it 'is unlikely to recur because it is shown, for example, that the act occurred because of immaturity, intoxication, coercion, or a desire to avoid military service'. Another section adds 'curiousity' (*sic*) to the list of extenuating motives. The regulation expressly states that 'The intent of this policy is to permit retention *only* of *nonhomosexual* soldiers who, because of extenuating circumstances engaged in, attempted to engage in, or solicited a homosexual act'. (All citations from *Watkins v. United States Army*, original emphasis.) Still, there are problem cases. Think what the Army would say about one lover of Watkins', who, asked why he had sex with Watkins every day, replied, 'Well, I like a good blow job, and the women downtown don't know how to suck dick worth a damn. But this man happens to suck mine better than anyone I have ever found in the world' (Humphreys, 1993, p. 371). We shall never know the Army's verdict, since Watkins did not name names. But the odds are that this man, who considered himself 'straight', would be retained by some reading of the rules. (Curiosity, as Aristotle informs us, is a regular self-renewing part of our human equipment.)

We might suppose that we are dealing here with the stuff of high comedy, or even farce. Such definitions, however, determine the course of many lives, not only in the military; and they create an atmosphere within which the violence endemic to American life can very easily direct itself against these people – whoever, more precisely, they are.

Can we ourselves define the category in a useful way? Any good definition should recognize that sexual orientation is itself multiple and complex. The biological sex of the partner may be just one part of what an individual desires in a partner. In many cultures, both historical and modern, biological sex is traditionally considered less salient than sexual role (e.g. the active or the passive) (Dover, 1986, *passim*; Nussbaum, 1994, *passim*). At the same time few real people would be willing to make love with any willing member of a given sex. Most people's 'orientation' has other desiderata, often inscrutable and complex: persons of a certain ethnic type, or a certain level of intelligence, or a certain way of laughing or a certain resemblance to a parent. In many individuals and cultures, such desiderata are at least as revealing and interesting as biological sex. American culture's focus on the sex of the partners seems no more timeless than its equally obsessive focus on their race. (In the case of both homosexuality and miscegenation it has been similarly argued that 'nature' forbids the unions in question: *Loving v. Virginia*.) However, to be crudely practical, let us define gays, lesbians and bisexuals, the class of persons with a 'homosexual or bisexual orientation' (now the most common formulation in non-discrimination law), as those who stably and characteristically desire to engage in sexual conduct with a member or members of the same sex (whether or not they also desire sexual conduct with the opposite sex) and let us adopt a difficult-to-ascertain but not impossibly broad definition of same-sex conduct, namely that it is bodily conduct intended to lead to orgasm on the part of one or both parties. Notice, then, that we are talking about the rights both of people who frequently perform these acts and also of those who desire to but don't. 'Stably and characteristically' is tricky still, but perhaps we can live with it, knowing that it excludes a person who experimented a few times in adolescence, or who hasn't desired such conduct for a good many years. On the other hand it includes people who regularly have sex with partners of both sexes, the so-called bisexuals. This definition clearly includes all the people against whom the Army policies are directed. Does it also include Watkins' friend, whom the Army would probably wish to retain? I think it should – he had regular access to women, but still repeatedly chose Watkins; on the other hand, notice that his desire, completely impersonal and self-referential, had little to do with Watkins' sex, – so he is in that way different from a person who has an actual *preference* for a partner of a certain sex. (It seems a bit odd for the Army to prefer him to Watkins, if indeed it would, just on the grounds of the total non-selectivity of his desire.) This definition, though it seems the best available at present, embodies no real understanding of people, and seems grossly inadequate as a conceptual basis for interference with real people's lives.

Why are lesbian and gay people as they are? (This question is rarely asked about heterosexuals, since that way of being is assumed to be neutral and natural.) Few questions in this area are more hotly disputed. There is considerable evidence in favour of some kind of biological explanation for sexual preference, though there are serious flaws with all the research done until now. But one thing that seems clear is that sexual orientation, if not innate, is formed very early in life, certainly before the age of ten, and after that time proves highly resistant to change, despite all the countless therapies that have been devised to change it. (It may, of course, not be exclusive, and, especially in these cases, it may alter with stages of life.) Another thing that is becoming increasingly clear from empirical research is that a child's sexual orientation is not a function of that of its parents or guardians (Posner, 1992, p. 418).

WHAT RIGHTS?

The right to be protected against violence

Gays, lesbians and bisexuals are targets of violence in America. Twenty-four per cent of gay men and ten per cent of lesbians, in a recent survey, reported some form of criminal assault because of their sexual orientation during the past year (as compared to general population assault rates in a comparable urban area of four per cent for women and six per cent for men). A Massachusetts study found that twenty-one per cent of lesbian and gay students, compared to five per cent of the entire student body, report having been physically attacked. An average of five recent US non-college surveys on anti-gay/lesbian violence show that thirty-three per cent of those surveyed had been chased or followed, twenty-three per cent had had objects thrown at them, eighteen per cent had been punched, hit, kicked or beaten, sixteen per cent had been victims of vandalism or arson, seven per cent had been spat on, and seven per cent had been assaulted with a weapon (data from Comstock, 1991, pp. 31–55). To live as a gay or lesbian in America is thus to live with fear. As one might expect, such violence is not unknown in the military. Most famous, but not unique, was the 1992 death of navy radioman Allen Schindler at the hands of three of his shipmates who, unprovoked, stalked and then fatally beat him – and later blamed their crime on the presence of gays in the military.

Who are the perpetrators? They are more likely than average assault perpetrators are to be strangers to their victims. Ninety-four per cent of them are male (as compared with eighty-seven per cent for comparable crimes of violence); forty-six per cent are under twenty-two years of age (as compared with twenty-nine per cent for comparable crimes); sixty-seven per cent are white. They do not typically exhibit what are customarily thought of as criminal attitudes. 'Many conform to or are models of middle-class respectability' (Comstock, 1991, pp. 91–2). The arresting officer in a Toronto incident in which five youths beat a forty-year old gay man to death remarked, 'If you went to [a shopping mall] and picked up any group of young males about the same age as these boys – that is what they were like. Average' (Comstock, 1991, p. 93). The data suggest that gay-beatings, including the most lethal, are often in essence 'recreational': groups of adolescent men, bored and intoxicated, seek out gays not so much because they have a deep-seated hatred of them as because they recognize that this is a group society has agreed to dislike and not to protect fully (Comstock, 1991, p. 94). A California perpetrator of multiple anti-gay beatings, interviewed by Comstock, cited as reasons for his acts boredom, the desire for adventure, a belief in the wrongness of homosexuality and, finally, attraction to the men he and his friends attacked. He told Comstock that '[we] were probably attacking something within ourselves' (Comstock, 1991, pp. 171–2).

Physical assaults are crimes as defined by the laws of every state in the US. In that sense, the right to be protected against them is a right that gays and lesbians have already. But there is ample evidence that the police often fail to uphold these rights. They may indeed actively perpetrate violence against gays, in unduly violent behavior during vice arrests, etc. Such violence is illegal if it exceeds the requirements of arrest, but it is widely practiced. Even more common is the failure of police to come promptly to the aid of gays and lesbians who are being assaulted. A Canadian study finds that in fifty-six per cent of cases in which gays sought police protection the behaviour of the responding officers was 'markedly unsatisfactory' (Comstock, 1991, pp. 151–62).

In numerous US jurisdictions, moreover, killers of gays have successfully pleaded 'reasonable provocation', alleging that the revulsion occasioned by a (non-coercive and non-violent) homosexual advance, or even by witnessing gay sexual acts, justified a homicidal response; there is no corresponding tradition of a 'heterosexual advance' defence. In a 1990 Pennsylvania case in which a drifter murdered two lesbians whom he saw making love in the woods, the court refused to allow this defence, saying that the law 'does not recognize homosexual activity between two persons as legal provocation sufficient to reduce an unlawful killing . . . from murder to voluntary manslaughter' (*Commonwealth v. Carr*). This is, however, the exception rather than the rule (Mison, 1992).

There is a good case for linking rights involving protection against violence to other facets of gay experience as yet not universally recognized. As long as no laws protect gays against discrimination in other areas of life and guarantee their equal citizenship, as long as their sex acts can be criminalized, as long they are disparaged as second-class citizens, we may expect the rights they do have to go on being underenforced, and violence against them to remain a common fact.

My discussion of violence has not addressed the emotional violence done to lesbians and gay people by the perception that they are hated and despised. This issue too can be addressed by law and public policy; for by enacting non-discrimination laws (such as the law recently enacted in my home state of Massachusetts, which forbids discrimination against lesbian and gay students in the school system) one can begin to alter the behaviour that causes this harm. Perhaps eventually one may alter attitudes themselves.

The right to have consensual adult sexual relations without criminal penalty

Consensual sexual relations between adult males were decriminalized in Britain in 1967. In the US, five states still criminalize only same-sex sodomy, while eighteen statutes (including the Uniform Code of Military Justice) criminalize sodomy for all. Five state sodomy laws have recently been judicially repealed, and, in addition, a Massachusetts law prohibiting 'unnatural and lascivious act[s]'. (But Massachusetts still has another law prohibiting 'crime against nature', *Symposium*, 1993, p. 1774.) These laws are rarely enforced, but such enforcement as there is is highly selective, usually against same-sex conduct. Penalties are not negligible: the maximum penalty for consensual sodomy in Georgia is twenty years' imprisonment.

Although sodomy laws are, as I have argued, both under and over-inclusive for same-sex conduct, it is frequently assumed that sodomy defines gay or lesbian sexual life. Thus the laws, in addition to their use in targeting the consensual activities of actual sodomites, can also be used to discriminate against gay and lesbian individuals who have never been shown to engage in the practices in question – as when Robin Shahar lost her job in the Georgia Attorney General's office for announcing a lesbian marriage. It was claimed that she could not be a reliable enforcer of the state's sodomy statute (*Shahar v. Bowers*). (All heterosexual intercourse outside marriage is criminal 'fornication' in Georgia, and yet there is no evidence that Bowers ever denied employment to heterosexual violators of either that law or the sodomy law.)

The case against sodomy laws is strong. Rarity of enforcement creates a problem of arbitrary and selective police behaviour. Although neither all nor only homosexuals are sodomites, the laws are overwhelmingly used to target them; and the fact that some of their acts remain criminal is closely connected with the perception that they are acceptable targets of violence and with other social exclusions as well. For example, '[t]here is . . . a natural reluctance

... to appoint to judicial positions people who have committed hundreds or even thousands of criminal acts' (Posner, 1992, p. 311) – unjustified as this reluctance may be, and also arbitrary, given that the judiciary is no doubt full of heterosexual perpetrators of sodomy and criminal fornication. (Laumann shows that the frequency of both oral and anal sex among heterosexuals increases with level of education, Laumann *et al.*, 1994.)

Most important, such adult consensual sexual activity does no harm. There is thus no public benefit to offset the evident burdens these laws impose. As Judge Posner concludes, such laws 'express an irrational fear and loathing of a group that has been subjected to discrimination' (1992, p. 346). We have no need of such laws in a country all too full of incitements to violence.

Should the age of consent be the same for same-sex as for opposite-sex activity? I am inclined to think that, in current American and European nations, 16 is a reasonable age for both. The biggest problem with age of consent law generally is the failure to discriminate between the act of two 15-year-olds and an act between a 30-year-old and a 15-year-old. In both same and opposite-sex relations, the law should (and often does) address itself to this issue.

The right to be free from discrimination in housing, employment and education

Gays, lesbians and bisexuals suffer discrimination in housing and employment. Many US states and local communities have responded to this situation by adopting non-discrimination laws. (Such laws have for some time been in effect in some European countries and in some Australian states.) Recently in the US, efforts have also been made to prevent local communities from so legislating, through referenda amending the state's constitution to forbid the passage of such a local law. The most famous example is that of Amendment 2 in the State of Colorado, which nullified anti-discrimination laws in three cities in the state, and prevented the passage of any new ones. I believe that there is no good argument for discrimination against gays and lesbians in housing and employment. (The repeated suggestion that such protection against discrimination would lead to quotas for this group and would therefore injure the prospects of other minorities was especially invidious and misleading; none of the local ordinances had even suggested quota policies.)

Along with the Supreme Court of Colorado (when it upheld a preliminary injunction against the law, laying the legal basis for the trial court judgement that found the law unconstitutional), I would make a further point. Such referenda, by depriving gays and lesbians of the right to organize at the local level to secure the passage of laws that protect them, thereby deprive them of equality with respect to the fundamental right of political participation. They, and they alone, have to amend the state constitution in order to pass a fair housing law in some town. Similar state laws have long been declared unconstitutional in the area of race. I believe that they are morally repugnant in this area as well.

The most serious issue that arises with regard to non-discrimination laws is that of religious freedom. Both institutions and individuals may sincerely believe that to be required to treat lesbians and gays as equal candidates for jobs (or as equal prospective tenants) is to be deprived of the freedom to exercise their religion. This argument seems more pertinent to some occupations than others. To hire someone as a teacher may plausibly be seen as conferring a certain role-model status on that person; to hire someone as an accountant can hardly be seen in this light. And it is not clear to me that a landlord's religious freedom is compromised by being forced to consider on an equal basis tenants he may deem immoral. (The US Supreme Court recently refused to hear an appeal of an Alaska decision against a landlord who refused to rent on religious grounds to an unmarried heterosexual couple.)

Various responses are possible. The Denver statute exempted religious organizations from its non-discrimination provisions. The American Philosophical Association refused to exempt religious institutions from its (non-binding) non-discrimination policy for hiring and promotion, except in the case of discrimination on the basis of religious membership. I believe that we should combine these two approaches: religious organizations should in some cases be allowed greater latitude to follow their own beliefs; but in publicly funded and in large professional organizations, with sexuality as with race, freedom to discriminate should be limited by shared requirements of justice. I recognize, however, that many people of good faith with deep religious convictions are likely to disagree.

Even in the sensitive area of education, there is no evidence to show that the presence of gay and lesbian teachers harms children or adolescents. Gays are at least no more likely, and in some studies less likely to molest children than are heterosexual males; nor is there evidence to show that knowing or respecting a gay person has the power to convert children to homosexuality (any more than being taught by heterosexuals has converted gay youths to heterosexuality). The sexual harassment of students or colleagues should be dealt with firmly wherever it occurs. Beyond that, what one's colleagues do in bed should be irrelevant to their employment.

One further educational issue remains: this is the right to have opportunities to learn about lesbian and gay people. This right is of special interest to lesbian and gay students, but it is also, importantly, a right of all students, all of whom are citizens and need to learn something about their fellow citizens, especially as potential voters in referenda such as the one in Colorado. The study of homosexuality – historical, psychological, sociological, legal, literary – is now a burgeoning field of research. Do students of various ages have the right to learn about this work? In the US the First Amendment makes a flat prohibition of such teaching unlikely (not impossible, since the First Amendment is not binding on private institutions), though teachers may be subtly penalized for introducing such material into their courses. In Britain, a 1986 law forbids local government to 'intentionally promote homosexuality or publish material with the intention of promoting homosexuality' or to 'promote the teaching in any maintained school of the acceptability of homosexuality as a pretended family relationship' (Local Government Act 1986, cited in *Symposium*, 1993, p. 7). This law would very likely be unconstitutional in the US. It is also, I think, morally repugnant for several reasons. First, it inhibits the freedom of enquiry. Second, it inhibits the freedom of political debate. Third, it creates just the sort of atmosphere of taboo and disgust that fosters discrimination and violence against gays and lesbians. Furthermore, I believe it to be counterproductive to the proponents' own ostensible goals of fostering morality as they understand it. For a moral doctrine to announce publicly that it needs to be backed up by informational restrictions of this sort is a clear confession of weakness. And Judge Richard Posner has cogently argued that such policies actually increase the likelihood that gay sex will be casual and promiscuous, presumably something the law's partisans wish to avoid. Deprived of the chance to learn about themselves in any way other than through action, Posner argues, young gay people will in all likelihood choose action earlier than they might have otherwise (Posner, 1992, p. 302). The atmosphere of concealment also makes courtship and dating difficult – so 'they will tend to substitute the sex act, which can be performed in a very short time and in private, for courtship, which is public and protracted' (Posner, 1992, p. 302).

The right to military service

It is clear enough that gays and lesbians can serve with distinction in the military, since many of them have done so (Shilts, 1992, *passim*; Posner, 1992, p. 317). Furthermore, the armies of quite a few nations have successfully integrated open homosexuals into the service: France, Germany, Israel, Switzerland, Sweden, Denmark, Norway, Finland, the Netherlands, Belgium, Australia, Spain and recently Canada. As Posner writes, 'The idea that homosexuals will not or cannot fight seems a canard, on a par with the idea that Jews or blacks will not or cannot fight' (Posner, 1992, p. 317). Nor are they security risks, if they openly announce their homosexuality. Nor are they to be excluded because they might commit acts of sexual harassment. (If this were so, in the wake of recent sexual harassment scandals in the US military we should first exclude all heterosexual males.) Sexual harassment should be dealt with firmly wherever it occurs; this has nothing to do with our issue.

The real issue that keeps coming up is that heterosexual males do not want to be forced to associate intimately with gay males, especially to be seen naked by them. The psychology of this intense fear of the gaze of the homosexual is interesting. (It has even been attempted as a legal defence in gay-bashing cases, under the description 'homosexual panic'.) This fear may have something to do with the idea expressed by Comstock's gay-basher, when he perceptively noted that his aggression assailed something within himself. It may also be connected with the thought that this man will look at me in the way I look at a woman – i.e. not in a respectful or personal way, but a way that says 'I want to fuck you' – and that this gaze will somehow humiliate me. What should be noted, however, is that this fear goes away when it needs to, and quite quickly too. As a frequenter of health clubs, I note that in that setting both males and females undress all the time in front of other patrons, many of whom they can be sure are gay; frequently it is clear through conversation who the gays and lesbians are. Nonetheless, we do not observe an epidemic of muscular failure. Straight men do not leap off the treadmill or drop their barbells in panic. They know they cannot root out and eject these people, so they forget about the issue. Moving on, we note that openly gay officers have been included in the police forces of New York City, Chicago, San Francisco, Los Angeles and probably others by now, without incident. During wartime, moreover, when the need for solidarity and high morale is greatest, toleration of gay and lesbian soldiers has gone up, not down (see Shilts, 1992). It seems likely that gays could be integrated relatively painlessly into the US Armed Forces, if firm leadership were given from the top. The unfortunate fact, however, is that, here as with the harassment of women, high-ranking officers do not give the requisite leadership. As Judge Posner writes, 'it is terrible to tell people they are unfit to serve their country, unless they really are unfit, which is not the case here' (Posner, 1992, p. 321).

The right to marriage and/or the legal and social benefits of marriage

Gays and lesbians in Denmark, Sweden and Norway can form a registered partnership that gives all the tax, inheritance and other civic benefits of marriage; similar legislation is soon to be passed in Finland. Many businesses, universities and other organizations within other nations, including the US, have extended their marriage benefits to registered same-sex domestic partners. Gay marriage is currently a topic of intense debate in Judaism and in every major branch of Christianity.

Why are marriage rights important to gays? Legally, marriage is a source of many benefits, including favourable tax, inheritance and insurance status; immigration rights; custody rights; the right to collect unemployment benefits if one partner quits a job to move to be where his or her partner has found employment; the spousal privilege exception when giving testimony; the right to bring a wrongful death action upon the negligent death of a spouse; the right to the privileges of next-of-kin in hospital visitations, decisions about burial, etc. (Mohr, 1994, pp. 72–3, Nava and Dawidoff, 1994, p. 155, citing Hawaii Sup. Ct, *Baehr v. Lewin*). Many gays and lesbians have discovered in the most painful way that they lack these rights, although they may have lived together loyally for years.

Emotionally and morally, being able to enter a legally recognized form of marriage means the opportunity to declare publicly an intent to live in commitment and partnership. Although many lesbian and gay people consider themselves married and have frequently solemnized their commitment in ceremonies not recognized by the state, they still seek to do so in a recognized manner, because they attach importance to the public recognition of their union.

As the Norwegian Ministry of Children and Family Affairs writes, supporting Norway's 1993 law: 'It can be detrimental for a person to have to suppress fundamental feelings concerning attachment and love for another person. Distancing oneself from these feelings or attempts to suppress them may destroy one's self-respect' (Norwegian Act on Registered Partnerships for Homosexual Couples, 1993). Noting that ninety-two per cent of gays and lesbians polled in a comprehensive Swedish survey were either part of a registered couple or stated that they would like to be, the Ministry concluded that the primary obstacle to stable marital unions in the gay community is 'negative attitudes from the social environment'.

These seem to be very plausible views. And yet gay marriage is widely opposed. On what grounds? On what account of marriage is it an institution that should remain closed to lesbians and gay men? The basis of marriage in the US and Europe is generally taken to be a stated desire to live together in intimacy, love and partnership, and to support one another, materially and emotionally, in the conduct of daily life. Of course many people enter marriage unprepared, and many marriages fail; but the law cannot and should not undertake a stringent enquiry into the character and behaviour of the parties before admitting them to the benefits of that status.

Many people do believe that a central purpose of marriage is to have and educate children. But (apart from the fact that many lesbian and gay people do have and raise children, whether their own from previous unions or conceived by artificial insemination within the relationship) nobody has seriously suggested denying marriage rights to post-menopausal women, to sterile individuals of any age or to people who simply know (and state) that they don't want children and won't have them. It therefore seems flatly inconsistent and unjust to deny these rights to other individuals who wish to form exactly this type of committed yet childless union.

No doubt the extension of marriage rights to gays and lesbians will change the way we think about 'the family'. On the other hand, 'the family' has never been a single thing in western, far less in world, history, and its nuclear heterosexual form has been associated with grave problems of child abuse and gender inequality, so there is no reason to sentimentalize it as a morally perfect institution. Studies have shown that homosexual households have a more equal division of domestic labour than heterosexual ones (Blumstein and Schwartz,

1983). So they may even have valuable contributions to make to our understanding of what personal commitment and marital fairness are.

The right to retain custody of children and/or to adopt

Gays and lesbians have and raise children. In a 1970s California survey, twenty per cent of male homosexuals and more than a third of female homosexuals have been married (Posner, 1992, p. 417), and many of those have had children. Lesbian couples can have children through artificial insemination or sex with a male; a gay man can obtain a child through some sort of surrogacy arrangement. Should these things be (or remain) legal? Experience shows that children raised in homosexual households showed no differences from other groups, either in sexual orientation or in general mental health or social adjustment. Indeed, there was evidence that children raised by an unmarried heterosexual woman had more psychological problems than others (Posner, 1992, p. 418). We need more research on these issues, clearly; samples have been small and have covered a relatively short time-span. But so far there is no evidence to justify a court in removing a child from its parent's custody on the grounds that he or she is living in a homosexual union. If one were to argue that such a child will inevitably be the target of social prejudice, no matter how well its parent is doing, it seems plausible that the Constitution will intervene to block that argument. In a 1984 case, *Palmore v. Sidoti*, in which a child was removed from its (white) mother's custody because she had remarried to a black man – grounds for change of custody being that such a child will suffer from public racial prejudice – the US Supreme Court returned custody to the child's mother, holding that the law may not give public legitimacy to private prejudices. This case was cited as a precedent in a 1985 Alaska decision granting custody to a gay parent (Mison, 1992, p. 175). In general, it seems especially important that children should not be removed from the custody of parents who love and care for them successfully, without compelling reason.

As for adoption and foster-parenting, I concur with Judge Posner that courts should take a case-by-case approach, rejecting a flat ban. Frequently, especially where foster-parenting is concerned, such a placement might be a child's best chance for a productive home life (Posner, 1992, p. 420). Once again, the reason for refusing a homosexual couple must not be the existence of public prejudice against homosexuality; and yet, no feature intrinsic to homosexuality as such has been demonstrated to have a detrimental effect on children.

COUNTERARGUMENTS: SCRUTON

It is frequently held, against gay rights of various sorts, that gay sex relationships are unusually likely to be promiscuous and/or superficial. This has rarely been claimed about lesbian relationships. But the image of the gay male bathhouse has often been paraded before voters as a scare image. What should we say about this?

To begin with, we have no reliable data. The only data about sexual behaviour in America that are even remotely reliable are those in the recent Laumann/Chicago survey (Laumann *et al.*, 1994). Because of funding difficulties resulting from conservative Congressional opposition to the study, Laumann could not study a large enough sample of homosexuals to draw conclusions about their number of sex partners. His results show, however, that many if not most common beliefs in this general area are false, and that most types of people have far fewer sex partners than popular belief supposes. (The alleged promiscuity of black males, for example, turns out to be a complete myth: black males and white males have exactly the same number of lifetime sexual partners.)

One might well hold that a person's promiscuity is not the business of the law, unless he harms others, and should not have any relevance to deliberations about basic legal rights. But large numbers of people do think that the alleged connection between male homosexuality and promiscuity is pertinent to deliberations about such rights as the rights to marriage and adoption, and perhaps certain employment rights as well. So we should address these concerns.

First of all, we should insist that straight men are allowed to get married and to obtain the legal, emotional and religious benefits of marriage; gay men are not, and their stable committed unions have to fight against public denial and opprobrium. Furthermore, no evidence about the behaviour of a group that is currently the target of social opprobrium and violence is a very reliable predictor of the way in which those same people would behave in better social circumstances.

Next, we have to note that we are talking about males raised in a culture that has generally taught men to value self-sufficiency and the uncommitted state, women to value intimacy and commitment. It is not surprising that sometimes putting two males together doubles the 'maleness' of the relationship – but should that be blamed on the same-sex character of the relationship, or its maleness? And is the remedy to be found (if one is wanted) in yet more measures against same-sex individuals, or in the reformation of the moral education of males?

In general, like any statistical argument, this cannot serve as a justification for denying any right to an entire group. If the mobility and assembly rights of all males were curtailed on the ground that males commit a high proportion of our society's violent crimes, we would view that as an outrage. So we should repudiate any attempt to deny rights to gays on grounds of the (alleged) promiscuity of some or even many gays. If the law wishes to discourage promiscuity, there are steps that can be taken without removing anyone's civil rights: tax incentives for married couples, public rhetoric of a hortatory sort, above all the legalization of gay and lesbian marriage. There is no need to target a group already targeted. It is inaccurate, and it is unjust.

An interesting variant of this argument, focusing on superficiality rather than promiscuity, has been made by my opponent Roger Scruton (Scruton, 1986, pp. 305–10). Scruton's argument is a pleasure to approach because it is expressed with a tentativeness and a lack of venom rare in these matters. The argument is as follows: when one makes love with someone of the opposite gender, one is dealing with a different, mysterious world; by contrast, the world of one's own gender is familiar and well known. (Scruton seems to me to give people undue credit for self-knowledge.) The willingness to put one's being at risk in the midst of a world so profoundly other is morally valuable and imparts depth to the relationship; same-sex relationships lack this risky openness, and this is connected with their (alleged) greater superficiality. This may help us to see that male gay sex (Scruton explicitly exempts lesbian relationships) is, if not perverted or depraved, still morally inferior.

A number of problems arise. First, Scruton uses the unclear notion of 'gender', rather than the somewhat clearer notion of biological sex. This is important, since knowing one's own gender is supposed to be a matter of not just knowing what it's like to have a certain sort of genital organ, but of knowing a whole way of being in the world. But even within a single culture, most individuals will find in themselves in both conformity and non-conformity with any list of gender attributes one might construct. And even if one's attributes on the whole conform to the stereotype, one need not find the other gender's world unfamiliar, if one works with many people of that gender and has intimate friendships with some of them. I suspect, in fact, that Scruton's idea that the world of the female is mysterious to men (an idea I have heard from quite a number of men) is not easily separable from its cultural context, in which single-sex education and the sparse representation of women in the professions have made it hard for men to have female friends.

Next, the argument is more sweeping than Scruton appears to realize, in two ways. First, if we follow it we shall be led to find superior moral value in any relationship in which a barrier of experiential difference is crossed. This ought to mean that relationships between the Chinese and the British, or the sighted and the blind or the aged and the youthful, have greater moral value than relationships between two Britons or two sighted people or two young people. I doubt that Scruton would actually hold this. I think Scruton is actually thinking not of qualitative differences of this sort, but of the mystery of intimacy with any world that is separate from one's own. But that is a challenge that exists in any intimate human relationship.

Second, if we really direct disapproval against those who are (for whatever reason) unwilling to be vulnerable and at risk in their sexual relationships, preferring contacts of a superficial sort, we will have to exclude from the targeted group many homosexuals, both female and male, and include many heterosexuals, well exemplified by Watkins' satisfied friend, whose desires were as superficial and narcissistic as anyone's could be. Indeed, attitudes just this self-centred, and even more possessive, have been common attitudes of men toward women throughout much of history.

Would it make any sense to say that people inclined to superficiality in sex could not serve in the armed forces? The US Navy's shameful Tailhook scandal (in which crude harassment of women was revealed as endemic to naval life) shows the broad sweep of promiscuous attitudes about sex, even at the highest levels of the services. Indeed, it appears that such attitudes are actively encouraged, in order to promote male group solidarity. It seems pathetic to lay all this at the door of the one group that is not allowed to serve and can least be blamed for the current situation. Where marriage rights are concerned, it might make *moral* sense to dissuade a person prone to superficial sexual contacts from marrying, given the likelihood that the partner might be disappointed. But surely this makes no *political* sense as a basis for the denial of the marriage licence. The enquiries that would then be required would be unmanageable and incredibly prone to abuse, vindictive ex-spouses offering testimony about their ex's superficial attitudes and his unwillingness to be 'at risk' toward the 'other', all to impede a marriage to the hated rival. Or, if a putative statistical correlation between (male) homosexuality and superficiality should be used as criterial, why not deny marriage licences to all males, on the grounds that they are far more likely than females to abuse their children? This is surely worse than superficiality. Where adoption is concerned, certainly let us look hard at the life of the individual couple – but let us look at the *individual* couple, and not assume beforehand what is perfectly false, that all and only same-sex couples are unsuitable. (Scruton already concedes the suitability of female couples, thus casting doubt on whether his argument is really about homosexuality at all.)

So: I think Scruton's argument gets at something deep about sex, when we take him to be talking about separateness or 'otherness' rather than mere qualitative difference. But the argument seems to have no bearing on the legal issues before us.

I believe that the rights of lesbians and gays are a central issue of justice for our time. It is my hope that fifty years from now the current situation of this group of citizens will look just as irrational and as repugnant to a shared sense of justice as the situation of blacks in America in 1950 now looks to virtually all of us.

8

GAY RESERVATIONS

Roger Scruton

There is a certain way of discussing sex, highly developed in America, but regarded with suspicion elsewhere, which summarizes the great matter of *eros* in a set of statistics and a bill of rights. The statistics are often phoney, the rights invariably liberal. And if the resulting morality is offensive to the conservative conscience, this seldom troubles those who propose it. On the contrary, it is the conservative conscience – the conscience which is prepared to condemn a great many of our erotic adventures in the interests of an idea of normal conduct – which appears as the villain in the story, the artificer of those 'mind-forg'd manacles' from which the new morality promises to free us.

If the issue of gay liberation is to be rightly understood, it must be seen as one 'moment' in the confrontation, not merely between an old and a new morality, but between an old and a new way of describing sex. The new language robs desire of its intentionality, and therefore of its essence. Instead it offers 'neutral' descriptions in which sexual organs occupy the foreground, and *eros* slinks in shame away. These descriptions provide a constant pornographic background, a reminder that, since sex is 'nothing but' the pumping and throbbing of those once embarrassing glands (embarrassing only because we decked them out with needless scruples), it would be absurd to prohibit its expression. But sex is altered with its own representation; as people acquire the taste for these new descriptions, so does sexual feeling change. We move towards a new human being, for whom a bill of rights contains the sum of sexual prohibitions, since all prohibitions are really permissions seen from the other side. The question is whether this new human being is viable: by which I mean not merely whether he is capable of reproducing his kind, but whether he is able to build a durable community, and a set of institutions, within which to seek and find his happiness. Professor Nussbaum does not answer this question; but then, nor does she raise it.

MILL, ARISTOTLE AND NUSSBAUM

The new morality has its origins in nineteenth-century liberalism, and in particular in John Stuart Mill's attempt to distinguish the private sphere of morality from the public sphere of law. If sexual activity is private (and what could be more private than our private parts?) then we have a legal right to engage in it, provided that we do no harm. Mill, who made the term 'harm' pivotal to his legal philosophy, never stooped to explain what he meant by it – and in consequence gave a hostage to fortune that his critics were quick to seize. Even so, in removing conduct from the sphere of legal prohibition, Mill did not intend to erase whatever moral stigma had attached to it, or to extend a permission more firmly rooted in our nature than a mere right in law. In modern America, however, where the entire business of social existence has been handed over to the law-courts, which have in consequence become the battle-ground for disputes which judges have no special competence to settle, questions of morality are invariably recast in legal form. Once it is discovered that we have a right (whether by statute, by common law or by the constitution) to do X, then all prohibition is at an end. Moreover, if there is a legal right to do X, there must be a right to encourage others to do likewise, to spread the good news of this permission, and to advocate the 'alternative lifestyle' of which X is the proud expression. That, it seems to me, is the gist of Professor Nussbaum's argument.

Nevertheless, it comes as a surprise to find that a philosopher, writing some one hundred and twenty years after Sir James Fitzjames Stephen's devastating criticism of Mill, could dismiss laws that forbid sodomy in the following un-nuanced words: 'Most important, such adult consensual sexual activity does no harm. There is thus no public benefit to offset the evident burdens these laws impose' (p. 97). It is not merely that these words, written in the era of AIDS, give a distinct impression of somnambulism; nor is it merely that they are left to stand as a bare assertion, without so much as a gesture of proof. It is also that they suggest a style of moral philosophy which flies in the face all that Nussbaum has elsewhere defended. The reader of *The Fragility of Goodness* and *Love's Knowledge* would have come away with the conviction that Nussbaum is some kind of Aristotelian, acutely aware that moral philosophy points us towards an idea of virtue, and therefore towards a theory of human nature, and of the ways and means whereby, knowingly or not, we frustrate or fulfil our lives as rational beings. It is not sufficient for us to be furnished with a set of permissions; we need dispositions that will guide us through the vale of chance, and prompt us not merely to choose what fulfils us, but also to know it as good and to want it for that very reason. As she rightly maintains, it is one of the glories of western literature that it points us towards those habits of perception, judgement and desire which are the core of virtue. And it is worth adding here (since the liberal conscience needs constantly to be reminded) that most people are neither students of philosophy nor open to the influence of the high culture which has nourished her (and my) emotions. Hence they stand in need of some other guide than these inconstant and garrulous companions – a guide which, whether in the form of religious scruples or of old-fashioned decency, will almost certainly be prodigal of prohibitions, and perhaps not so far removed from the conservative conscience which speaks audibly, if faintly, from her more judicious pages. Certainly, the Nussbaum who discusses Plato, Henry James and Aeschylus would be loath to write, in this *a priori* and unthinking way, about the 'harm' of sexual conduct – as though we had some means of estimating such a thing, without a reasoned philosophy of vice and virtue.

THE NEW LANGUAGE

My argument, however, is not *ad hominem*. I wish to begin from the question of language; and in doing so I shall be confronting not Nussbaum only but the entire culture which speaks through her, and which has so effectively begged the question of sexual morality in its favour. Putting Nussbaum's argument to one side, I consider instead one of the authorities to whom she defers: Judge Richard Posner, whose *Sex and Reason* typifies the approach to human sexuality that Nussbaum seems to espouse.

Posner wishes to subsume sex under the sole theory of practical reason that he acknowledges – namely economics, conceived as the analysis of rational choice under risk and uncertainty. Hence he describes sex as a commodity, the pursuit of which is rational whenever the benefit outweighs the cost. For Posner, therefore, the moments of measurable excitement begin to take on a supreme importance, so much so that he builds them into his very description of sexual conduct. His first chapter opens with the following sentence: 'There is sexual behaviour, having to do mainly with excitation of the sexual organs' (1992, p.13). Concerning this excitation, Judge Posner is something of an expert, having pursued his researches through countless statistical reports and studies, the unwitting comedy of which informs his many footnotes. In reality sexual behaviour has to do with courtship, desire, love, jealousy, marriage, grief, joy and intrigue. Such excitement as occurs is excitement of the whole person. As for the sexual organs, they can be as 'excited' (if that is the word) by a bus journey as by the object of desire. Nevertheless, it seems to me, Posner's simplifying language is essential to his aim: only if sexual desire is shorn of its intentionality (and so brought down from the realm of emotion to that of sensation) will it yield to the utilitarian reasoning which, for Posner, is the only form of practical deliberation that exists. The ends of sexual activity, he says, are 'procreative, hedonistic, and sociable', and the hedonistic rewards of sex he compares to 'scratching an itch, or to drinking water when one is thirsty' (Posner, 1992, p. 111). This recalls the Socrates of Xenophon's *Memorabilia*: 'Socrates . . . said he thought Critias was no better off than a pig if he wanted to scratch himself against Euthydemus as piglets against a stone' (i, 229 f). We recognize in that picture of Critias' lust not true desire, but one of its infantile perversions. When John desires Mary he does not seek to 'scratch the itch' of his sexual excitement. For in that case why choose Mary? Why not Elizabeth, Henry or anything else at hand – a rubber doll say?

Well, why not? Certainly, if desire is the thing that Posner describes, there can be no conceivable distinction between its normal and its perverted expression, no conceivable place for desire in personal relations other than as a kind of hospitality – like that offered by Nussbaum's Sergeant Watkins to the person whom she chooses to describe as his 'friend' (on the incredible ground that he regularly used Watkins, or rather Watkins' mouth, as a means to his narcissistic pleasure). This latter-day Critias is a pervert – not because he uses a man, rather than a woman, in order to excite his sexual organs, but precisely because he *uses* someone, in order to *excite* his *sexual organs* – in other words, precisely because Posner's description of sexual conduct is an accurate description of what he does. Moreover, as the soldier's testimony indicates, he himself thinks of sex in just this way – he is a graduate of the sexological culture, whose desires have been shaped by the language which comes as naturally to him as it comes to Kinsey and Posner. And that is one reason *why*, for him, the sexual act has been divorced from its inter-personal intentionality, and has ceased to be an expression of an interpersonal desire. Take him through a class in economics, and he would discover himself in Posner, who describes the 'costs' of sexual gratification in language like this:

> One is the cost of search. It is zero for masturbation, consid-ered as a solitary activity, which is why it is the cheapest of practices. (The qualification is important: 'mutual masturba-tion', heterosexual or homosexual, is a form of nonvaginal intercourse, and its search costs are positive.)
>
> (1992, pp. 119–20)

Posner proceeds to consider hypothetical cases: for example, the case where a man sets a 'value' of 'twenty' on 'sex' with a 'woman of average attractiveness', and a 'value' of 'two' on 'sex' with a 'male substitute' (1992, p. 121). In this way, by constructing a slightly mad, and in any case perverted, fiction in the place of normal sexual desire, Posner is able to endorse the implicit *Weltanschauung* of Watkins' 'friend', and to persuade himself that ordinary procedures of economic reasoning might explain and justify the vast expendi-ture of human energy on this pursuit, which his language, however, makes quite incomprehensible.

Professor Nussbaum is entitled to cite whichever authority she should choose. But I am struck by the fact that, just as she unthink-ingly adopts the discredited language of John Stuart Mill, so does she find no reason to distance herself from that of Posner. If you consider the words that I quoted – the numerical 'value' attached to 'sex' with a 'woman of average attractiveness', for whom, however, there might be a (male) 'substitute' – you will begin to marvel that a woman, and a feminist, could tolerate the soul that uttered them. Here, in all its raw untutored nastiness, is the view of woman (and man too) as 'sex object', of sex as a 'commodity' and of the human being in his abject, instrumentalized and alienated condition, as a slave of sensory pleasure. It is the job of a philosopher in our time not to endorse Posner's language, but to interrogate the mind that finds nothing wrong with it. It seems, however, that Nussbaum is so steeped in the sexological culture that she too finds nothing wrong. Thus she defines 'same-sex conduct' as 'bodily conduct intended to lead to orgasm on the part of one or both parties': a definition which has just the effect of Posner's bleak descriptions, in reducing sexual desire to a pursuit (whether alone or in company) of the sexual commodity. It is perhaps true that my *Sexual Desire* was a *mega kakon*; nevertheless, I am surprised that someone who has read that book should fail to understand sexual arousal as the core component in the expression of desire, and fail to see that arousal is already an interpersonal reaction, with the epistemic intentionality that raises it from the sensory to the moral sphere.

However, an explanation occurs to me as to why Nussbaum should find so little wrong with Posner's language. By 'de-moralizing' sex, Posner also moralizes it, in a liberal direction. If sex is the neutral activity that he describes, then what conceivable point is there in controlling or forbidding it? Everything goes, at least between consenting adults (though why stop at adults?). If this or that practice is to be avoided, it is not because it is 'perverted', still less because it is wrong. The only questions concern cost and benefit, and in such questions the true experts are not the moralist or the philosopher, but the economist, the sociologist and the sexological researcher, as he counts the spasms and orgasms that occupy his thin obsessions.

It is not surprising, therefore, to find that Posner is persuaded by Foucault's *History of Sexuality*, according to which it is only in certain civilizations that the sexual act has been moralized, when the construction of sexual morality has been dictated by the needs of 'power'. But once we recognize that the object of desire is a person, who judges and is judged in the very moment of arousal, we see that what Foucault called the 'problematization' of the sexual act is part of its nature. If sex were not moralized, it would cease to be the thing that it is: the interpersonal force around which our life-choices congregate. Anyone who takes a second look at the history over which Foucault casts his first self-seeking glances will discover that there has never been a civilization worth the name which did not surround the expression of sexual desire with prohibitions, and instil shame and hesitation into the very impulse to express it.

But, you might say, sex *has* ceased to be moralized. The new human being has chattered himself into existence, and now stalks triumphant across this once sacred territory, loudly proclaiming his rights. Henceforth there are to be no 'forbidden pleasures', and the sexual commodity is offered in a free market, to be tasted by anyone, and in any company. It is unrealistic to impose prohibitions whose meaning derives from a vanished form of life, and another kind of human psyche. All that remains are the legal rights that protect our private pleasures: the rest is up to us.

Let me say, before turning to Martha Nussbaum's argument, that I do not think we have yet entered this Brave New World. The new kind of human being has an uncanny way of lapsing into the old, when the reality of sex is borne in upon him. Young women, encouraged to view the sexual commodity in the manner of Sergeant Watkins' Critias, are in the habit of waking up the morning after and, in their shame and confusion, cancelling the consent of the night before. And since these young women are often American liberals, brought up in the belief that their true moral guardian is neither God nor conscience but the court of law, they wonder what offence it is of which they are the victims. I do not endorse the invention of these strange torts and crimes – sexual harassment, date rape, and the rest – whereby women seek to obtain through law what can be guaranteed only by custom. But their spontaneous eruption into the forum of American litigiousness is testimony, I believe, to the enduring reality of sexual desire as a compromising force, the expression of which is not a contract for pleasurable sensations, but an existential choice. And even if modern Americans have suffered that 'decline in the sentiment of sex' to which Henry James referred, to such a point that the new human type really has edged its way to dominance, it is no part of a philosopher's role to endorse this fact, or to curtail his arguments merely because they describe the existing state of things as a falling off from some higher possibility.

'GAY RIGHTS'

But this brings me to Nussbaum's argument, which contains, along with the statistics and the rights, a great many empirical, legal and occasionally philosophical claims. The statistics speak to the contention that homosexuals are persecuted in the United States:

> Twenty-four per cent of gay men and ten per cent of lesbians, in a recent survey, reported some form of criminal assault because of their sexual orientation during the past year. . . . A Massachusetts study found that twenty-one per cent of lesbian and gay students, compared to five per cent of the entire student body, report having been physically attacked. . . . A Canadian

study finds that in fifty-six per cent of cases in which gays sought police protection the behaviour of the responding officers was 'markedly unsatisfactory'.

(pp. 94, 95)

Now I do not wish to dismiss these statistics. However, we should recognize that they concern allegations, not cases established by law. Like most of Nussbaum's data, they are taken from a far-from-unbiased source (Gary David Comstock's *Violence against Lesbians and Gay Men*); and in some respects they are internally inconsistent. (For example, we are told that those who violently assault homosexual men are more likely than other assailants to be strangers to their victims – in which case, how did they know that the victims are gay?) Moreover, neither Comstock nor Nussbaum raises the question of whether the violence against homosexuals has *increased* or *decreased* since their campaign to raise the consciousness of Middle America. Until this question is addressed, then it is hard to know whether homosexuals have been well served by their liberation.

If we are to settle the question of gay liberation by a bundle of statistics, we should be a trifle more searching than Nussbaum. We should examine the degree to which homosexual relations are promiscuous, temporary or casual; the propensity of homosexual conduct to induce diseases; the relative tendency of homosexuals towards paedophilia; and a host of other things which she barely mentions. These statistics too are available, although the most convenient summaries are contained in sources as *parti-pris* as those referred to by Nussbaum. (See, for example, Stephen Green, *The Sexual Dead End* (1992).) Nevertheless, if we do not examine them, we cannot share her conviction that the hostility towards homosexuals has no foundation in fact.

Disapproval of the homosexual lifestyle does not justify violence towards those who engage in it, and if it is true that homosexuals have been victimized in the way that Nussbaum describes, things are not as they should be. But what follows? The attitude of the English law is simple: each person has an equal right to be protected against crime; in no sense could this right be qualified by the victim's sexual orientation. And if the right is not enforced by the police, because of their attitude to the victim, then this in turn is a crime, for which the police must be prosecuted. The mechanics of law-enforcement are not a philosopher's concern – but if this is what the demand for gay rights amounts to, I do not see that any philosopher could dissent

115

from it. Intellectually speaking, the issue of criminal violence is surely settled in advance.

However, Nussbaum has other rights in view: the right to have consensual adult sexual relations without criminal penalty is the first of them, and for many people this is the crux of the matter. Again, however, the attitude of the English law is simple. Consensual relations between adults in private are not the business of the criminal law – so it was decided by the Sexual Offences Act 1967, which established a legal right to engage in homosexual acts. Of course, nothing follows from this as to whether there is also a moral right to do so. There is a legal right in England to commit adultery, to be a prostitute, to live the life of a Don Juan or a Casanova.

But an Englishman is likely to be suspicious of the rights that Nussbaum adds to that first undisputed pair. First, the right to non-discrimination in housing, employment and education. We have now left the realm of the criminal law, where rights are one-sided permissions, and entered that of the civil law, where your right is my duty. The issues are no longer clear-cut, and it is uncertain what Nussbaum means by asserting that homosexuals have the right to such non-discrimination. Does she mean that US law already grants the right? Or does she mean that it *ought* to grant the right – which means to enforce it against, and therefore coerce, those who are in the business of providing housing, employment or education?

The issue is even more unclear with the next alleged right – the 'right to military service'. In English law there is no such right – although there is a duty to serve, when called upon. I doubt that there is such a right in US law either – although Supreme Court judges may one day discern one. Nussbaum conjures this right from the metaphysical ether, and then argues, from egalitarian assumptions, that since homosexual orientation does nothing to incapacitate a person as a soldier, it cannot be used to deprive him of the right to serve. If, however, there is no such right, the argument ceases to be a question of justice, and becomes one of utility. It must then be conducted with far more attention to the facts than Nussbaum allows. How, for example, do heterosexual soldiers respond to the presence of practising homosexuals in the ranks beside them? What are the findings of military history – if there are any? The survival of a society depends upon the functioning of its army: to compromise military effectiveness merely for a fictitious right would be to threaten all our rights together.

116

With the fifth right we enter new and strange territory. For Nussbaum homosexuals have a right to marriage, and its legal benefits. There is, of course, such a right in English law – but only to marriage as traditionally defined, between monogamous partners of opposite sex. (In this respect, as in every other so far as I can see, homosexuals and heterosexuals have exactly the *same* rights in English law.) But Nussbaum wishes to extend this right to 'marriages' between partners of the same sex. There is no such positive right in our system of law; and no philosopher of natural law, to my knowledge, defends a natural right to same-sex marriages.

It is true that marriage is a legally defined condition, to which legal rights (and also legal duties) attach. But it is only the new human type which sees marriage exclusively in this way, and for the new human type marriage is a vanishing option. The marital relation was traditionally conceived, not in terms of legal rights and privileges, but in terms of a vow: the partners gave themselves to each other before God, and 'until death do us part'. The sacramental character of marriage was an endorsement of the sacrifice involved in it – the sacrifice of the self for something larger. This larger thing – the family – is dismissed by Nussbaum in two journalistic sentences, and with a flippant reference to the 'more equal division of labour' in the homosexual household. It is clear from these sentences that she has little conception of what is at stake, when the institution upon which our civilization has depended for its continuity is suddenly deprived of its sacramental character, and made into a merely legal partnership, with no essential connection to the generation of children. Certainly, the issue needs more thought than Nussbaum is prepared to give it: yet her style suggests that she is so deeply attached to her liberal prejudices, that she can no longer see the need for an argument that would justify them.

LAW, RIGHT AND CONSTITUTION

There is a feature of Nussbaum's reasoning which makes it hard for me to confront it directly. While her case is conceived in terms of rights, she says nothing about the *kind* of rights she has in mind. It is normal to distinguish a legal or positive right – a right created by the law – from a 'natural' right, a right that exists in the nature of things, whether because God prescribed it, or because practical reason has discovered it. Nussbaum's silence regarding this distinction is made less noticeable (to an American at least) by the existence of a third kind of right – a right granted under the Constitution, where the Constitution is conceived as Americans tend to conceive it, as having a higher authority than any legal enactment. Often, when an American author asks the question: 'Is there a right to X?', he means 'Is there a constitutional right to X?'. And because this question is one for the Supreme Court, whose reasoning ranges as widely as jurisprudence itself, the answer may seem to have the authority of a natural law. This in turn enables American jurists to prescribe rights and duties for all mankind, when they are really describing only the legislation of a body of American judges, whose deliberations are frequently inspired, but as frequently distorted, by a document the meaning of which has all but vanished beneath its interpretations.

It seems to me that it matters very much what kind of right Nussbaum is defending. If there is a natural right to do X, then there is something morally wrong with a legal system that forbids it. And if there is a constitutional right, then X is *already* permitted, even if there is no statute or judgement which says so. Consider, however, Nussbaum's fifth kind of 'right' – the 'right' to same-sex marriage. Nothing that she says establishes a natural right to this condition; nor do her arguments point to a right under the American Constitution. Her arguments amount to nothing more than a few snatches of *a priori* social science, with which to support the conclusion that the sum of human happiness would be increased were the legal privileges of marriage extended also to unions between people of the same sex. And if I were to venture a piece of *a priori* social science in return, I should suggest that institutions like marriage and the family, which have evolved over centuries, guided by the invisible hand of our deepest interests, and animated by a myriad consensual transactions, ought not to be tampered with lightly, merely because of some hair-brained scheme for human emancipation. (Nor is this piece of social science entirely *a priori*, as any student of the French or Russian revolutions will recognize.) In short, I do not think that Nussbaum has mounted an argument for the existence of any rights, other than those legal rights which are already contained in English law.

SEXUAL MORALITY

But this brings me back to my starting point. What is the purpose of this talk about rights, when we are offered such a thin account of the

activities which are to be protected by them? Nussbaum makes passing remarks about an argument of mine – although I do not think
that she identifies the core of it. I argued that sexual desire is desire
for another person, conceived as a member of a sexual kind (where
the conception in turn involves the idea of gender). You desire John
as a man, Elizabeth *as* a woman. And I suggested that the strangeness
of the sexes to each other plays an important part, not only in building the concept of gender and the associated division of psychic labour
between man and woman, but also in imbuing desire with the hesi-
tations which shape sexual union according to a moral idea – which
is the idea of marriage as a 'substantial' union, to use Hegel's illumi-
nating term. I went on to give a tentative explanation as to why the
homosexual act (though, of course, not the inclination) is perceived
as perverted. However, I found no proof that it really *is* so.

Looking back at this discussion, as Nussbaum obliges me to do,
I note that she ignores all the phenomena to which traditional sexual
morality emerged as a consensual response and which formed the
background to my argument. Of course, I was describing the old
type of human being. Nevertheless, the best authorities on sex – the
poets and prophets – have had no other type of human being to
discuss. And they present us with desire, shame, lust, love, obscenity,
arousal, modesty, jealousy and all the many things that have 'prob-
lematized' the course of sexual union, and made it the thing that it
is. No reference to these phenomena occurs in Nussbaum's pages,
and therefore it is impossible to say whether the rights that she
conjures from the void are anything more than prejudices as
unthinking as those against which she argues.

It seems to me that we must see the matter in the very Aristotelian
terms which Nussbaum elsewhere defends. And this means seeing
sexual conduct in the full context of the life that is shaped by it.
Traditional morality did not merely lay down a system of Kantian
prohibitions: it sought to inculcate feelings of hesitation, revulsion
and shame, the last of which was aptly described by Max Scheler as
a *Schutzgefühl* – a protective feeling. A woman, whose sexual feeling
once aroused tends to make her existentially vulnerable to its object,
has reason to hesitate. She therefore has need of the *Schutzgefühle* –
shame being one of them – that guard her against the intemperate
'yes'. It is the lack of such feelings – and of the moral education that
induces them – which has left young women so exposed, leading
them to seek futile vengeance through law, for a fault which lies too
deep for any legal remedy.

The traditional revulsion against homosexuality can also be seen as a *Schutzgefühl*. Like many of our sexual revulsions (those towards incest and paedophilia, for example) it is inspired by the thought of arousal. Sexual arousal is a reciprocal experience, wilfully generated between persons; the *Schutzgefühl* is triggered by the thought of this experience inhabiting 'flesh of a single kind'. It is because of this that many people have seen the homosexual act as obscene, and therefore perverted. The question is not whether such an act should be permitted by law, or whether homosexuals should enjoy the rights that are conferred on others. (To both those questions I am inclined to answer 'yes'.) The question is rather one of moral education. Ought we to induce in our children, or allow them spontaneously to acquire, the revulsion towards homosexual conduct which has been so striking a feature of traditional sexual morality? This question is touched on by Nussbaum only in the course of a peremptory attack on the English Local Government Act 1986, which forbids local governments to 'promote the teaching in any maintained school of the acceptability of homosexuality as a pretended family relationship'. This piece of legislation she regards as morally repugnant. Yet she does not consider the situation to which it was a response. The children of the lower classes are conscripts, and the state, which has taken charge of their education, is answerable to the parents from whom they have been purloined. These children were subjected to sexual propaganda of a kind that their parents judged to be obscene. Of course, there must be freedom of debate: and maybe those parents, the mere majority, were morally in the wrong. But one purpose of law in a democracy is to protect people against gratuitous violence to their moral feelings. It could be that the majority condemnation of adultery would not stand up to the kind of refined moral scrutiny which a philosopher would advocate. But it may be right nevertheless to forbid teachers from representing adultery as a viable moral option, in front of children whose parents are both deeply outraged by such a doctrine, and at the same time powerless to remove their children from the classroom.

And here we reach what seems to me to be the nub of the question. There is a great difference between the advocacy of 'gay rights' – meaning the right to possess and express homosexual inclinations – and the instigation of educational programmes designed to eradicate our feelings of revulsion, to 'normalize' the homosexual act, and to present the 'culture of transgression' as a viable alternative. There is a legal right to do many things which the normal conscience abhors

– not only to commit adultery, to seduce and betray or exploit another's brief attraction, but also to sponge off one's friends, to be gratuitously rude to the inoffensive, to fart and belch in public, to smear one's food on one's face and stick one's tongue out at strangers. The ethical education of children aims at good habits – whether of manners or of morals. And a person of good habits is motivated by feelings which are not acquired automatically, but must be transmitted by the surrounding culture. In the modern world, it is a good habit to respect the right to bad habits – but that does not mean that we have a right to inculcate bad habits, or to endorse them as valid 'alternatives'.

The real question, therefore, is whether the feeling of revulsion towards the homosexual act is justifiable. This question can be answered only by a patient examination of the nature of sexual feeling, and its place both in the life of society, and in the life of the individual. I shall conclude with an outline of the case for thinking that the revulsion to which I have referred is a legitimate *Schutzgefühl*, the perpetuation of which is a human good. To the extent that this is so, then the public representation of homosexuality as a fully legitimate option threatens human fulfilment: it 'liberates' us from something which it is in our common interest to retain.

First, let us consider the social arguments. Among the more important, it seems to me, are these four:

(1) Traditional sexual morality is constructed around a conception of normal conduct. This idea has a social function, reinforcing the desire of one generation to sacrifice itself for the next. The family embodies this spirit of sacrifice, translating sexual attraction into a commitment to offspring, which is at the same time a commitment to home. Sexual feeling acquires a solemn character, for the very reason that the unborn and the dead have an interest in it. The greatest social artifice has been deployed in order to bolster this solemnity – to prevent the easy gratification which will annul the experience of sexual passion as an eternal commitment. That is why sexual unions were traditionally enshrined in vows rather than contracts. 'Normal' sexual feeling came to enjoy the dignity of a sacrament.

The liberal view, even when unpolluted by the language of a Kinsey or a Posner, sees the sexual bond as an agreement between individuals – 'consenting adults' – who write the terms of the contract according to their own desires. Other generations are not intrinsically involved in the transaction, and the sacrifices which some people feel mysteriously impelled to make for the sake of future generations, or from an obligation to ancestors who are no longer around, come to seem optional and arbitrary. Why go to so much trouble, merely for the sake of sexual pleasure?

The idea that home-building is the normal result, and the justifying goal, of sexual attraction is so widespread and enduring that we might be tempted to conclude – on grounds of natural selection – that my functional justification of it is empirically confirmed. At any rate, the loss of this 'regulative' idea must surely be regarded with a measure of apprehension. A society depends upon continuities that are more easily destroyed than created, and cannot easily brook the severance of sexual passion from the commitment to past and future generations.

(2) According to the traditional conception, which I defend in *Sexual Desire* (1986), the sexual act involves passing a threshold, a moving outwards from the self, into a realm that is partly unknown and in the normal case not fully knowable. Sexual possession is also a spiritual awakening, and a peculiar sense of responsibility comes from knowing that you have awakened feelings that could never be yours. The heterosexual therefore makes himself vulnerable in the sexual act, and is a solicitor for love and understanding. This vulnerability is socially useful, since it is the foundation of the mutual dependence which causes marriages to last.

(3) There is in homosexual union between men a vector which tends to promiscuity. Unimpeded by the shame which governs women, the male homosexual hastens to arouse in another those feelings which he knows in himself. The natural predatoriness of the male is shared by both partners, and the body of the one holds no mystery for the other. When the experience of the other is so familiar and predictable, it can easily become the subject of a contract, and if both parties consent, why should the contract not be acted upon?

That piece of *a priorism* would be reprehensible if it were not capable of a deeper philosophical defence (such as I give elsewhere), and if it were not (*pace* incidental remarks by Nussbaum) abundantly confirmed by observation. And it points to a deep disorder in a society that regards homosexual and heterosexual union as morally on a par. For such a society must school itself to regard promiscuity – with all that it means by way of social breakdown, impermanence and the loss of care – as morally neutral.

(4) It is undeniable that certain people in any generation are attracted to their own sex, and especially to children of their own sex. The *Schutzgefühl* prevents them from expressing this attraction in desire, perhaps even from acknowledging it as sexual. At the same time, in searching for an outlet for their now 'sublimated' feelings, they tend to take a non-familial and generalized interest in the young. They become priests, teachers, scoutmasters and coaches. They acquire the character of 'father' or 'mother' to everyone's children, and their role is that of *paideia* in the Greek sense. If you were to wonder why homosexual tendencies tend to be reproduced, here is a functional explanation: societies benefit from the emergence of this priestly caste, which in turn benefits from sublimated homosexual feeling and the chastity that it imposes. Homosexuality can confer this benefit, however, only if it is felt as forbidden – and that, I believe, is what Plato perceived, in his wonderful celebrations of the love that bears his name.

Even if all that is true, however, an Aristotelian would scarcely be satisfied with it. For he would want to know how the *Schutzgefühl* is part of virtue – which is to say, how the habit of responding in this way promotes our happiness. It is not enough to describe the actual unhappiness of homosexuals in our society: for it may be that this is merely contingent, a result of social circumstances which could be altered without damage to the whole. It is necessary to show that our nature as rational beings is fulfilled only in those circumstances where homosexual conduct retains its 'forbidden' character. Let me make a suggestion, therefore. It is *only* a suggestion, and I am confident that Nussbaum will be quite unpersuaded by it. Nevertheless, my aim is to shift the onus of proof back onto the liberator, who must reassure the conservative that those attitudes and institutions which have so far offered us the way to happiness, will survive the great psychic upheaval involved in destroying the regulative idea of normal sexual conduct.

The individual rational agent it seems to me, has a reason to acquire those prohibitions – against promiscuity, obscenity, bestiality, paedophilia and, I believe, homosexuality – which guarantee his proximity to, and right conduct towards, the rising generation. This right conduct is of two kinds, as Plato saw – the ordinary way of child-rearing, and the way of *paideia*. Without it, a person remains fixed in the circle of his own life, aiming at nothing beyond his own desires. The 'liberation' of our sexual appetites involves a vast curtailment of our projects, a reduction of *eros* to something transient and unfruitful: and it is this curtailing of our moral ambitions that is registered most vividly in the new language through which sex is represented in America. If we refuse to adopt this language, and speak instead of sexual desire in all its civilized complexity, then we see that the onus lies not on the conservative, to defend the way of life that has grown from traditional prohibitions, but on the liberator, who wishes to cancel those prohibitions, and who must think seriously – far more seriously than Nussbaum – about the consequences of doing so.

9

NUSSBAUM'S REPLY

Roger Scruton is right in divining that we are in a substantial measure of agreement about many of the ethical issues that arise in the sexual domain. Both of us attach great importance to the interpersonal intentionality characteristic of sexual arousal, and both of us feel that the valuable dimensions of sex can best be realized in a relationship of some depth, characterized by mutual trust and some degree of commitment. We are both drawn to an odd combination of romanticism with marital friendship that may be difficult to instantiate in the real world, but which seems valuable as an ideal. Scruton romanticizes the traditional family more than I would. His claim that it is among the 'institutions which have so far offered us the way to happiness' (p. 123) seems to me not evidently correct. The situation of women who have been involved in that institution in many parts of the world could not easily be described as one of happiness, given that it is characterized by great inequalities in basic nutrition, health-care, employment and education rights, and political voice. All these inequities the institution of marriage has helped, frequently, to perpetuate. On this topic as on so many, John Stuart Mill offers profound insight.

However, the questions I want to press here do not concern the status of women, since that is not our topic. Let us suppose that Scruton's moral ideal is agreed to be valuable. Two questions are now before us: (1) does valuing that ideal give us any reason to look negatively on homosexual relationships? and (2) what does any of this have to do with legal and political rights of the sort under discussion?

But first, three remarks about sources. Scruton writes that Gary David Comstock's *Violence Against Lesbians and Gay Men* is a 'far-from-unbiased source' (p. 115). What does he mean? This is a well-received work published in a refereed series by a major university press; the data cited in it come from surveys published in major refereed sociological journals and other public sources. I can only suppose that Scruton has the suspicion that Comstock is a gay man (a proposition for which the book offers no evidence at all), and supposes that a gay man is 'biased' on the subject of violence against gays. This is innuendo parading as argument. Besides, if every author is assumed to be biased in favour of his or her own sexual orientation, then nobody, including Scruton and Nussbaum, can engage in rational argument or good scholarship in this area. I believe that proposition to be false. As to the alleged 'inconsistency' in Comstock (if the assailants are strangers, how do they know their victims are gay?), Scruton could find out the answer by reading the book, and many other sources: they observe gestures of affection, they hang around outside gay bars, they identify people by their dress or manner, and so forth. In the lesbian case I described, the attacker lurked in the woods and observed the two women making love before he shot them. He remained, nonetheless, a stranger.

Second, Posner. Posner's economic theory of sexuality is not only not a necessary prop in his defence of libertarian principles, it is actually in considerable tension with those principles, as I pointed out in my review in the *University of Chicago Law Review*.[1] Posner has now granted this point.[2] For reasons related to Scruton's, I am highly critical of the reductive bioeconomic theory, and I imagine Scruton would be in sympathy with the criticisms I expressed. I therefore did not rely on Posner for the part of his view that I have attacked and repudiated, but, rather, for empirical information that seemed to me correct, and also for libertarian arguments that are logically independent of (and in tension with) the bioeconomic theory.

Third, Mill. Scruton's criticism of J.S. Mill seems to me hasty and unfair. Mill has a rich conception of qualitative distinctions in plea-sure, and is really more of an Aristotelian eudaemonist than a utilitarian. Moreover, *The Subjection of Women* reveals an unusual degree of insight into the social deformation of sexual intentionality by unequal structures of power. Scruton might do worse than to ponder these arguments.

Scruton's complex arguments about intentionality, while valuable, still seem to me to have nothing to do with homosexuality as such. Scruton never criticizes same-sex relations among females. The link between his moral view and opposition to homosexual acts comes through the alleged promiscuity of gay males. But here Mill shows us the way: for the same reasons that the abilities of women could not be known in 1869, when they were deprived of equal social opportunities, the marital inclinations of gay men cannot be known in 1995. To observe people who are forbidden to marry, and who are offered every obstacle to the formation of lasting stable unions, and then to assert that they should not have these rights because they are promiscuous, seems to me just the sort of pseudo-argument Mill exposed in *Subjection* (women should not be educated because they are empty-headed things . . .). Scruton offers no reply to my suggestion that the problem of promiscuity, if it is one, comes from the moral education of all males in our society. He offers me no reason to think that straight men are especially monogamous, and I am sure he will agree with me that they are not. Nor, moreover, does he give me any reason to think that promiscuous male behaviour is rooted in innate mechanisms, rather than in moral education. He suggests, in fact, that moral education is the primary source of norms of promiscuity. He should, I think, conclude that we need to ponder our norms of maleness, not our views about sexual orientation as such.

In fact, as I said, an overwhelming majority of gay males polled in Sweden, a nation that comes as close as any to respecting them as equal citizens, said that they wished to form a lifelong partnership. Such partnerships can certainly have a 'sacramental' character if that is what the parties wish: all major Christian and Jewish denominations are debating this issue at the present time, and there is none that does not contain some segment supporting gay marriage. But I must also remind Scruton that marriage has long been a secular legal institution, and what gays are most urgently demanding is the basic legal right to be counted as the spouse of one's lifelong partner, in matters such as hospital visits, decisions about burial, etc. Many such couples have amply demonstrated that they have Scruton's central qualification for marriage, namely a capacity for 'the sacrifice of the self for something larger' (p. 117). If, then, we should agree that society should discourage promiscuity and promote marriage, it seems bizarre to do so by denying social and legal rights to the one group whose failure to marry results not from choice but from legally imposed barriers.

One further point about moral education. Scruton suggests that teaching a revulsion with homosexuality will produce more heterosexuals – at least I think this is his argument. But there is overwhelming evidence that sexual orientation is formed very early in life and is highly resistant to change. So teaching children to be revolted by homosexuality is teaching them to have disgust either toward themselves or toward their gay and lesbian peers. How does this make anyone's life better? As the parent of a bisexual child, I can assure Scruton that such teaching causes untold misery and pain. It would seem best to teach all children to respect themselves and others as human beings, regardless of the traits with which they happen to be born. Then we will be far more likely to produce a society of people who are capable of respect and commitment.

Now we reach the issue of rights, which was our topic. I am sure Scruton and I can agree that many things that are morally desirable should not be legally enforced. If we prefer politeness to impoliteness, generosity to stinginess, modesty to ostentation, we have no inclination to burden those who lack these virtues with legal and political disabilities. Suppose, now, that we single out only the homosexuals who can be shown to engage in behaviour of which Scruton morally disapproves – that is, the promiscuous ones. (For it seems quite unfair to include lesbians, whom he holds to be non-promiscuous, or those among gay men who don't have the trait of which he disapproves.) Let us, to be fair, put with them the promiscuous heterosexuals (as even God did, if we are to believe Dante's account of Purgatory, where the lustful of both orientations are punished fully symmetrically). Should we now deny these people various legal rights? Scruton agrees that their consensual sexual acts should not be illegal. Good. That means that he is for radical legal reform in the US, and that he would have been for radical change in the Britain that imprisoned Wilde and so many others. He agrees, too, that there is reason for social outrage if the police do not give them the equal protection of the law. Good again; and once again there is some reason to suppose that, in the US at least, this is a radical position.

Where, now, do we disagree? Marriage we have already discussed. On non-discrimination, what I mean is that communities ought to grant such rights, *and* that when they vote to do so, a statewide referendum (as in Colorado) should not be permitted to prevent them. I held that such rights should not be enforced against religious organizations, which are frequently exempted in such ordinances.

Scruton finds my remarks about military service obscure. But I can assure him that the rights in question are all too palpable: they are the right not to be tossed out of one's military job on account of one's sexual orientation, the right to get a diploma from the US

Naval Academy if one has satisfied all the graduation requirements, the right to keep one's ROTC scholarship and so forth. Courts have long been hearing cases dealing with these rights. The point is not that everyone has a right to be in the army; there is no general right to be a typist either. But if someone who is a qualified typist is fired on account of race or gender, that is a violation of one's constitutional right to the equal protection of the law. It has been argued that similar issues are at stake in the sexual orientation cases in the military, and this is what concerns me. I assume, furthermore, that Scruton, to be fair to the gays and consistent with his argument, would be in favour of tossing out all and only the promiscuous soldiers, not all and only the gay and lesbian soldiers. I shall look forward with interest to Scruton's proposals for military reform.

NOTES

1　" 'Only Grey Matter?" Richard Posner's Cost-benefit Analysis of Sex', *University of Chicago Law Review*, 59 (1993).
2　R. Posner, *Overcoming Law* (Cambridge, Mass.: Harvard University Press, 1995).

BIBLIOGRAPHY

BOOKS AND ARTICLES

Blumstein, P. and Schwartz, P. (1983) *American Couples: Money, Work, Sex*, New York: William Morrow.

Comstock, G.D. (1991) *Violence Against Lesbians and Gay Men*, New York: Columbia University Press.

Dover, K. (1986) *Greek Homosexuality*, 2nd edn, Cambridge, Mass.: Harvard University Press.

Foucault, M. (1984) *Histoire de la Sexualité*, Paris: Editions Gallimard.

Green, S. (1992) *The Sexual Dead End*, London: Broadview Books.

Humphrey, M.A. (1993) 'Interview with Perry Watkins', in W.B. Rubenstein (ed.), *Lesbians, Gay Men, and the Law*, New York: The New Press.

Laumann, E. *et al.* (1994) (indexed under Robert T. Michael), *Sex in America*, Boston: Little Brown.

Mill, J.S. (1991) 'On Liberty', in J. Gray (ed.), *On Liberty and Other Essays*, Oxford: Oxford University Press, first published in 1859.

Mison, R.B. (1992) 'Homophobia in Manslaughter: The Homosexual Advance as Insufficient Provocation', *California Law Review*, 80, 133–78.

Mohr, R.D. (1994) *A More Perfect Union: Why Straight America Must Stand Up for Gay Rights*, Boston: Beacon Press.

Nava, M. and Dawidoff, R. (1994) *Created Equal: Why Gay Rights Matter to Americans*, New York: St Martin's Press.

Norwegian Act on Registered Partnerships for Homosexual Couples (1993), Oslo, Norway: Ministry of Children and Family Affairs.

Nussbaum, M. (1986) *The Fragility of Goodness*, Cambridge: Cambridge University Press.

—— (1990) *Love's Knowledge*, Oxford: Oxford University Press.

—— (1994) 'Platonic Love and Colorado Law: The Relevance of Ancient Greek Norms to Modern Sexual Controversies', *Virginia Law Review*, 80 (October).

Posner, R. (1992) *Sex and Reason*, Cambridge, Mass.: Harvard University Press.

Rubenstein, W.B. (ed.) (1993) *Lesbians, Gay Men, and the Law*, New York: The New Press (includes *High Tech Gays, Watkins* and other cases).

Scheler, M. (1957) 'Über Scham und Schamgefühl', in M. Scheler (ed.), *Schriften aus dem Nachlass*, 2nd edn, Berne, Switzerland.

Scruton, R. (1986) *Sexual Desire: A Moral Philosophy of the Erotic*, New York: The Free Press.

Shilts, R. (1992) *Conduct Unbecoming: Lesbians and Gays in the US Military*, Harmondsworth: Penguin.

Stephen, J.F. (1967) *Liberty, Equality and Fraternity*, Cambridge: Cambridge University Press, first published in 1871.

Symposium on Sexual Orientation and the Law (1993), various authors, *Virginia Law Review*, 79 (October).

Xenophon (1965) *Memorabilia and Oeconomicus*, trans. E. Marchant, London: Heinemann, and Cambridge, Mass.: Harvard University Press.

CASES

Baehr v. Lewin, 852 P. 2d 44 (1993) Hawaii.

Bowers v. Hardwick, 487 U.S. 186 (1986).

Commonwealth v. Carr, 580 A. 2d 1362 (Pa. Super. 1990).

Evans v. Romer, Civ. Nol. 92–7223 (District Court, City and County of Denver, Colorado, decided 14 December 1994).

High Tech Gays v. Defense Indus. Sec. Clearance Office, 895 F. 2d 563 (9th Cir. 1990).

Loving v. Virginia, 388 U.S. 1 (1967).

Palmore v. Sidoti, 466 U.S. 429 (1984).

Shahar v. Bowers, 836 F. Supp. 859 (D Ga.993).

Watkins v. United States Army, 837 F. 2d 1428 (9th Cir. 1988) *amended*, 847 F. 2d 1329, *different results reached on reh'g*, 875 F. 2d 699 (9th Cir. 1989) (en banc), *cert. denied*, 111 S. Ct. 384 (1990).

Part IV

CHILDREN'S LIBERATION

10

LIBERATING CHILDREN

John Harris

Despite an avalanche of interest in and legislation concerning children's rights in the last decade and an increase both of interest in, and in the incidence of, child abuse, little of value has emerged concerning the acute problem of how to reconcile the increasing emphasis on and respect for children's rights with the increasing need to protect children from abuse.

There is the hint of a paradox here. For rights and protection are often incompatible. Insofar as I have a right to do something, you are not entitled to prevent me from doing it or to protect me, against my will, from its harmful effects. Rights protect liberties. The two classic anti-libertarian approaches to morality are essentially protectionist in character. They are *paternalism* and *moralism*. Paternalism claims the right to control the behaviour of another for that other's own good while moralism asserts that right to protect others from wickedness. The characteristic call of the paternalist is: 'Don't do that, it will harm you!', that of the moralist is: 'Don't do that, it's wicked!'.

If we are concerned about children's rights and hence concerned to protect children from abuse, we cannot ignore the question of whether or not they have a right to choose either to be abused, paradoxical as this might sound, or, to choose a context which, though 'abuse' occurs, is preferable from their perspective to any likely alternative.[1]

In the brief space available here I want to try to do three things. They are, first to articulate, though not defend,[2] a principle of respect for persons which expresses children's rights in their strongest form. Then I will show how, at least in principle, this is not incompatible with a principle of protection. Finally, I will set out some general principles about the nature of autonomy and the scope and limits of paternalism.

135

CHILDREN'S RIGHTS AND RESPECT FOR PERSONS

If, as I believe, children's rights can only be coherently defended as a dimension of human rights, that is as part of a general theory of the rights of persons, then certain interesting and alarming consequences flow.

No one in the history of political theory has succeeded in answering the puzzling question as to where rights come from. However, we can say something about those on whom they fall, about the possessors of rights.

I believe there are really only two alternatives here. Either rights are possessed in virtue of the type of being in question – a human say, or they are possessed in virtue of the capacities possessed by that being. In either case we have big problems. Let me explain:

Rights are possessed by natural kinds

If rights are possessed by types of beings, then there are two types possible. Either they are possessed by natural kinds of beings, like humans, or they are possessed by beings defined in terms of their properties. For example the category *persons* is often defined in terms not of species-membership but, following the English seventeenth-century philosopher John Locke, in terms of the possession of properties like self-consciousness and rationality. These are, of course, possessed not in virtue of an individual's identity as a particular kind of being *per se* but in virtue of that being's capacities – our second type.

Now, if rights are possessed by 'natural kinds' of creatures they are certainly possessed by humans. It is not possible (despite the best endeavours of some) to deny that children are humans and so children have whatever rights are distinctively human rights.

I refer you to the Universal Declaration of Human Rights and the European Convention on Human Rights for further (if bizarre) insights as to what these might be in fact.

From this it follows that all children, and almost certainly foetuses as well insofar as they are live and human ones, have full human rights.

Rights are possessed by beings with certain capacities

This view, which I believe, for reasons I do not have space to detail here[3], to be the right one, yields conclusions almost equally complicated from the perspective of the paternalistic control and protection of children. For if rights are possessed by beings with certain capacities, then it follows that those who possess the capacities have the rights. On any analysis of the way rights, either generally or particularly, may be linked to capacities, this is a disaster. For many adults will lack the relevant capacities and have to be deprived of substantial rights and many children will possess the capacities which confer the most powerful of rights. We cannot in consistency be selective, either we must deny many adults substantial rights and freedoms in order to preserve the right to paternalist control and protection of children, or, we will have to grant substantial rights to all children and full rights, including the franchise, to all children who have capacities relevantly comparable to any adults also granted the franchise and other rights.

Either model of rights I believe implies a revolution in our thinking about children which we might well call *children's liberation* on the model of women's liberation.[4] Both imply that children have in most cases the same moral and political status as most adults. Moreover, from the perspective of rights, they are entitled not only to the same concern, respect and protection as is accorded to any other member of the community, no more and no less, but also are entitled to the same freedoms and self-determination.

DOES CHILDREN'S LIBERATION IMPLY LOSS OF PROTECTION?

One very important and persuasive argument seems poised to undermine the conclusions so far reached. It achieved perhaps its clearest and most powerful articulation in the work of the famous nineteenth-century jurist James Fitzjames Stephen, who argued that 'if children were regarded as the equal of adults . . . it would involve a degree of cruelty to the young which can hardly be realized even in imagination' (Stephen, 1967). The spectre raised by Stephen of cruelty to and perhaps exploitation of young children on a new, vast and unprecedented scale must be taken very seriously. He had in mind things like the exploitation of children in the labour market, sending them down mines, up chimneys; low pay, long hours and so on. He would also doubtless have been aware of the huge problem of child prostitution which today would perhaps be regarded simply as one dimension of the problem of child abuse. If these were to be the consequences of the emancipation of children, then the price would be one no civilized society should be prepared to pay. But is this where my suggestions have been leading?

If Stephen is taken to mean that unless children are protected from predatory and exploitative adults they will be cruelly used, this might well be true – but it need not concern us. For my suggestion is simply that the only defensible views as to which sorts of creatures possess rights involves the idea that all persons, adult or child, are entitled to equal concern, respect and protection, including equality before the law and other civil rights. But any principle of equality worthy of the name and certainly the idea towards which we have been arguing, is itself a principle of protection. If children are genuinely regarded as the equals of adults, then they are regarded as being entitled, among other things, to equal protection. To regard people as equals is to recognize that they may well not be equally able to protect themselves and their interests. It is rather to recognize that their wishes and interests matter as much as anyone else's, regardless of their ability to protect them or further them unaided. It is when people are not regarded as the equals of others that they are in danger of arbitrary or ill usage, tyranny and exploitation.

To regard people as the equals one of another is to take a stand on how they are entitled to be treated, not to make a remark about their capacity to obtain that treatment by their unaided efforts. It is to recognize that there is something about them in virtue of which they are justified in claiming and receiving the same political status as others, irrespective of their ability to achieve that status for themselves.

Indeed, if the point of Stephen's argument is well taken, it might be argued against his conclusion that it is precisely because children have been treated as children and not as equals that they have been fair game for adults, exploited, abused, and even tortured and arbitrarily done to death. And perhaps irrespective of the merits of the case for their being accorded equality with adults, we should grant this status merely out of paternalistic concern for their welfare.

The recognition of full rights for children does not then necessarily imply a cruel disregard of their needs and interests. It is rather a claim that they are entitled to the same concern, respect and protection as are adults and in particular, and this is crucial, that any claim that a certain child cannot make his or her own choices and assert and demand aid in protecting his or her own rights, in short any claim that a particular child is not competent, must be established in the same way that it would have to be for an adult about whom similar claims were made.

THE STATUS OF CHILDREN

What we might call the status of children, the way they are treated and the freedoms or privileges they enjoy, in all societies reflects the almost universally held belief that children are incompetent to exercise the responsibilities and discharge the obligations of full citizenship.

In consequence of this supposed incompetence adults have felt entitled to place children in what amounts to protective custody. In addition to the comprehensive list of legal disabilities imposed on children – inability to vote, to initiate or defend legal proceedings on their own account, to consent to sexual relations, to see and read uncensored material and so on – they find their lives positively controlled by the preferences of adults. This control finds dramatic and public expression and reinforcement in the system of compulsory attendance at and obedience in schools.

While the supposed incompetence of children is the ground for the imposition of political and legal disabilities, protective custody is justified both on the grounds of the incompetence of children and also as the measure required most effectively to remove that incompetence and to allow children to proceed, without danger or mishap, to the stage where they will shed their incompetence and be sufficiently autonomous to join the community of self-determining adults.

Now, if it is supposed that it is the comprehensive possession by adults of capacities lacked equally comprehensively by children that sustains and justifies the disabling of children and their control by adults, then the supposition is quite clearly and obviously false. False because we all know that there are numerous children whom it would be implausible to regard as incompetent, and numerous adults whom it would be implausible to regard as anything but incompetent, so that if we really care about protecting the incompetent we would have to take many adults into protective custody. And, if we believe that those individuals who possess whatever range of capacities it is believed that most normal adults possess, should be 'licensed' fully

139

to participate in decision-making and should enjoy whatever free-doms are granted to full citizens, then we would have to enfranchise and grant adult freedoms to very many children.

The idea of taking many adults (or many more adults)[5] into protective custody is as abhorrent to most people as is the idea of enfranchising millions of children. To know whether either or both of these 'horrors' should be supported we need to be clearer about just what it is that entitles adults to determine their own fates and to take upon themselves the determination of the fate of their children and of children generally. The umbrella under which that 'something' or range of 'somethings' that it is believed adults comprehensively[6] possess and children equally comprehensively lack is the idea of autonomy. Equally it is the idea that many children are obviously autonomous and many adults obviously are not that seems to require that in consistency we should enfranchise many children and take into protective custody many adults. Clearly it is time to be clearer about what we mean by autonomy.

AUTONOMY

I have set out elsewhere[7] an account of the defects that can occur in an individual's autonomy and what follows is an abbreviated but importantly modified and I hope improved account of these defects. And of course when we are clear or at least clearer about what tends to undermine an individual's autonomy, we will also be clearer about what autonomy is.

While the list of possible defects in autonomy is not intended to be exhaustive it is useful to think of the ways in which autonomy can be undermined under four general headings.

These are, then:

1 *Control*: the individual may not be in control or in complete control of either her desires or actions or both.
2 *Reasoning*: this ability may be impaired in many ways which affect the individual's capacity to make genuine decisions.
3 *Information*: this may be defective in many ways which affect decision-making.
4 *Stability*: an individual's preferences may change over time and 'mature' in various important ways which seem to affect the reality of her choices.

If we look at each of these in turn we will see how they each bear upon the question of whether or not the individual can be said to be in autonomous control of herself.

Defects in control

We are all familiar with the idea that people literally lose control of themselves and that when this genuinely occurs they may not be responsible for what they 'do' while out of control. Such loss of control may afford a defence in law as in the case of 'guilty but insane' or 'diminished responsibility' verdicts in trials. Mental illness of various kinds is often thought to be a source of such loss of control. Another important case occurs where the individual finds his behaviour controlled by desires he does not wish to have. The classic case here is that of addiction where the addict desires to take drugs but wishes he didn't. The loss of control involves the first-order desire for a fix controlling the second-order desire not to be an addict. With something like heroin addiction we are accustomed to thinking of the addict as literally controlled by his habit, but whether even this is true may be doubtful. However, 'addiction' is a much abused term. Someone who wishes to lose weight but who cannot resist another cake may be said to have their first-order desire to lose weight controlled by their second-order desire for another delicious mouthful. However, there is some ambivalence here and it is unclear that many people who seem to lack self-control in cases like this have really worked out where the balance in the priority of their desires lies. The issue is further complicated by the fact that addiction itself is not destructive of autonomy. We are all addicted to lots of things fully voluntarily. When I choose to play squash or study philosophy, my autonomous choice is in no way defective because, although I am conscious that I cannot give these activities up, or at least that it would be extraordinarily difficult for me to do so, I have no desire at all to do so.

Children are thought to be particularly prone to being controlled by desires that either they do not wish to have, or, more commonly, desires it is thought that they would not wish to have if their reasoning or information were better. We will postpone discussion of the plausibility of such claims until we have considered these other supposed defects in autonomy.

Defects in reasoning

This is a broad category which subsumes many ways in which an individual's autonomy may be vitiated or weakened by defects in her ability to reason or be 'rational'. Some examples will help to make clear what is involved here. Someone who could not draw inferences or appreciate the connection between cause and effect would have substantial difficulties in making autonomous choices. If they failed to see that smoking was dangerous, or that alcohol impaired their ability to drive safely, they would end up by doing things that they didn't want to do – like endangering their own lives and those of others.

Similarly, where people allow received opinion or gut reaction to form the basis of their values or when they make judgements based on manifestly implausible 'facts', their autonomy is undermined, as it is when through something like 'bad faith' they refuse to admit or recognize something they know to be true.

Defects in information

Where someone's beliefs or choices are made on the basis of false or incomplete information they will to that extent be less autonomous simply because they will be in danger of doing something they wouldn't do if their information were better or more complete. Under this heading comes also the sort of 'information' which it is very hard to categorize. This is like a cross between reasoning and information. I have in mind that elusive thing called experience. Those who have what is called the relevant experience will be less in danger of making non-autonomous choices than those who lack such experience – or so experience tells us.

Defects in stability

This may be an unfamiliar category to many but the problem it highlights will not be. It is simply that our particular preferences, and indeed often our whole pattern of preferences, tend to change over time so that the choices I made when 12 or 14 say, may come to seem absurd, and even absurdly misjudged, when I look back on them in my forties. Some of them may even be bitterly regretted, for they have shaped my life and if I had my time over again I would behave differently. This instability in our preferences is often cited as a justification for paternalism. 'I'm only doing this for your own good and one day you'll be grateful.' Since we all change not only our minds but our personalities over time, it is hardly surprising that there is a sort of in-built instability in our preferences. The sort of people we are and the things we choose will change over time as the things we choose modify the sort of person we are. If the very confident prediction that we will later regret what we now choose to do were to be a justification for paternalism and a reason to believe that our present decisions were somehow less than fully autonomous, then full autonomy would only be achieved (if ever) in extreme old age. Apart from the absurdity of this it reveals a fundamental mistake about the nature of autonomy. An autonomous individual is one who governs herself, who runs her life the way she pleases. If what pleases her changes over time this provides no evidence at all that there was something spurious about her earlier preferences. They were not less genuinely hers – just different.

Autonomous persons

Now that we have reviewed the various types of defects which may count against the autonomy of an individual's decision we are in a position to draw some conclusions. We should note to start with that the four apparent categories of defect in the autonomy of our decision-making have reduced to three. The last category considered, that of the instability of our preferences, was found on inspection to provide no grounds for supposing that a decision was defective from the point of view of autonomy merely because the individual might (or even would certainly) regret it later. This is a risk of all decision-making.

CONCLUSION

We may (and should) conclude that where children's decisions or preferences cannot be shown to suffer from any of the defects that render decisions non-autonomous, they should be given absolute control over their own destiny exactly as are adults and for the same reasons.

Consider the rationale given for control of children. In the first place, most instances of the control exercised by adults over children could not plausibly be claimed to be for the protection of their lives or of any equally valuable interest. Second, such control is usually exercised comprehensively, and not merely for so long as any defects in autonomy remain. Third, it is standardly exercised without the taking of any steps to see whether it is required in the first place; that is, without adults trying to see whether the individual child is capable of choosing autonomously in the particular case, and without their trying to ascertain what steps are required to remedy what may be purely 'technical' defects in autonomy, like lack of an easily supplied and comprehended item of information.

Think of the daily interaction between almost any adults and any children that occurs to you, parents and their children or teachers and pupils for example, and the truth of these remarks will be obvious. Parents or teachers unthinkingly, and absolutely as a matter of course, presume to regulate the lives of the children 'in their charge'. The children are told what to do and how to behave, to talk or not to talk, are sent on errands for the convenience of the adults; they may be told what to wear and how they may arrange their hair or otherwise present themselves to the world. They are in short ordered about in all directions, and all without any claim at all that such control is somehow necessary for the children's welfare or indeed because they lack autonomy with respect to all or any of these things themselves.

Where it is claimed that control of children is justified because they necessarily fail, or fail fully, to comprehend the dangers that may face them we again usually fail to make a relevant distinction between adults and children. What is it to fail, or fail fully, to comprehend a danger? What counts as a remedy for the defects in autonomy that generate such lack of comprehension?

Consider fairly standard adult actions and choices; the woman who smokes cigarettes or the man who eats a high cholesterol diet, or those who refuse to give up alcohol when its abuse is killing them and endangering others. Can such people be said to comprehend, or comprehend fully, the danger they are in? Whether or not they comprehend the danger, what follows? Are we entitled or obliged to impose abstinence or a modified diet upon them?

Certainly we are obliged to point out, and to do so quite unequivocally, the dangers. This is simply because to fail to do so would be to partake in the responsibility for their coming to grief. Where the individual knows the dangers (or at least knows that the consensus of informed opinion is that there are dangers) and both wishes to persist in the life-threatening practice and wants to have a long and a happy life, then clearly their decision-making is defective.

144

Obviously the decision-making of very many adults indeed is defective in precisely this way and yet it is seldom suggested that this fact constitutes grounds for paternalistic control. If the very same grounds are thought of as justifying the control of children then we require some additional argument which would distinguish the two cases. One way out of this problem is shown by remembering that it is possible autonomously to accept certain defects in autonomy, but the consequences of bearing this in mind are far from providing the necessary distinguishing argument.

THE AUTONOMOUS ACCEPTANCE OF DEFECTS IN AUTONOMY

In the circumstances we have described, an individual can autonomously decide to live with some defects in the autonomy of her decision-making. And it is clearly better, from the point of view of autonomy, for the individual to do this than live subject to the paternalist control of others. Where the individual has so chosen, the paternalist cannot claim to be acting in the interests of the individual's autonomy when she claims the moral right to control that person's behaviour for her own good.

If this is right, it is precisely the same for adults as for children and the only question is simply whether or not the individual in question, adult or child, has autonomously chosen to live with some defects in autonomy. Whether they are capable of such autonomous choice will be a question of fact in each case.

That it is a matter of fact, or at least a matter of judgement, in each case as to whether or not an individual is capable of autonomous choice, provides a framework for dealing with the consequences of recognizing the ageism of the accepted approach to the treatment of children. In short it provides a framework for beginning the process of children's liberation. I cannot elaborate that framework now but its outlines will surely be clear. They are that it is decisions which are autonomous, not people. Autonomy is not an existential state – a state of being. Rather, persons make decisions which either are, or are not, autonomous. Those who respect persons will respect their autonomous decisions at whatever age such decisions are made and will not assume, or be permitted to act on the assumption, that a decision is not autonomous because of the chronological age of the decider.[8]

NOTES

1 The use of the term 'abuse' of course begs the question as to whether, if the child consents, it can be abuse strictly speaking. However, I will continue to use the term 'abuse' to cover cases which many would consider at least *prima facie* cases of abuse.

2 There won't be time.

3 See Harris, 1990.

4 Indeed there are many interesting parallels with women's liberation; particularly, the arguments that have been used to deny women's rights are remarkably similar to those which have been used to deny children's rights. See Harris, 1983.

5 I say 'many more' since substantial numbers of adult people are compulsorily detained under various sections of The Mental Health Acts.

6 With the exception noted above.

7 In Harris, 1990, ch. 10.

8 For more on respect for persons see my 'Euthanasia and the Value of Life', in John Keown (ed.), *Examining Euthanasia: Ethical, Legal and Clinical Perspectives* (Cambridge: Cambridge University Press, 1995).

11

CHILDREN'S LIBERATION: A BLUEPRINT FOR DISASTER

Laura Purdy

THE ARGUMENT FROM AUTONOMY

Children's liberation holds that children have the same right to run their lives as adults. The basic argument for children's liberation, as laid out by John Harris and others, is clear and eloquent. Given the perennial appeal of freedom, children's liberation is an attractive position. It has some drawbacks that suggest that we should be slow to embrace it, however, and so, much as it pains me to argue against any form of liberation, I conclude that neither his argument nor any other I have seen is tenable.

Harris starts by asserting that the most reasonable conception of rights implies that children should have the same rights as adults. Why? Because adult rights are predicated on the assumption that they are capable of making autonomous decisions about their own welfare. Hence their decisions can be interfered with only where they risk serious harm to others. But children, Harris claims, are no less autonomous than adults; hence it is unjust to deny them equal rights on this ground.

Harris assumes but does not argue for the thesis that autonomy is the ground of equal rights. Nor does he provide much argument for the view that children are as autonomous as adults: he simply asserts that this is true. In his view, decisions – including children's decisions – are to be viewed as autonomous unless they can be shown to be otherwise. Even apparently non-autonomous decisions may really be autonomous since it is possible autonomously to choose to live with some defects in one's decision-making patterns.

Harris believes that autonomy involves three components: control, reasoning and information.[1] *Control* involves power over one's actions and desires. Thus, for example, the control element of autonomy

147

requires that children learn to defer gratification or do distasteful things in order to enjoy their desired fruits. *Reasoning* has many dimensions, ranging from simple inferential logic and an understanding of the familiar fallacies to epistemological sophistication and the willingness to face reality. So children need to learn both the logical rules that protect them from fallacious thinking, and appropriate scepticism about knowledge claims. *Information* means having some grasp of relevant facts and circumstances. This criterion requires of children not only a sufficiently large stock of true beliefs, but also a plausible worldview that helps them make sense of those beliefs.

Many people would want to add something like *stability of ideas and desires* to the definition of autonomy; but Harris rejects this on the grounds that our ideas evolve in part as a result of our prior decisions. He says that he views as autonomous an individual who 'governs herself, who runs her life the way she pleases. If what pleases her changes over time this provides no evidence at all that there was something spurious about her earlier preferences. They were not less genuinely hers – just different' (p. 143). Here Harris is quite rightly pointing out that stability of ideas and desires over time is not necessarily a sign of autonomy: people often change their minds about what they think and what they want. I will consider shortly whether that is the whole story.

Harris thinks that our failure to accord children equal rights has devastating consequences. He writes:

> children are told what to do and how to behave, to talk or not to talk, are sent on errands for the convenience of adults; they may be told what to wear and how they may arrange their hair or otherwise present themselves to the world. They are in short ordered about in all directions.
>
> (p. 144)

He maintains that nobody even tries to make the case that this treatment is necessary for children's welfare or that they are incapable of autonomous choices with respect to them.

Lack of equal rights has still more significant consequences. Consider that the guardians who provide for children have a corresponding right to choose their names, religion and type of education, as well as to decide where they live and what they eat. A guardian can censor books and movies, and even has a right to a child's wages. As schools are considered *in loco parentis*, they too can adopt a variety of regulations intended to ensure a good learning situation. Among those the courts have found acceptable are dress codes, restrictions on hair length and prohibitions of secret societies. More generally, children are also subject to curfews, as well as limits on their work, on visits to dance and pool halls, on driving, drinking and access to pornography. Some acts, 'juvenile status offences' are crimes only when they are committed by minors. They include running away from home, being ungovernable, being truant, having sexual intercourse and becoming pregnant. Children cannot marry, vote, make a will or make a valid contract (Purdy, 1992, p. 3).

Comparable limits on any other group would be viewed as oppression. So if autonomy is the basis for equal rights and if children are truly autonomous, justice requires that such distinctions between adults and children be eradicated.

AUTONOMY'S LIMITS

Harris writes with admirable clarity and conviction. However, I believe that his approach ignores a number of important issues. For one thing, he lives in the sharp-edged world of classical liberals, a world of atomistic rational contractors seeking the best deals. Glaringly absent from it is the clutter of real human existence, with needy babies, toddlers, loving mums or the infirm. Also, his autonomy-based moral world seems devoid of important competing values.

Let us start by questioning Harris' assumption that children are autonomous. Autonomy is, as we have seen, a complicated issue. I agree with Harris that control, reasoning and information are all important elements of autonomy. However it should be emphasized that these characteristics are not absolutes, such that you either have them or you don't. On the contrary, very young children start with little control, reasoning or information, and then usually go on to acquire them in much greater degree. Even precocious children know more at age 13 than they did at age 7. Adults, too, vary tremendously in the extent to which they possess these attributes. Furthermore, the components of autonomy don't necessarily develop evenly, so a particular child may be strong on information, but weak on control, or vice versa. Hence, an individual's 'autonomy profile' can consist of many widely varying capacities and tendencies. All of this means that autonomy admits of degrees, and it seems appropriate to describe people with relatively low levels of control, information and reasoning as only weakly autonomous. It would also be plausible to argue that even one weak link often drags overall behaviour down to that level.

Harris' rejection of stability as a component of autonomy is also problematic. I am less willing than he is to assimilate all instability of ideas or desires to simple mind-changing. Changes in direction can, in some cases, represent lapses of autonomy. For example, people, especially young people, sometimes fall under the spell of charismatic cult leaders under whose influence they give up all their previous pursuits. However, if they are abruptly removed from that leader's presence, they return to their old lives. Should we really maintain that these individuals are behaving autonomously? Or that these decisions are equally sound? I believe that doing so weakens the concept of autonomy almost beyond recognition and obscures the distinction between more and less mature decisions.

Harris' conclusion that children deserve equal rights rests on the assumption that children's decisions are (contrary to popular belief) no less autonomous than those of adults. One problem with this approach is that most of us neither see older children as so totally non-autonomous, nor adults as so totally autonomous, as Harris asserts. Autonomous decision-making is not an all-or-nothing enterprise, but develops gradually over time. Deciding whether people are autonomous is therefore not a matter of picking out some magic moment at which they become so, but rather of deciding where to draw an admittedly somewhat arbitrary line on a continuum.

Harris recognizes this fact in part by focusing on autonomous decision-making, rather than autonomous persons, and in part by his stand that we can autonomously choose to live with some defects in our decision-making patterns. Both are consonant with the more sophisticated contemporary understanding of autonomy that acknowledges how imperfectly humans function and tries to respect and work with less than complete autonomy. But it may be inefficient to have to do this for every decision, so it makes sense to set up general guidelines for different kinds of situations. Thus society may decide that children below a certain age, incarcerated adults or women in labour, are capable of only limited autonomy. These guidelines are admittedly imprecise and open to error.

Harris wants us to believe that society has grievously misjudged children's capacity for autonomy; to remedy that mistake, children should be offered the same rights as adults. Because he proposes no lower age limit for these rights, it is clear that he accepts a very undemanding conception of autonomy. But even if we did recognize some such weak notion, serious difficulties remain.

Autonomy with respect to major life decisions tends to be inadequate in children even as old as 10. Take Sean, for example. He has always been resistant to direction from parents and teachers, preferring to do things his own way. Often the price is high. For example, because he prefers games to homework, his grades are low and he is not acquiring the background knowledge he needs to keep open a broad array of future choices. He says he is aware of this problem, but argues that since he wants to be a racing car driver he'll be fine. When confronted with statistics about how few openings there are for racing car drivers, he answers that since he is well co-ordinated, he will get one of them and if he doesn't, he'll cope. He maintains that as he is prepared to live with the consequences of his current choices he should be free to do as he pleases.

What is Harris to do with this case – or the still more disturbing ones where a 14-year-old proposes to continue a pregnancy, drop out of school or run away from home? If he denies their autonomy, he eviscerates his own position. So he must have to argue that they constitute a legitimate exercise of autonomy. Yet all involve wishful thinking, lack of information and weak control; their autonomy is questionable. Given deleterious effects of such low-level decision-making on both the children in question and society at large, it would be a serious mistake to see it as the basis for equal rights.

HARRIS FIGHTS BACK

Harris' rebuttal is to point to silly and self-destructive behaviour on the part of adults. There is, of course, no lack of such behaviour. However, I believe that we have higher standards for adults, so that the same epithets do not necessarily refer to the same low level of autonomy as for children. Adults also usually have more resources (both mental and physical) to help them recover from their lapses.

In any case, few situations in life or law permit us reliably to draw exceptionless lines between two categories. The rest of the time, we must decide whether the exceptions are so significant that they make a mockery of the distinction we are trying to make. If there are significant exceptions, it is necessary either to give up on the idea of drawing any useful line at all, or accept that it will in some cases be arbitrary. I believe that only a utilitarian analysis can tell us which approach makes the most sense in a particular situation. In other words, it is necessary to compare the consequences of the two competing approaches, and to choose the one that is, on balance, most beneficial. So in this case we need to compare the consequences of treating all but a very few clearly non-autonomous individuals, including children, as if they were autonomous, with the consequences of assuming that children are generally non-autonomous and assuming that adults are generally autonomous. Given the facts of human development and the reality of human interdependence, there are excellent reasons for choosing the latter course and recognizing a line between children (for whom the burden of proof will lie in showing their decisions to be autonomous) and adults (for whom the burden of proof lies in showing their decisions to be non-autonomous).

How can this approach deal with those in-between cases – proficient children and deficient adults – where the system breaks down and decisions begin to seem arbitrary? There is no doubt that many children are capable of quite autonomous decisions on some issues, and that a few children are capable of a good deal more. Naturally, this gift often reaps its own rewards, as children who have it tend to be better at getting what they want. But I would agree with Harris that these children deserve greater freedom than the average child. Good parents are already aware of their children's characteristics, and treat them according to their natures. However, 'official' recognition of their status would also be appropriate, since not all parents are sensitive to their children's needs, and bureaucratic institutions like schools are not generally geared to them either. In the last twenty years, children's legal rights have been significantly expanded in the United States. Expanding them still more would create some problems, but they are no more insurmountable than many others we already cope with, and are less daunting than many others that would be caused by children's liberation.

So much for precocious children. What about deficient adults? In part society's response does – and should – depend on the nature of their deficiencies. If the deficiencies are fundamental, then those persons need continued protection for their own welfare, as well as for the protection of others.[2] If an individual's problem is more limited, doing nothing may be the best response. For example, quite a few people have trouble thinking ahead, or subordinating their present desires to future benefits. Although this trait undermines their welfare and risks harming others, it would be impossible to limit their decision-making powers without confining them to an institution. Some live short, unhappy lives; others may eventually develop the skills they need to function reasonably well.

Does the existence of a few proficient children and a few fundamentally deficient adults undermine the attempt to draw a meaningful line between children and adults? I don't believe that it does, once we compare the advantages and liabilities of the conflicting policies. In this case, the choice is between a policy that distinguishes fairly sharply between children and adults (leaving some anomalous cases at the centre) and a policy that relies on those (relatively few) anomalous cases to refuse to uphold any but the weakest dividing line between them. Setting a fairly high standard avoids the worst injustices done to precocious children if coupled with expanded opportunities for recognizing their autonomy. It can allow weakly autonomous adults inappropriate freedom, but prevents some of the most serious harms by protecting those with the most deficient autonomy. Setting a very low standard sidesteps these messy accommodations, but only at the cost of still worse consequences. It refuses to recognize that because autonomy develops over time and because contemporary society offers a tempting array of unwise paths, children will quite often imprudently choose paths that fundamentally and irreversibly undermine their own long-term welfare. Furthermore – and liberationist arguments fail to recognize this fact – large numbers of individuals making unwise personal decisions make life worse for everybody.

MORAL ISSUES

I have just argued that if children are, for the most part, only weakly autonomous, children's liberation would be harmful. But even if children were quite autonomous, contra Harris, it would not follow that they should have equal rights. For social creatures like humans, autonomy is not a sufficient condition for letting people loose in society on their own: moral sensitivity to the needs of other is also necessary for society to function in a desirable way, indeed, to function at all. The capacity for moral behaviour, like the capacity for autonomy, develops over time. This is, in part, because moral action depends on some of the same characteristics as autonomy. Society can thus be expected to function significantly worse if children join it as equal players before they become somewhat morally sophisticated, and significantly better if they must wait until a majority of them do meet that criterion.

Harris does not appear to notice this crucial point because he focuses so fully on autonomy as the overriding social value. Indeed, the roots of children's liberation tend to lie in liberal – even libertarian – theories that treat human societies as groups of egoistic, rational calculators freely choosing their commitments. This conception of society has recently been criticized as both cognitively and morally inadequate. On the one hand, it underestimates the trust and altruism necessary to keep a society functioning at all. Imagine, for instance, how difficult life would be if we could *never* assume that our belongings were safe from theft.[3] And how in the world would children get reared if nobody took time out of their busy schedules to feed them, change their diapers or teach them to read? On the other hand, this conception of society tends to focus so much on individual autonomy and self-realization that concern for the common welfare has a way of dropping out of the picture altogether. The underlying assumption is that life would be just fine if everybody did only what they perceived to be in their own interest. On the contrary, things would be even worse than they are for many people if everyone behaved that way, and many people would live much more satisfying lives if there were a generally higher standard of moral action.

Because of these liberal underpinnings, proponents of children's liberation seem unconcerned about children's moral development, touching upon it, if at all, in only the most cursory way (Cohen, 1980; Harris, 1982). Oddly enough, the same is true for many critical discussions of children's liberation. Joel Feinberg, for example, argues in the liberal vein that children's liberation is untenable because it closes off children's future choices (Feinberg, 1980). Yet failing to consider the consequences of children's liberation for children's moral development implies that either morality is unimportant, or that it is part of autonomy. Neither alternative is plausible. There is no reason to think that anything like a livable society results from individuals making decisions about their own welfare in the absence of explicit concern about consequences for others. Nor is there any hint in Harris' definition of autonomy about such concern; at most, one might discern enlightened self-interest. But morality makes more demands than enlightened self-interest.

So accepting children's liberation on Harris' terms seems to mean that we resign ourselves to a world where many more people are less prudent than is now the case, and where they take still less account of the needs of others. I believe that if there were many more imprudent or morally deficient individuals it would be still more difficult than at present to cope with the problems facing humanity. Given the gravity of these problems, it is questionable whether future generations can count on anything like a decent life. In fact, if we as a species don't start behaving significantly more prudently and morally, it is beginning to seem likely that human civilization will regress to much more primitive conditions, and human survival is by no means assured. If, on the contrary, we attempt to inculcate higher standards of prudence and morality in rising generations, we might survive and even prosper. Given all this, adopting a narrow conception of justice that requires equal rights for children would seem most unwise, all things considered.

THE FIXITY OF CHILDHOOD

Thus far my argument depends on the fact that the average child is at present less prudent and moral than the average adult. But perhaps if we treated children differently, they would be sufficiently prudent and moral to justify children's liberation.

There are some grounds for believing that if children were treated differently, they would behave more maturely. If children were routinely offered more explanations and fewer orders, it would be more difficult for the adult world to impose indefensible rules on them. I also believe that children could also be expected more easily to understand, obey and internalize reasonable rules. Children would also be likely to benefit from a carefully graduated expansion of freedom if accompanied by appropriate responsibility. One can see these factors at work when children, like prefects in private schools or members of student government, are entrusted with special responsibilities. Additional treatment of this kind would help them develop their capacity for autonomous and moral action in an environment that protects them as much as possible from irreversibly harmful consequences. Moreover, many children need more help dealing with, and sometimes escaping from, abusive family situations. Children have a right to this kind of help and making sure they get it should be a top social priority. But these rights neither assume nor imply children's liberation.

Whether children would respond constructively to equal rights at an early age is an entirely different matter. The most direct evidence one could have about this question would be experimental. But it would obviously be difficult to arrange this kind of experiment and it would not give us answers for at least a generation. It would also be immoral to attempt such a thing without first gathering indirect evidence about the probability of a good outcome. I believe that there is sufficient evidence of this kind to suggest that children's liberation would not be a good idea.

A look at models of human development may shed some light on the question whether children (and society) would flourish with children's liberation. Proponents of children's liberation rarely say much about this matter. Shulamith Firestone is an exception who articulates the position that seems to be at the core of much children's liberation thinking (Firestone, 1970, pp. 76ff.).

Firestone relies on the work of Aries and others who maintain that children lived much more like adults before the recent 'invention' of childhood. Ariès argues that:

In medieval society the idea of childhood did not exist; this is not to suggest that children were neglected, forsaken or despised. The idea of childhood is not to be confused with affection for children: it corresponds to an awareness of the particular nature of childhood, that particular nature which distinguishes the child from the adult, even the young adult. In medieval society, this awareness was lacking.[4]

Firestone, building on this view, asserts that 'The best way to raise a child is to LAY OFF' (Firestone, 1970, p. 91). The underlying suggestion is that the adult world interferes with children's natural development when it protects limits or coerces, and, that left alone, internal forces would speedily render them capable of adult life. In other words human nature flowers from within, developing relatively independently of the environment (although the 'wrong' environment can obviously interfere with 'proper' development).

This view harks back to the so-called 'growth' model long associated with Rousseau. The growth model says that development in humans is determined by an internal plan and so there is no need for external shaping in the form of education. Such assumptions about human nature are still widely believed, for example, by those who are attracted to biological determinism. They are in contrast with the notion of a more externally-driven model of development, something like the *tabula rasa* associated with Locke; this approach assumes that all mental development is a result of experience. Both the growth model and the *tabula rasa* are, of course, extreme views without much credibility today. Much more plausible is some

156

interactionist position, and most of the contemporary controversy arises with respect to the degree of influence exerted by each factor. At present many thinkers are more inclined toward the biological end of the spectrum – consider society's continuing fascination with sociobiology, the most recent incarnation of internalist thinking,[5] and the enormous resources now being poured into the Human Genome Project on the assumption that it will, among other things, reveal the wellsprings of human behaviour. However, I believe that there is evidence that environmental factors are extremely important in human development.[6] This is, of course, a major debate that cannot be resolved here. However, one factor in my conclusion here is the weakness and inconsistency in Rousseau's own thinking (Purdy, 1992, ch. 3). Another is that this model predicts that freer children would develop well on their own, but that is not borne out by experience.

It is important to keep in mind that even were a biologically determinist model to be substantiated, it would not necessarily support children's liberation. It could turn out to be true that children need a certain number of years (or experiences) to develop the kind of responsibility essential for exercising adult freedoms as well as adults. That fact would undermine both justice-based and utilitarian arguments for children's liberation.[7] Conversely, a more Lockean understanding doesn't necessarily undermine children's liberation. Although it would presumably rule out any extreme version of it, at least for those with utilitarian leanings, it may well be true that certain kinds of early experiences could prepare children for adult freedom and responsibility much more effectively than current child-rearing approaches.[8]

DEVELOPMENTAL EXPERIMENTS

What evidence is there for freedom's bad effects on children's development? A great deal of useful information can be found by gleaning information from a variety of sources, such as historical experience, psychological studies and contemporary sociological trends. Only a quick survey of these matters is possible here.[9]

In one historical experiment, eighteenth-century British parents attempted to provide their children with what they understood Rousseau to be recommending: complete freedom from ages 2 to 12, including freedom from academic studies. They were to have 'natural' surroundings, and consequences, not parental demands, were to be their teachers.[10] As Christina Hardyment writes in her book on the history of childrearing advice:

> unfortunately, parents and educators rapidly became disillusioned by their experiments with nobly savage children. Richard Lovell Edgeworth's boy became so unmanageable that he was sent away to boarding school. David Williams described one little child of nature who, aged 13, slept on the floor, spoke 'a jargon he had formed out of the several dialects of the family', could neither read nor write, and was 'a little emaciated figure, his countenance betraying marks of premature decay, or depraved passions; his teeth discolored, his hearing almost gone'.
>
> (Hardyment, 1983, p. 19)

Obviously, this account does not by itself give us much evidence, but it certainly suggests a need for caution. A more fully documented twentieth-century experiment in so-called psychoanalytic pedagogy is more informative, however. Based on the Freudian idea that repression is the cause of neurosis, psychoanalytic pedagogy sought to prevent neurosis in children by leaving them free to develop with minimal interference from adults. This movement culminated in a series of experiments; most were short-lived and were regarded as unsuccessful.[11] Liberation, including by the way sexual liberation, was to have produced creative, contented individuals. Instead, the children remained distressingly infantile. They showed relatively little interest in the world about them, preferring to daydream, and were not toilet trained. They were uncooperative, balking at the most minimal demands by adults about timetables, mealtimes, table manners and ordinary hygienic measures. In addition, they were irritable, could not concentrate and were subject to obsessions and depression; nor did they show any special creativity (Purdy, 1992, p. 95).

This regime is remarkably similar to what children's liberation would prescribe for young children. Its results suggest the need for great caution in implementing anything like children's liberation. This conclusion is reinforced by psychological studies that consistently link *laissez-faire* permissiveness – childrearing that leaves maximal decision-making power to children – with impulsiveness, irresponsibility, disorganization, aggression, and intellectual and behavioural immaturity. On the contrary, high control coupled with warmth and rational explanation are related to the opposite traits.[12]

The underlying explanation probably goes something like this. Behaviour is primarily a function of learning, rather than some purely internal process. Desirable traits are harder to learn than undesirable ones, since they involve self-control, and the willingness to put off gratification and sometimes to give it up altogether. Unless children get help in learning how to do these things from parents and other respected adults, they will tend to choose immediate gratification over more long-term benefit, and will tend to prefer their own interests to those of others. When parents set standards and encourage children to meet them, in part by setting limits for them, children experience success and praise. That helps them internalize the standards, and develop the kind of self-esteem that allows them to value themselves and resist pressures for self-destructive and immoral behaviour. Children who do not develop in this way will have a harder time with others and in school, and will be more vulnerable to destructive peer pressure.[13]

This position is based on a solid array of psychological and sociological studies. Such studies are subject to the usual caveats about research on humans; however, while there is undoubtedly more to be said on the subject, it would be foolish to ignore the evidence that *laissez-faire* permissiveness undermines the development of desirable traits. Surely the burden of proof is on those who argue for this kind of permissiveness to show either that the evidence is flawed or that the relevant traits are undesirable.

If adopting children's liberation is likely to reduce rather than enhance prudence and morality in children, its overall consequences would be most disheartening. Children's liberation could be expected to make family life still more difficult than it already is, undermine the educational system and increase exploitation of children and other workers.

There is no space here to develop any of these arguments at length.[14] But consider briefly some of the more obvious problems. First, children's liberation makes schooling optional, for adults are not required to go to school. Furthermore, it would interfere with children's right to work (or just 'hang out' if they have the resources to do so). Therefore schooling cannot be required of children.

Now it is undeniable that most school systems are far from ideal; however, despite some calls for their abolition (Illich, 1971), it would seem much more sensible to concentrate on improving them instead. Where else can we count on children learning the academic and cultural things they need to know to function well in advanced technological societies? Where else could they learn critical thinking – if we as a society made that subject no priority? Furthermore, despite the radical accusation that schools only reproduce social hierarchy, schools can help children climb out of poverty. They could do it more consistently if society wanted them to do so. Given the reality of inadequate home environments, school is some children's best hope. In general, much of what is wrong with schools can be traced to problems in society: weakening schools attacks the wrong enemy.

If compulsory schooling were abolished, many fewer children would receive schooling. But lack of education would not be equally distributed. Relatively large numbers of middle and upper-class children would probably continue to go to school, but for poor children, the pressure to earn money, together with the apparent lack of opportunity for improving their lot by means of education, would probably lead to an even higher dropout rate than is now the case. Yet dropping out tends to lock them into poverty. Abolishing compulsory schooling would also probably accelerate the loss of support for state schools already evident among the wealthier classes, leading to still more inadequate state schools for those who cannot afford private ones. So this consequence of children's liberation would undoubtedly widen and harden the gap between rich and poor.

Second, opening the labour market to young people would also create serious problems. On the one hand, only the brightest and best-situated young people (middle-class white boys) would likely benefit from the new opportunities. It is true that a few less well-off children might escape the negative influences of school and thus take full advantage of their natural talents. And some children who think school pointless might see it through new eyes after a period of work. Getting practical experience in 'the real world' might also help some individuals pick suitable fields. On the other hand, children disadvantaged by poverty, race or gender would face a flooded labour market. Lacking skills, they would be competing for minimal wages and risking exploitation. As the benefits of children's liberation could probably be achieved by other means, including intelligent work study programmes, its drawbacks seem overwhelming.[15]

CONCLUSION

These potentially disastrous consequences of children's liberation are by themselves sufficient grounds for rejecting it. As I argued earlier, still broader future-oriented concerns are another reason. Decisions about children's place are inextricably linked with our goals for them. Those goals are in turn tied to our hopes for a given society, and for humanity as a whole. It is impossible to determine on the basis of one limited factor like autonomy what constitutes justice for children, as Harris attempts to do. Children are not mere instruments for achieving a particular vision of the future, but neither can we decide what is best for them in isolation from society. Our best hope is to adopt higher standards for new generations, not lower ones. Arguing that this is unfair is no more sensible than arguing that it is unfair for children to have to learn more biology in 1995 than in 1895.

NOTES

1 Harris' understanding of autonomy here is significantly more sophisticated than his earlier emphasis on instrumental reasoning. See Harris, 1982. For an extended response to the views expressed in this piece, see Purdy, 1992, esp. ch. 2.

2 In the past, society has dealt with them by a variety of mechanisms, many, like insane asylums, cruel and inadequate for their needs. However, that history does not preclude more appropriate ones now.

3 Unfortunately, in some living situations people must already live with that assumption.

4 Ariès, 1962, p. 125.

5 For an excellent refutation of this theory's application to humans, see Philip Kitcher's *Vaulting Ambition: Sociobiology and the Quest for Human Nature* (Cambridge, Mass.: MIT Press, 1985).

6 It is important to keep in mind that there is a moral and political dimension to this debate. Conservative thinkers tend to be attracted to the various forms of biological determinism, for it sees human development as relatively unchangeable. It follows that social programmes that aim at a more egalitarian society will be ineffective, since less talented individuals will inevitably drift to the bottom of the ladder. Conversely, progressive thinkers tend to be attracted to environmental explanations of human development that offer more opportunity to intervene in favour of a more egalitarian society. Thus egalitarianism makes spending on such programmes morally mandatory.

7 Harris' argument is justice-based: it relies on the principle that injustice occurs when like cases are treated differently, together with the claim that children are like adults in the relevant ways. A utilitarian argument looks at the consequences of granting equal rights to children.

8 However, the experiences in question may involve more control at some stages, rather than more freedom. Consider, for example, a study comparing Danish and American families that supports the hypothesis that learning self-control early is possible. Danish families are strict with young children but permissive with adolescents. Those adolescents are

more self-disciplined and autonomous than the American children who have lived in a more consistently permissive environment. See Kandel and Lesser, in Bronfenbrenne, 1972.

9 Purdy, 1992, ch. 3 takes these questions up in much greater detail.

10 How accurately these precepts represent Rousseau is another question. However, they are useful for our purposes because they have much in common with what children's liberation would recommend.

11 Many of their authors emigrated to the United States, where they proceeded to criticize progressive education on the grounds that it lacked the structure, limits and authority that children need to develop well (Purdy, 1992, p. 97).

12 Diana Baumrind distinguishes between 'democratic' and 'laissez-faire' permissiveness. The former requires parents to supply justifications for rules, and underlines the importance of discussion with children; however, where parent and child disagree on important issues, parents can overrule a child (so perhaps 'democratic' is the wrong label here). The latter lets children go their own way even where a parent has strong objections (Purdy, 1992, pp. 100ff.).

13 I consider these issues in much greater detail in Purdy, 1992, ch. 3.

14 For much more detailed discussion, see Purdy, 1992, esp. Part II.

15 One might contend that precisely the same argument about unemployment, etc., could be used to try to keep women out of the labour market. However, justice requires that women be offered equal opportunity in work, whereas that is not true for children. Therefore society's response to the same objections may be different.

12

HARRIS' REPLY

Purdy claims that I assume but do not argue for the thesis that autonomy is the ground of equal rights. I do not assume this and so the fact that I do not argue for it is unsurprising. What I *do* do is rehearse two different views about where equal rights might come from. I suggest that either it is thought that rights are (in some mysterious way!) possessed by 'natural kinds' in which case since children are as much members of the natural kind that human beings are as adults, they qualify on that ground; or rights are possessed by individuals with a certain range of capacities. I indicate what this range of capacities might be thought to be. Principal among them would be self-consciousness and autonomy but not principally autonomy. I then point out that insofar as these capacities are possessed by sorts or creatures, they are also possessed in significant measure by children. So autonomy is not the ground to equal rights. The ground is either membership of a natural kind or the possession of a range of capacities, among them autonomy. My strategy is to indicate that one or other of these views is widely held and that neither of them give grounds for the exclusion of children.

Next Purdy complains that I do not provide much argument for the view that children are as autonomous as adults and that I simply assert it as true. Again this is not quite fair. The form my argument takes is rather to issue a challenge to the effect that if it is claimed that children do differ systematically from adults in respect of their autonomy or degree of autonomy, then this needs to be sustained and in the absence of detailed evidence in particular cases, it is not a plausible hypothesis.

Then Purdy goes on to challenge, in more detail, my assumption that children are autonomous, and I am glad that it has moved to being an assumption rather than an unsupported assertion; this is nearer the truth. She points out that autonomy is not an absolute. This I agree with and argued specifically for in my book *The Value of Life* (1990). There I suggested that it is not persons that are either autonomous or not but rather that decisions are either autonomous or not, and that autonomy is established by a web of features of decision-making which may be present wholly or in part in any particular case. Hence I agree with Purdy that autonomy is not an absolute and I think I have argued, more subtly than she has done, for the ways and the reasons why it is not.

She suggests, by posing a rhetorical question, that there are only a few proficient children and only a few fundamentally deficient adults. Impressionistic evidence, admittedly, strongly indicates the contrary. It is surely plausible to suppose that a large proportion of children, say between 14 and 18 years of age, are highly competent and the law now widely recognizes this in some aspects. It permits children increasingly to consent and refuse medical treatments, sexual relations and so on. This is certainly more than just a few proficient children. Equally, we are aware of very large numbers of not particularly proficient adults – depending on how demanding one's standards are.

Purdy then makes a rather extraordinary claim in her section headed *Moral issues*. She says, and I quote,

> But even if children were quite autonomous, contra Harris, it would not follow that they should have equal rights. For social creatures like humans, autonomy is not a sufficient condition for letting people loose in society on their own: moral sensitivity to the needs of others is also necessary.
>
> (p. 153)

Whilst I agree that moral sensitivity is not only highly desirable but necessary for cohesion in society, it does not follow that it is one of the grounds of individual rights. People who, for example, do not exhibit moral sensitivity do not thereby lose their rights. Indeed it is fairly standard to insist on and even emphasize and protect the rights of those who have conspicuously demonstrated, by criminal acts perhaps, their lack of moral sensitivity. The rights, particularly the civil rights, of such individuals are always defended; and rightly so. It is not thought that they have lost their civil rights merely because they have not demonstrated moral sensitivity.

She then seeks to discredit my argument by citing some rather bizarre historical experiments in which children were left 'free to develop with minimal interference from adults' (p. 158). Children's liberation does not require that adults do not take an active role in the lives of children any more than women's liberation requires that men do not take an active role in the lives of women. The point is that such a role should be taken as between equal partners. Children's liberation would allow adults to persuade, cajole, criticize, rebuke and so on; what it would not do is give them the freedom to coerce. So when Purdy says 'Unless children get help in learning how to do these things [making difficult decisions, relationships and so forth] from parents and other respected adults they will tend to chose immediate gratification over more long-term benefit, and will tend to prefer their own interests as to those of others' (p. 159), she is probably speaking the truth. But no one, least of all me, is suggesting that children should not get help in learning from adults and indeed from other children. We should all get help in learning from each other, just as I have received considerable help from Purdy by reading her criticism; and I am grateful to her for it!

BIBLIOGRAPHY

Archard, D. (1993) *Children: Rights and Childhood*, London: Routledge.

Ariès, P. (1962) *Centuries of Childhood*, trans. R. Baldick, London: Jonathan Cape.

Baumrind, D. (1967) 'Childcare Practices Anteceding Three Patterns of Preschool Behavior', *Genetic Psychology Monographs*, 75 (1967), 43–88.

Blustein, J. (1982) *Parents and Children: The Ethics of the Family*, Oxford: Oxford University Press.

Bronfenbrenner, U. (1972) *Influences on Human Development*, Hinsdale, Ill.: Dryden.

Cohen, H. (1980) *Equal Rights for Children*, Totowa, NJ: Littlefield Adams.

Condry, J. and Siman, M.L. (1974) 'Characteristics of Peer- and Adult-Oriented Children', *Journal of Marriage and the Family*, 36 (August 1974), 543–54.

Elkind, D. (1984) *All Grown Up and No Place to Go: Teenagers in Crisis*, Reading, Mass.: Addison-Wesley.

Feinberg, J. (1980) 'The Child's Right to an Open Future', in W. Aiken and H. LaFollette (eds), *Whose Child? Children's Rights, Parental Authority, and State Power*, Totowa, NJ: Rowman & Allenheld.

Firestone, S. (1970) *The Dialectic of Sex*, New York: Bantam.

Gross, B. and Gross, R. (eds) *The Children's Rights Movement: Overcoming the Oppression of Young People*, New York: Anchor/Doubleday.

Hardyment, C. (1983) *Dream Babies: Three Centuries of Good Advice on Child Care*, New York: Harper & Row.

Harris, J. (1983) 'The Political Status of Children', in Keith Graham (ed.), *Contemporary Political Philosophy: Radical Studies*, Cambridge: Cambridge University Press.

—— (1990) *The Value of Life*, London: Routledge.

—— (1992) *Wonderwoman and Superman: Ethics and Human Biotechnology*, Oxford: Oxford University Press.

Houlgate, L.D. (1980) *The Child and the State: A Normative Theory of Juvenile Rights*, Baltimore: Johns Hopkins University Press.

Illich, I. (1971) *Deschooling Society*, New York: Harper & Row.

Keown, J. (1995) *Examining Euthanasia: Ethical, Legal and Clinical Perspectives*, Cambridge: Cambridge University Press.

LaFollette, H. (1980) 'Licensing Parents', *Philosophy and Public Affairs*, 9 (Winter 1980), 182–97.

Locke, J. (1968) *The Educational Writings*, ed. J.L. Axtell, Cambridge: Cambridge University Press.

Maccoby, E. (1980) *Social Development: Psychological Growth and the Parent–Child Relationship*, San Diego: Harcourt Brace Jovanovich.

Minow, M. (1986) 'Rights for the Next Generation: A Feminist Approach to Children's Rights', *Harvard Women's Law Journal*, 9, 1–24.

O'Neill, O. and Ruddick, W. (1979) *Having Children: Philosophical and Legal Reflections on Parenthood*, Oxford: Oxford University Press.

Palmeri, A. (1980) 'Childhood's End: Toward the Liberation of Children', in W. Aiken and H. LaFollette (eds), *Whose Child?*, Totowa, NJ: Rowman & Allenheld.

Purdy, L.M. (1992) *In Their Best Interest? The Case Against Equal Rights for Children*, Ithaca NY: Cornell University Press.

Rousseau, J-J. (1979) *Emile, or On Education*, trans. A. Bloom, New York: Basic Books, first published 1762.

Scarre, G. (ed.) (1989) *Children, Parents, and Politics*, Cambridge: Cambridge University Press.

Skolnick, A. (ed.) (1974) *Rethinking Childhood: Perspectives on Development and Society*, Boston: Little Brown.

Stephen, J.F. (1967) *Liberty, Equality and Fraternity*, Cambridge: Cambridge University Press, first published 1871.

Wald, M.S. (1979) 'Children's Rights: A Framework for Analysis', *University of California Davis Law Review*, 12 (2), 255–82.

Zelizer, V. (1985) *Pricing the Priceless Child*, New York: Basic Books.

Part V

ANIMAL LIBERATION

13

FOR ANIMAL RIGHTS

Andrew Linzey

Of all the possible subjects for liberation from oppression, the case of animals may at first strike us as strange. The most obvious reason for this is that animals have far too infrequently been on the moral agenda – at least until comparatively recently. That is not to say that many great minds in western philosophy and theology have never concerned themselves with animals or that there have not been powerful voices for animals within western thinking – indeed there have been (see e.g. Primatt, 1776; Ryder, 1989; Sorabji, 1993).

If we ask why animals – their claims and rights – have been historically so little on the agenda of human affairs, there is another equally obvious reason. It is because in almost all human societies and cultures, it has been usual for humans to exploit animals. So much so that it is difficult to think of *any* human endeavour in almost any field that has not used, or rather abused, animals. Today we hunt, ride, shoot, fish, eat, wear, cage, trap, exhibit, factory farm and experiment upon billions of animals worldwide every year. Human life and culture as we have received it depends upon the relentless and frequently ruthless exploitation of animals.

Because all of us are party in some way to animal exploitation and the gains that this exploitation has procured for us, it is difficult to be impartial about animals. As one recent philosopher has put it there is a 'limited human capacity for impartiality in giving consideration to the interest of animals' (Brown, 1988, p. x). This is a simple point but one worth reminding ourselves of at the outset. When it comes to the exploitation of human subjects most of us rightly sense that *their* liberation will not adversely affect *us*. We may of course be wrong about our sense of what other liberation movements may cost us – at least eventually – but when it comes to animals we can be fairly certain that *their* liberation is not going to be cost-free to their exploiters – in which camp we must include, I believe, almost all human beings.

Because of our common indebtedness to animal exploitation, we need to work hard even to *think* impartially about animals. I am reminded of that line of Bertrand Russell: 'Few English people think, indeed most English people would rather die than think – and most of them actually do.' Now, I am not suggesting that only animal liberationists think impartially about animals – though I certainly do think it is the case that many who do exploit animals haven't thought seriously about the issue at all.

THREE EXAMPLES OF OPPRESSION

But what precisely should animals be liberated *from*? Let us begin by focusing on three practical examples of how we use animals today – in farming, sport and science. Needless to say, almost all animal liberationists would regard them as examples of oppression.

The first example I choose is that of battery hen production. There are about thirty million hens in battery conditions in the United Kingdom and around nine billion in the United States. Each battery cage holds five birds. The space allotted to each bird is less than one A4 piece of paper. They stand on sloping wire mesh, in semi-darkness, five to a cage. Their diet consists of dry mash which contains artificial yolk colouring. The mash occasionally or frequently is treated with antibiotics to prevent disease. Hens stay in these batteries on average for one year: eighteen to seventy-two weeks. Because violence and cannibalism are not uncommon, hens are occasionally de-beaked with hot pincers. After seventy-two weeks, they are transported to slaughter where they are hung upside down, pre-stunned with an electric shock, have their throat cut electronically and are then put into scalding water to make their feathers fall off. (Just in case you are wondering what happens to their male counterparts, within seventy-two hours of hatching male chicks are gassed, suffocated or homogenized, that is, fed through chopping machines *en masse*).

The second example I choose is drawn from the world of sport, namely deer hunting with hounds. There are four packs of stag hounds in England (stag hunting is illegal in Scotland). Altogether they kill approximately 200 deer a year. Generally, they chase three kinds: big stags, red hinds and the spring stags, during differing periods between April and October of each year. Deer of both sexes are hunted and the law allows hunting while the female is pregnant. The average length of a hunt is three to four hours during which time the deer are progressively weakened and exhausted. While the deer are usually cornered by the hounds, occasionally they are brought down by the hounds before being shot by the huntsmen. Most commonly, deer are killed as they move downhill, progressively weakened, and are caught in the riverbeds.

The third example I choose is drawn from the world of science, namely the patenting of the now famous 'oncomouse'. The onco-mouse is a mouse genetically altered so that it 'naturally' develops cancer. Whereas in the past, scientists frequently induced cancer arti-ficially in animals, the oncomouse effectively offers them a genetically designed laboratory tool ready to hand. The oncomouse, or its equiv-alent, has already been patented in the United States and has recently been patented by the European Patent Office. In practice this means that the patent holders legally 'own' the animal in the same way as human artefacts are owned. This is the first time that animals have been legally classified as human inventions (see Linzey, 1994). The purpose of patenting is legally to secure one's rights to the property and also, of course, to benefit from the financial return in the trade in new commodities. It is frequently overlooked that the European patent actually covers 'all non-human mammals', so it may only be a question of time before we have the oncopig, the oncochicken, the oncosheep or, indeed, the oncochimp.

NEGATIVE THEORIES OF THE STATUS OF ANIMALS

If we ask *why* it is that these practices – to take only three examples – are currently regarded as morally acceptable in most western coun-tries, then we need to address the underlying thinking about animals which justifies such treatment. As has often been said, 'there is nothing so practical as a good theory'. I begin by looking at two negative theories and one potentially progressive one.

Humanocentric theory

According to this view, animals have no moral status. Humans have no direct duties to animals except insofar as some human interest is involved. Wanton cruelty may be wrong not because it infringes the rights of animals but because cruelty brutalises human beings, or leads to similar activity in relation to human subjects. Morality, strictly speaking, only concerns what humans do to humans, or to other subjects insofar as they affect human subjects.

This theory may also be called the classical, or Aristotelian–Thomist view. In terms of systematic theology, it was the virtually unchallenged Christian view until the eighteenth century. As late as the middle of the nineteenth century, Pope Pius IX forbade the opening of an animal protection office in Rome on the grounds that humans had duties to other humans but none to animals. It finds its clearest continuing expression in Roman Catholic moral theology, for example: 'Zoophilists often lose sight of the end for which animals, irrational creatures, were created by God, viz., the service and use of man. . . . In fact, Catholic moral doctrine teaches that animals have no rights on the part of man' (Palazzini, 1962, p. 73).

There are two main philosophical/theological justifications for this view both derived, at least in part, from Aristotle and systematized in the Christian tradition mainly through the work of St Thomas Aquinas. First, animals are by divine providence and nature our slaves – given for our use. 'Hereby is refuted the error of those who said it is sinful for man to kill brute animals; for by divine providence they are intended for man's use according to the order of nature. Hence it is not wrong for man to make use of them either by killing or in any other way whatever' (*Summa Contra Gentiles*, pp. 220–4). Second, animals are by definition non-rational creatures, they cannot therefore possess a mind, or an immortal soul, and are not persons possessing rights. Their *raison d'être* is to serve the higher intellectual species, namely human beings.

Recent Roman Catholic teaching may have modified this stark Thomistic perspective. The *Catechism of the Catholic Church* does acknowledge that we owe animals 'kindness' after the example shown by the saints. But the same *Catechism* reaffirms the major elements of Thomist thought. God still destines 'all material creatures for the good of the human race'. It is '*contrary to human dignity*' (but only it seems contrary to *human* dignity) to cause animals to suffer or die needlessly, and 'it is likewise unworthy to spend money on them [animals] which should as a priority go to the relief of human misery' (*Catechism*, 1994, pp. 81; 516–17; my emphasis).

Are the interests of animals dealt with impartially or adequately by this theory? Quite obviously they are not. Indeed the telling presumption of this theory is that animals aren't worth anything *in themselves* at all. Moral considerability arises only within the human sphere – that is the obvious point and intention of this approach. But it should also be equally obvious that this view begins with the very assumption, or assumptions, which require justification. It needs to be shown *why* human rationality or human personhood – for example – should be regarded as the main or exclusive grounds for postulating moral worth.

The humanocentric view would certainly be supportive of the three practices we have described: hen batteries, sport hunting and animal patenting. It may be that some forms of Thomism might object to transgenic engineering of animals on the grounds that it alters the given order of creation; but even here what would finally determine the morality of what we do to animals is simply whether humans would benefit. Once that benefit is established, moral justification follows automatically.

Contractualist theory

According to this view, rights and duties flow from persons who are capable of making contracts or entering into mutual obligations. In short: no duties, no rights.

This is a variant of the standard Aristotelian–Thomist position. Aristotle held that justice required rational friendship – a quality he judged was impossible between those who were not equals (and hence slaves and animals, to take only two examples, were excluded from the moral community) (*Nicomachean Ethics*, 1161a–b). Aquinas held likewise that friendship was only possible between rational creatures (*Summa Theologica*, Part 1, Questions 64.1 and 65.3).

Perhaps the best contemporary defence of contractualism is found in the work of John Rawls. He concludes that animals are 'outside the scope of the theory of justice' and that it is not possible for a contractualist theory to 'include them in a natural way'. The 'considered beliefs' that we owe duties to animals apparently depend upon a metaphysical view of the world separate from contractualist doctrine (Rawls, 1972, pp. 504–12). To be fair to Rawls, his theory is a limited project; his overwhelming concern is with justice to human beings (and he therefore seeks to frame a theory that will most secure his objective in relation to human subjects) but it is nevertheless telling that he finds it possible to articulate a conception of justice that so clearly excludes animals.

Notice again how utterly self-serving such a moral theory is in practice. It is we humans who decide the moral rules of the game (inevitably, I hear you say) but in such a way that impartial consideration of the status of other beings is excluded. In short: contractualist theory in itself provides no basis for opposing any practices which cause suffering or death to animals. The hen batteries, stag hunting and the oncomouse patenting would continue.

Before I move on to consider another theory, it is important to grasp what these negative theories *leave out* of their moral reckoning. They leave out any notion that other individuals of other species have intrinsic value – value, that is, *in themselves*, distinct from their usefulness to human beings. Only humans are so classified. They also leave out any direct consideration of the issue of sentiency (a shorthand term which has come to mean – albeit slightly inaccurately – the ability of a being to experience pain and suffering). That animals can and do suffer more or less analogously to individuals of our own species is not considered as morally relevant.

I now turn to the third theory, one which also has considerable contemporary currency and which appears to offer a potentially positive view of the status of animals.

Humanitarian theory

There are two key elements. First, that humans should prevent unnecessary cruelty and promote kindness to sentient beings, and second, that humans should exercise benevolence or philanthropy towards inferior creatures – especially for their own (humans') sake.

This theory, or rather sensitivity, was characteristic of what is now called the humanitarian movement especially dominant in the nineteenth and twentieth centuries and which gave rise to such organizations as the Humanitarian League, the English and American Societies for the Prevention of Cruelty to Animals and the Friends of Animals League (see Turner, 1980; Thomas, 1983). This movement was in conscious or unconscious reaction to Thomist scholasticism which failed to include animals, at least directly, within the sphere of human moral responsibility.

The RSPCA, for example, was founded by an Anglican priest, Arthur Broome, in 1824. He penned the first Prospectus of the Society in which he argues:

> Our country is distinguished by the number and variety of its benevolent institutions ... all breathing the pure spirit of Christian charity ... But shall we stop here? Is the moral circle

perfect so long as any power of doing good remains? Or can the infliction of cruelty on any being which the Almighty has endured with feelings of pain and pleasure consist with genuine and true benevolence?

(Broome, 1824, pp. 203–4)

The underlying argument is that cruelty to humans or animals is incompatible with the Christian faith; indeed the Society recorded in its First Minute Book a resolution that it was a Christian Society based specifically on the Christian faith and on Christian principles (see Turner, 1980).

Perhaps the most progressive exponent of this general theory is Humphry Primatt. His *Dissertation on the Duty of Mercy and the Sin of Cruelty to Brute Animals*, published in 1776, maintained that: 'We may pretend to what religion we please, but cruelty is atheism. We may make our boast of Christianity, but cruelty is infidelity. We may trust to our orthodoxy, but cruelty is the worst of heresies' (Primatt, 1776, p. 288).

This theory is an advance on the two previous ones. Most obviously it takes into account that other non-human creatures can suffer; what we do to them falls to some degree within the domain of justice. Moreover it accepts – albeit in those philanthropic terms so characteristic of nineteenth-century reforming movements – that the special place of humankind involves special responsibility to other creatures. But despite these advances – and advances in their historical context, where cruelty to animals was rife, they certainly were – this theory suffers from one continuing weakness characteristic of the early theories it sought consciously, or unconsciously, to oppose. And that weakness is the way in which humankind is still the dominant criterion of what constitutes moral goodness in relation to animals. It is that animals suffer, *and* that such suffering offends or dehumanizes humankind, that are the two pivotal points of this approach. It assumes that the infliction of 'necessary' pain (necessary because humans benefit from it) can be justified, and altogether leaves to one side whether human interests should, judged impartially, always come out on top in the way supposed.

When it comes to our three practical examples then, humanitarian theory, we need to remind ourselves, opposes *unnecessary* cruelty. Not all infliction of pain and death on animals is wrong – only that which is by definition wanton, without justification in relation to human betterment, namely 'cruel'. In practice, the humanitarian theory might exclude some aspects of hen batteries (certainly not commercial animal farming in general: even Primatt, despite his eloquence, was not a vegetarian) and even rule out deer hunting, but the oncomouse would probably be deemed 'necessary' cruelty.

POSITIVE THEORIES OF THE STATUS OF ANIMALS

I now turn to the three main positive theories of the status of animals.

Welfare theory

Weak welfare theory is almost indistinguishable from humanitarian theory but I shall concentrate here on the strongest utilitarian version propounded by Peter Singer. There are three key elements: first, sentiency is the only defensible boundary of moral concern between species. Second, once it can be reasonably supposed that a being is sentient, its suffering should be taken into account morally. Third, all sentient beings human or animal, have an *equal* claim to have their interests considered as individuals (see Singer, 1979; Linzey, 1976). Perhaps it is worth pointing out that Singer appears to draw the line at molluscs; everything above is sentient life.

The welfare theory has a number of advantages over its rivals: it unambiguously recognizes sentiency in the animal world (about which there is little scientific dispute – see e.g. Rollin, 1981; Rodd, 1990 and for a discordant view, Carruthers, 1992). It focuses quite specifically on *individual* sentient subjects and takes their right to be spared suffering seriously into account. Moreover its 'sentiency criterion' (see Linzey, 1976; cf. Frey, 1980, 1983) offers a more impartial means of assessing the respective interests of animals and humans alike. Although Singer has no desire to offer a *Christian* theory as such, it is not perhaps irrelevant that the emphasis upon suffering here envisaged can commend itself to philosophers and theologians alike.

One major difficulty with this brand of the welfare theory, however, is the way in which it is tied to a utilitarian ethical position. Whilst it insists that animal suffering must be treated with the greatest seriousness and that all sentient beings have an equal claim to moral consideration, this does not commit utilitarian welfarists to an absolutist position. A utilitarian position is always open to the weighing up of consequences. As Singer himself writes in his *Practical Ethics*:

> if one, or even a dozen animals had to suffer experiments in order to save thousands [presumably Singer here means thousands of the same species], I would think it right and in accordance with equal consideration of interests that they should do so.
>
> (Singer, 1979, p. 58)

In other words, if it could be shown that the suffering of some animals could save the suffering of many more, it would be justifiable to make them suffer – according to the utilitarian version of this theory.

Some of us who are non-utilitarians (and in this category I unambiguously include myself) find this kind of reckoning difficult. Quite apart from whether utilitarianism is a decent ethical theory, such a welfare theory effectively justifies the use of one or more creatures *as means to another's end* without their consent. This means in practice that individual animals can be treated in an unjust manner if the relevant utilitarian calculations are against them. Thus despite the emphasis on the moral significance of suffering, such welfare theory can and does justify the infliction of suffering in, for example, the use of sentients in laboratory experiments. The practical upshot then is that this welfare theory would oppose hen batteries and deer hunting and might oppose patenting in principle (where it causes unjustified suffering) but it would not be opposed to the use of all animals even in painful research. The oncomouse might stay.

Is there a better moral theory inclusive of animals? I now turn to another positive theory of the status of animals which tries to meet the very weakness embodied in utilitarian theory.

Rights theory

Again, there are three key elements: first, animals are ends in themselves and must not be regarded as means to human ends, as resources, commodities, laboratory tools or units of production. Second, all animals which are – in the words of Tom Regan – 'subjects of a life' have inherent value and therefore possess rights (Regan, 1983, pp. 232–65). Third, those beings which possess inherent value possess it *equally*, so it is normally wrong to infringe the rights of *individual* animals, no matter the consequences.

179

There are secular and theological doctrines of animal rights. The secular philosophical view enumerated by Regan argues that animals are complex beings with emotions, desires and interests to such an extent that they bring subjectivity to our world. It is this subjectivity which makes them beings with inherent value. Regan argues that all mentally normal mammals of a year or more have rights equal to that of humans (Regan, 1983, p. 78).

The theological basis of rights (Linzey, 1987, 1994) holds that while all creation has value, some beings have rights by virtue of their Creator's right. Animals who are 'Spirit-filled, breathing creatures, composed of flesh and blood, are subjects of inherent value to God' (Linzey, 1987, p. 69). According to this view, animals have 'theos-rights' (literally 'God-rights') because it is the right of God which establishes the specific value of some living beings. In this sense, rights are not awarded, accorded or bestowed but *recognized*. 'When we speak of animal rights we conceptualise what is objectively owed to animals as a matter of justice by virtue of their Creator's right' (Linzey, 1987, p. 97).

The attainment of animal rights' goals would certainly require a transformation of human society as we know it. Such a society would be characterized by minimal disturbance to animal life and an end to all institutional abuse of animals in agriculture, science and sport. In short: no hen batteries, no hunted deer, and no oncomice.

There are a number of advantages to the rights theory. First, it underscores the view of the welfare theory that animals are subjects of moral worth. Second, it makes clear that what is owed to them is a matter of direct and objective moral obligation. Third, and most importantly, it holds that there are fundamental moral limits to what we may do to them – limits that are analogous to those we accept in the case of fellow humans. In short, like the humanitarian theory and the welfare theory, except more so, it ensures that animals are included within the sphere of moral justice. Rights language, in my view, is highly desirable precisely because it reminds us that what we owe animals is basically *the same kind of obligation* which we owe fellow human beings. Rights language focuses for us the question of justice to individual animals – that is, I believe, its overwhelming justification and merit – and in doing so provides checks and markers *en route* to living a less exploitative way of life with other creatures.

Nevertheless, there are problems with a rights approach (see the critique in Linzey, 1987, pp. 94–7). It is difficult to argue that rights theory is the *only* theory of moral obligation or, indeed, that it is, by itself, a *comprehensive* one. Although there are philosophical, theological – not to mention rhetorical benefits in using rights language, it is impossible to say that rights language conveys everything that there is to say about animals from a moral perspective. Talk of sensitivity, gentleness, compassion, duty, love, generosity are also, surely, essential. Because of this some thinkers have argued that for the elaboration, definition and pursuit of the good with animals we require more terms than rights language can provide (Linzey, 1987, p. 95).

Like so much pro-animal literature, talk of rights or liberation can offer us at worst only a narrow view of morality as preventing the worst rather than promoting the best. This leads us naturally to our third positive theory, which seeks to provide a vision for our relations with animals that maximizes the potential for moral good.

Generosity theory

Drawing on the humanitarian theory, one theological view argues that what humans owe animals requires even more than an acceptance of their rights. According to this view, humans have a duty not only to respect the rights of animals but also to be morally generous. 'Drawing upon the notion of divine generosity exemplified in the person of Jesus, I suggest that the weak and defenceless should be given not equal, but greater, consideration. The weak should have moral priority' (Linzey, 1994, p. 28).

The key elements of the argument are as follows: first, humans are the deputized moral agents of God in creation, with a God-given responsibility to care for the earth generally and animals in particular. Second, this human power or 'dominion' over animals should take as its model the Christ-given paradigm of lordship manifest in service. Third, the logic of this Christological paradigm is that the 'higher' should sacrifice itself for the 'lower' and not the reverse. Fourth, animals have an analogous status to that of children; adult humans have a special responsibility to both, and, finally, animals, like children, should be seen as having not equal claim but greater claim upon us precisely because of their greater vulnerability and relative powerlessness.

The practical upshot then of the generosity theory is that not only is it not right to use hens in batteries or mice as laboratory tools or deer for sport, but moreover humans have a responsibility not just to prevent the worst but also to promote the good, which means in practice an ethic of costly care. In short: our very moral agency should provide the grounds for morally superior behaviour towards animals.

One advantage with this theory is the way in which it gives voice to the sense that animals are a special case analogous to that of dependent children. That specialness consists in various factors – that they are innocent, that they need others to protect them and that they are so easily abused by the powerful. One continuing danger with both the utilitarian welfare theory and the deontological rights theory is that they can both become the means by which we draw lines around our moral obligation so that we fail to address the radical specialness – and the radically appropriate response that such specialness demands – in the case of the vulnerable and the weak, both human and animal. The generosity theory opens us to the possibility that we may yet owe more, much more than our current calculations and theories allow. It's a theory that allows for the specialness of humankind to be demonstrated and manifested supremely through *extra*ordinary acts of generosity and self-giving.

As will have become clear, I do not think that any *one* of these theories *by itself* offers a wholly adequate, entirely rationally satisfying account of our moral obligations to animals – even and especially the ones I have advanced myself. I think the animal movement needs the humility to go on defining, redefining and formulating theories that seek to do justice to animals. There is certainly a long way to go and a lot more hard – and impartial – thinking yet to be done. Nevertheless, it does seem difficult to avoid the conclusion that the last three positive theories represent a real advance in terms of understanding the moral status of animals. The first two negative theories – and even arguably the third – continue to keep animals arbitrarily out of the sphere of moral justice.

A THEOLOGY OF ANIMAL LIBERATION

Some people may have been struck by the way in which theological considerations have played a significant part in the various theoretical discussions about animals. Part of the answer is historical. The Christian tradition has historically granted animals a very low status; the humanocentric tradition has flourished and triumphed and with it has gone the various notions that animals have no mind, reason, rational soul, moral status, or even, sometimes, any sentience. Many of these ideas continue to dominate western thinking about animals. It is against this background that the contemporary movement for animal liberation has acquired its identity and purpose. The view of Peter Singer that 'the Judeo–Christian tradition is our foe' (Singer, 1987, p. 7) whilst not generally the view of all animal liberationists, certainly expresses the sense of underlying tension. Specifically, it has been the Catholic, and latterly Protestant, denial of rights to the non-human that has made animal rights the issue it is. Despite the fact that the language of rights and responsibilities has had a distinguished provenance within the Christian tradition, this language has been almost universally affirmed in the case of humans but consistently denied to animals. In this sense, animal rights is a specifically Christian, indeed theological, problem.

Yet it doesn't take much to see that the dominant ideas which have emanated from the Judeo–Christian tradition are themselves open to challenge – not least of all in their own theological terms.

In this last section, I want to show how the tradition which has historically been guilty of legitimizing the maltreatment of animals can also provide a convincing theoretical basis for taking seriously the cause of animal liberation. There are five main issues:

Humanocentricity v. theocentricity

At the beginning, I referred to the practical problem of achieving impartiality in our assessment of animal interests. The humanocentric theory, as we have seen, tends to end up judging the worth of animals from the standpoint of their utility or otherwise to human beings. But this, admittedly powerful, moral humanocentricity must be challenged in strictly theological terms. The most obvious point to make is that if animals matter then theologically they matter to God the Creator. If we are to grapple with theology, then we must abandon purely humanocentric perspectives on animals. To argue that the value and significance of animals in the world can be circumscribed by their value and significance to human beings is simply untheological. I make this point strongly because there seems to be a misconception – even and especially among contemporary liberal advocates of the Christian faith – that theological ethics can be best expressed by a well-meaning, ethically enlightened humanism. Not so. To attempt a theological understanding must involve a fundamental break with humanism, secular and religious. God alone is

183

the source and value of all living beings (see the same critique in Linzey, 1994, 1995).

Instrumentalism v. intrinsic value

If what is created is by definition sustained and loved by God, then we need the strongest possible ethical language to express God's own interest or rights in creation itself. In this regard, the strong language of rights and generosity is one of the best ways of doing justice to the divine deontological imperative. Animals are God's creatures. It is God the Creator's justice that we have to contend with. It is, I judge, a sign of our myopic humanocentricity that we think God's right as Creator is concerned only with events or relationships within the human sphere.

Resources v. sentiency

Some people may respond by saying that God may well value all creation but that some creatures are more valuable in God's sight than others. I do not dissent from this view; I do not espouse the currently fashionable ecoview that all life forms (plants, insects, animals and humans) have the same value in the sight of God. But this doesn't mean that humans alone have intrinsic value. There are good reasons for supposing that the capacity for sentiency is theologically significant.

To give one example. At the heart of Christian life and experience is the symbol of the cross. From a theological perspective, the Cross of Christ is God's vindication of innocent suffering. To inflict suffering on innocent, undefended, unprotected beings – provided that the suffering is unmerited and undeserved as of course it always is in the case of animals – is nothing less than intrinsically evil. It finds its strongest expression theologically in the Oxford sermon of Cardinal Newman in which he argued that suffering inflicted on innocent animals is morally equivalent to that inflicted upon Christ.

> There is something so very dreadful, so satanic in tormenting those who have never harmed us, and who cannot defend themselves, who are utterly in our power, who have weapons neither of offence nor defence, that none but very hardened persons can endure the thought of it.

And he concludes: 'Think then, my brethren, of your feelings at cruelty practised upon brute animals, and you will gain one sort of feeling which the history of Christ's Cross and Passion ought to excite within you' (Newman, 1868, pp. 136–8).

Despotism v. dominion

Some may complain that the foregoing makes insufficient reference to the traditional notions that humans are made in the image of God and are given power or 'dominion' over animals. In fact both notions, properly interpreted, are essential to the gospel of animal liberation. To possess the divine image and to rule creation is a highly accountable affair. What it doesn't mean is that humans are made the gods of creation and can do with the earth what they like. Secularists may claim that power is itself the sufficient justification for our use of it. But Christians are not so free. No appeal to the power of God can be sufficient without reference to the revelation of that power exemplified in Jesus Christ. Much of what Jesus did about slaves, women or animals remains historically opaque. But we can know the contours even if the details are missing.

Spirituality v. scholasticism

The great spiritual writer Charles Péguy once wrote that 'Everything begins in mysticism and ends in politics'. Péguy may overstate the case, but the notion that there are new spiritual insights to be learnt – and that they should affect our lives – is part and parcel of the Christian doctrine of the Holy Spirit (see Murray, 1992). For the business of the Spirit is to anticipate the world order for which all creation longs and sighs – and in the case of animals actually 'groans and travails' (*Romans* 8: 18–28). When people today press the case for animals and their moral significance they may not directly utilize theological language (except when arguing *against* animals and therefore referring to souls and dominion!) but they are often expressing some fundamental moral insights which have their deepest roots in our Judeo–Christian heritage.

I suggest that the progressive theories of animal liberation and rights have their spiritual basis in the recovery of moral insights which while present have often remained dormant within the Judeo–Christian tradition. Overwhelmingly, what gives the present animal movement its force and power is the recovery of an ancient perception of the intrinsic value of sentient life. Animal liberationists have not themselves dreamt up the notion of the lion lying down with the lamb – that is, the vision of the peaceable kingdom found in *Isaiah* 11. Neither have animal liberationists invented the notion of a world freed from parasitical suffering – that is, the redeemed creation envisaged by St Paul in *Romans* 8. Neither have animal liberationists been responsible for the idea of the covenant between God and humans and all living creatures – as witnessed by the saga of Noah in *Genesis* 9. Neither have animal liberationists plucked from the air the idea that God originally willed humans – and animals – to be vegetarians – as described by the first book of the Bible, *Genesis* 1: 29. (For a scholarly review of the theme of the peaceable kingdom in scripture, together with a detailed exegesis of these texts, see Murray, 1992.)

Enlightened movements for liberation are not just human affairs about moral ends and means (though, of course, in one sense such movements are all-too-human affairs as anyone who has been involved in them can readily testify!). One test of authenticity, however difficult to apply, has to be how far any new movement of sensibility embodies sufficient insight to be taken seriously as a movement for spiritual renewal. Despite all the crankiness, self-righteousness, obsessiveness, fanaticism and craziness of the animal rights movement – paralleled only by the history of the Christian Church itself – despite all this, I believe that the change of perception which this movement represents is the result of spiritual vision. We must beware of course of claiming the Holy Spirit as the final authority of any reforming movement, however benign or well-intentioned. Nevertheless, if the Spirit of Christ is the spirit of peace we should be open to the possibility that freedom from violence to other forms of life is the beckoning of the same Creator Spirit.

In conclusion, I am well aware that some may be daunted by the prospect of the moral and social change required of us if we are even to approximate the peaceable kingdom on earth. All of us can bring to mind moments of sharp conflict between human and animal interest, and all of us are doubtless only too cognizant of how frail and weak a vessel the human conscience truly is. I never tire of repeating the line from Albert Schweitzer that a clean conscience is an invention of the Devil. As I indicated at the beginning, we all need to recognize that we are compromised in our dealings with animals and that currently there is no pure land on earth.

Nevertheless, I believe that there is a convincing strategy available to us and that is for each of us to adopt a programme of 'progressive disengagement from injury' (see Linzey, 1987, pp. 104–49). All of us can move some way to living in a more peaceful way with animals. We don't all have to be agreed on precisely the same means (though see my caveat below), or even the same theory (though I think some theories are more adequate than others), but I do propose that living free of injury to animals is a prima facie obligation which should be realized whenever we have the moral freedom to do so. At the very least, we can all live happy and healthy lives without battery hens, hunting deer for sport or patenting the oncomouse.

Sadly, one final caveat seems essential: animal rights thinking which eschews the use of sentient animals as means to human ends must also, logically, eschew the use of fellow humans as means to (even moral) ends as well – which means in practice that violence in pursuit of animal rights is morally self-contradictory and self-defeating.

14

BRUTE EQUIVOCATION

Michael Leahy

THE CASE TO ANSWER

Andrew Linzey's defence of animals is clear and straightforward. Many will think him to be, as they say, obviously on the side of the angels (which, for a clergyman, is as it should be). The skeleton of his argument goes like this:

Animals have a gruesome time at the hands of human beings. 'We hunt, ride, shoot, fish, eat, wear, cage, trap, exhibit, factory farm and experiment upon billions of animals worldwide every year' (p. 171). The suffering is rubbed in with typical horror stories – battery egg production, stag hunting and the somewhat anti-climactic 'onco-mouse'. The public, he argues, has been complacent about these gross exploitations and it is only in recent years that the issues have been taken seriously.

Three justifying theories are then mooted. The first owes much to Thomas Aquinas and plays variations upon the main theme of *Genesis* (1: 26–7) that the animal kingdom is created simply to serve its human masters. The second has specifically to do with *rights* and *duties*. The former (rights), typically in the sphere of human relations, must be *earned* by fulfilling relevant duties. Both theories are inadequate, Linzey argues, to protect animals from exploitation and the second, contractualism, rules out rights for creatures who have no sense of contractual obligation. The third theory will commend itself to many readers, although it is often scoffed at by liberationists as a Victorian relic. This is humanitarianism: the view that we have a duty to be kind to innocent beings and avoid their unnecessary suffering. Linzey damns all three on the grounds that they sanction the pre-eminence of *human* interests over those of brutes (e.g. *we* decide what constitutes 'unnecessary' suffering).

Three 'positive' arguments redress the balance to complete Linzey's rehabilitation of animals to equal moral status with human beings. Welfare theory introduces Peter Singer, the guru of liberationists, who stresses an absolutely central concept in the debate upon which Linzey is strangely almost silent. The 'innocent beings' of humanitarianism (see above) are morally demarcated or graded on the basis of their *sentience* (thus a worm, with its minimal perceptual apparatus, merits less consideration than a chimpanzee). But Linzey objects to Singer's utilitarianism, which allows that animals may be killed if human interests are pressing and paramount. A 'rights theory', owing much to Tom Regan (another luminary) allies sentience with a metaphysical creation of 'inherent value' which reinstates allegedly inalienable rights, and which Linzey buttresses with his own theological importation of 'theos' rights (and who can argue with God?). All of this leads to Linzey's final contention, his 'generosity theory', that we have an obligation actively to promote the well-being of brutes ('an ethic of costly care' as he puts it): 'animals are a special case analogous to that of dependent children' (p. 182). Like Regan, and unlike Singer, Linzey is uncompromising in his call for the total abolition of all of the liberationists' alleged abuses of animals, however imperative the human competition.

EQUIVOCATIONS

Early in his essay Linzey stresses that it is not easy to think beyond ones prejudices about animals and he quotes, rather incongruously, the *bon viveur* and no lover of animals, Bertrand Russell: 'Few English people think, indeed most English people would rather die than think.' Linzey adds, with a coy air of self-congratulation, 'I am not suggesting that only animal liberationists think impartially about animals' (p. 172). I agree with Linzey that it is both rare and difficult to think sensibly about creatures both like, and even more *un*like, ourselves. But, I shall argue, his above quotation is a fatal hostage to fortune. His own case, and those of his fellow travellers, trades upon equivocations ('to use ambiguous words to conceal the truth') and I will construct my counterarguments around some of his most spectacular and notorious examples.

Animals

Our basic subject matter is equivocal. What is imperative for chimpanzees, highly developed mammals biologically akin to ourselves, is inappropriate for cattle or lower species. But enthusiasts like Linzey talk of animals as if they had the species-solidarity of apes or birds. Furthermore the concept of 'human beings', with its range of competences, is similarly open to abuse; as we shall see in discussing 'innocents' (below).

Exploitation and abuse

Linzey's list of alleged abuses is highly dubious. Even if the images of factory farming disturb most people, the same is not true of horse-racing, which the beast often relishes, or exhibiting creatures in zoos (where life expectancy is far greater than in the wild). And it has yet to be established that the painless killing of animals in medical experiments or for food (a practice that I will highlight) involves suffering; and, if so, whether it compares with that of human beings. Thus 'suffering' also begins to lose touch with its paradigm base.

The protection of innocents

Central to Linzey's conclusion is the contention that we have the duty to protect brutes with the same moral zeal that we would our human innocents, such as mental deficients and babies; and these are genuinely fruitful comparisons which need careful disarticulation to reveal their implications. But consider the perverse logic in Linzey's 'Theology of Animal Liberation', where the suffering of beasts is claimed as the moral 'equivalent to that inflicted upon Christ'. I am not a theologian, and such special pleading is enough to confirm my reluctance ever to be so, but Christ's reputation is that of a man with a mission, aware of its pitfalls and dangers, and prepared to confront them. He is a subversive in the dock; his 'innocence' light-years from that of young children and other creatures. It is with these last damaging comparisons that I begin to paint an alternative picture.

MORAL PATIENTS

The ethics underpinning the adult treatment of babies, infants and children are deeply felt. Our obligations to our young are

peremptory and often overriding. Ethologists will argue, with justification, that they are rooted in our instinctive responses to other
creatures; a legacy of our own brute ancestry. It is a favourite strategy
of liberationists to recycle, some would say hijack, our ethics of childcare such that animals enjoy equal protection on roughly similar
grounds. Animals are likewise compared with mental incompetents;
another group (or series of groups, to allow for sufferers from Down's
syndrome, who may learn to read and write, and microcephalics,
whose competence is that of vegetables) for whom feelings run high.
That a maternity unit lets babies with vestigial brains and no obvious
potential simply die, occasions less hostility, and even constructive
approval, than if mongoloids were similarly fated. Yet if it were
known that microcephalic babies were regularly sold for invasive
procedures in research laboratories, the outcry would be predictable.
Were it known further that other poor wretches were being sold
surreptitiously to gourmet restaurants to satisfy the demands of
avant-garde cuisine, politicians and the National Guard would be
needed to placate the liberal conscience. But many radical vegetarians and vegans cite the 400 million animals eaten annually in the
UK (far higher in the USA) and view it in much the same light as
the killing and cooking of mental incompetents. It can even be argued
that with animals the outrage is *more* extreme. The abilities of food
animals and birds to fend for themselves, to care for their offspring
and to interact with their own and other species, far surpass those
of the 2-year-old child or the microcephalic with whom they are
bracketed.

Stephen Clark, a British liberationist, argues in the spirit of Linzey's
'generosity theory', in his article 'Animal Wrongs':

> We know that we ought to care for the subnormal precisely
> because they . . . are weak, defenceless, at our mercy. We *ought*
> to consider their wishes and feelings, not because we will be
> hurt if we don't, but because *they* will be hurt. And the same
> goes for those creatures like them who are of our kind though
> not of our species. . . . If the one is wrong (as it surely is), so
> is the other, for they are, in moral terms, the very same act.
>
> (Clark, 1978, p. 149)

Clark here brings together explicitly, and by implication, children,
incompetents and animals in terms of 'the very same act'. This significant tripartite constituency makes up what Tom Regan calls 'moral
patients' in his formidable *The Case for Animal Rights* (1983), to

mark the contrast with 'moral agents'; viz. human beings like ourselves. This is the first set of arguments, owed to Clark and Regan, on behalf of animals. We will need to return to it to consider its shortcomings.

PETER SINGER AND SENTIENCE

Singer's *Animal Liberation*, first published in 1975, was an influential source of the present obsessional interest in the treatment of animals. Its utilitarian premises, harking back to the eighteenth century, nonetheless marked out the line of battle for the struggles to come with politicians, cosmetic corporations, medical researchers, veterinarians, zoo curators, farmers, furriers, hunters, carnivores and petshops around the world.

Jeremy Bentham, Singer's illustrious predecessor, writing in 1789, provides the persuasive characteristic which bridges the interests of human beings and animals. Welcoming the fact that black slaves now enjoy the benefits of positive law (Bentham had no truck with so-called 'natural' or 'human' rights) and hoping for the inclusion of 'the rest of the animal creation' he continues:

> But a full-grown horse or dog is beyond comparison a more rational, as well as a more conversable animal, than an infant of a day, or a week, or even a month, old. But suppose they were otherwise, what would it avail? The question is not Can they *reason*? nor Can they *talk*? but *Can they suffer*?
>
> (Bentham, 1960, p. 411n.)

That Bentham *is* concerned with legal rights (i.e. positive law) is underlined, in the same footnote, by his approval of eating meat. He was no radical in this respect.

Suffering gives rise to interests of alleviation and consolation. It is a minimal notion since it can dispense with those interests which arise from reasoning and speech; but it needs to be thus qualified if it is to legitimize the interests of infants and mental incompetents. This then is the foundation of an ethics of 'sentience', taken in the sense (not altogether correctly) of a capacity for suffering, which is the stock-in-trade of all contemporary liberationists. But it is possible to build cumulatively upon this foundation with consequent augmentation of interests and possibly legal rights. First of all we can add the powers of sense-perception ('sentience' proper). It is only mildly controversial to claim that many brutes, certainly mammals, see, hear, smell, taste and touch, whilst being sceptical about their sense *contents*. Second, we can climb in the company of both Singer and Regan to the dizzy heights of attributing to animals *self*-consciousness and rationality and what goes with them (variously memory, intentionality, emotions, aspirations and forward planning). Singer goes so far as to claim explicitly that some brutes are *persons* (1979, p. 76):

> Some nonhuman animals appear to be rational and self-conscious beings, conceiving themselves as distinct beings with a past and a future. When this is so . . . the case against killing is strong, as strong as the case against killing permanently defective human beings at a similar mental level.
>
> (1979, p. 103)

Chimpanzees are Singer's 'clearest case of nonhuman persons' but he includes other apes, whales, dolphins, monkeys, dogs, cats, pigs, seals and bears as probable candidates. If he is right, then the creatures that qualify as persons would enjoy protection from almost every alleged exploitation, since the human defectives he refers to would need to be rational and self-conscious; perhaps as advanced as mature mongols. Full animal rights would be on all fours with human rights; if humans have them.

AGAINST THE RIGHTS VIEW

Two arguments have been mobilized. The first is the substance of Clark's quotation (above), aided by Regan's notion of *moral patients*, which caters to a popular view which denies any relevance to distinctions we draw between subnormal people and other creatures. To harm either is 'the very same act'. Despite its supporters there are signal grounds for suspicion:

(1) Not only are its implications implausibly catholic – in the wrong hands it could be used to promote worms and sea-anemones – but it ignores the obvious discriminations we make *within* the animal kingdom. The casual shooting of an ape or a zebra is surely criminal by contrast with stepping on a beetle or setting traps for mice. All are weak and defenceless but there is no question of 'the very same act'.

(2) Clark does not help his case by generalizing the class of human subnormals. Our care for the teenager with Downs Syndrome is more than a matter of mere 'wishes and feelings'. It is influenced by his

or her plans and aspirations. That none of this is within the competence of brutes (certainly beef cattle and most laboratory subjects, as we shall see when discussing 'sentience') would make fatuous the claim that killing a sheep and a mongoloid was 'the very same act'.

(3) Should Clarke have restricted the human analogues to microcephalics and their like, where the lack of language and its behavioural prototypes would ameliorate the comparison with animals? That we fail to treat at least mature mammals with the same respect that we do such ill-omened humans is, for Singer, speciesism (his animal variant of racism, sexism, ageism and the rest) in its starkest form. One can meet this charge, first of all, by denying that all forms of species solidarity are mere bias. That the normal generality of *homo sapiens* is unequivocally demarcated from brutes would seem to justify according a form of honorary status to those people enfeebled through age or retardation. The laws and conventions of most countries reflect this in, for example, the elaborate rituals required for the disposal of human corpses. But, indeed, perhaps there *is* a case for using non-sentient humans for important research; a view to which Singer (see above) seems to subscribe (1979, p. 103).

AGAINST SENTIENCE: ANECDOTES AND ANTHROPOMORPHISM

Liberationists of every hue, whether utilitarians (Rollin, Midgely, Hearne and the thinking public) or hard-liners (Regan, Clark, Linzey and the fanatics-in-orbit), all adopt a variety of Bentham's ethic of sentience, but invariably draw from it highly optimistic implications. We have noted that Singer attributes rationality and self-consciousness to some mammals and the consequent status of *persons*. What is his evidence? Lacking a developed language (more on this later) the only appeal can be to brute *behaviour*. This is given significance by anecdotes often of creatures performing typical routines (bees collecting honey, swallows migrating) or, more often, exceptional performances in quasi-experimental circumstances (apes manipulating signs, dogs or dolphins seeming to exhibit foresight), which, it is claimed, *require* that human attributions be employed to make sense of what is going on. That the famous chimpanzee Washoe is able, for example, to sign 'Me Washoe' to her reflection when provided with certain cues and rewards is Singer's warrant of her self-consciousness (1979, p. 94), although it is uncertain how cattle or pigs might be expected to exhibit such distinction without Ameslan (American sign language which substitutes for vocalization). Regan uses this strategy even more prolifically: mature mammals are 'individuals who, like us, have beliefs and desires' (1983, p. 78) such that they can be said to have intentions, expectations, a full perceptual and emotional life, and can be aware of what they are doing and why they are doing it; all of this without language.

The basic problem with the above methodology is its susceptibility to the charge of *anthropomorphism*; wishful thinking in the face of recalcitrant data for which alternative theories are available. Even Aristotle and Descartes found no difficulty in accounting for animal behaviour in language not dissimilar from that of twentieth-century ethologists, endocrinologists and psychologists, from Skinner, Thorndike and Tinbergen to J.B. Hutchinson and W.H. Thorpe, who find it straightforward to translate a cat's stalking a bird into the vocabulary of social releasers, pheromones, fixed action patterns and adaptation. But the Linzeys of the world will have none of this. Anthropomorphism is bred of their naive faith in the univocality of language. Rabies experts describe the virus as being 'extraordinarily clever', the cash value of which (we all know) is not that it bears comparison with Einstein, or the erstwhile KGB bent on world conquest, but that it has something to do with its virulence; in this case the timing with which it replicates in nervous tissue and then enters the saliva. If it is quite in order for a scientist to talk in this way about a virus without misconstruction, then we ought similarly to accept that much of our psychological talk about more complex creatures is, as it were, hedged in by emphatic but inexplicit contextual implication. This brings into prominence the philosopher Ludwig Wittgenstein's seminal notion of *language-games*. Thus we describe the hyena as foraging for food as an appetitive *function* driven by instinct and unaware that that is what it is doing, like but yet *un*like the human down-and-out who peers into garbage cans explicitly aware of what he is doing and what he hopes to find. Identical descriptions have dissimilar meaning; different language-games are played.

THE PRE-LINGUISTIC PROTOTYPES

Anthropomorphism is not the exclusive preserve of confused philosophy. It is a trap awaiting all language-users. The animal psychologist Donald Griffin describes tits and chickadees as obtaining milk from bottles by 'pecking through their shiny coverings with the conscious intention of obtaining food' (1984, p. 35). Clearly he thinks he is using 'conscious intention' as we would of a normal person stealing milk, otherwise he would fail to arouse his average reader's curiosity and sympathies. We may still, if we allow due weight to *context*, talk of dumb brutes 'consciously intending' or 'being extraordinarily clever' or 'compassionate' but we will be diverging from the human analogue and marking only the similarity of behavioural prototypes in the absence of self-consciousness.

Wittgenstein, in typically gnomic fashion, comments upon these prototypes in two related passages on pain behaviour (1967, p. 95e):

> It is a help here to remember that it is a primitive reaction to tend, to treat, the part that hurts when someone else is in pain; and not merely when oneself is . . .

> But what is the word 'primitive' meant to say here? Presumably that this sort of behaviour is *pre-linguistic*: that a language-game is based *on it*, that it is the prototype of a way of thinking and not the result of thought. (original emphasis)

The final lines are the significant ones. Language-users may interrupt, consider, argue over and elaborate upon their prototypical behaviour (e.g. when convulsed in pain or fleeing from a mad bull) upon which the pattern of language-games is *based*. But animals, demonstrating as they do our pre-linguistic ancestry, manifest only the prototypes.

Many intelligent animal lovers, and not just liberationists, will protest against my several references to brutes lacking language. They cite as counterevidence the varieties of so-called natural communication by which creatures hoot, howl, hiss, gibber, squeak, stridulate, and the contexts in which these performances play a part. There is also interaction through posture, gesture and odour; the implications of tail-wagging, for example, vary between species. Ethologists document the complexities to which performances like teeth-baring or birdsong give rise; for example, gulls emit a specific call which attracts others nearby if corn is thrown to them, but if the offering is fish they invariably issue a variant of greater range. But the fur flies when assessing whether this behaviour is a mark of intelligence or, indeed, whether it is misleading to describe it as 'communication' at all, with its redolence of language. Ethologists converge upon explanations in terms of stimulus–response, on grounds of the behaviour's limited adaptive potential, its equivalents being present in the lowest of life forms, its inflexibility (which is why birdsong so readily identifies species) and its stereotypical triggering by precise causes. Now on this causal view (to which I subscribe) it could be misleading to talk of monkeys *warning* each other, or of the gulls being *generous* for inviting the others to share their fish (unless as casual childtalk). The intercourse resembles in some ways the 'communication' that takes place in electronic devices or organic systems like the body. If the causal view of the ethologists is correct then natural communication, far from giving the lie to my claim that animals lack language, in fact provides the most authoritative example of pre-linguistic proto-types in favour of it. Human subjects qualify; the stereotypical babbling of babies is not language but the *sine qua non* from which it progressively springs.

(The potential of the Ameslan apes like Washoe might continue to trouble some readers. Despite its fascination the issue must be side-stepped, although I discuss the issue at length in *Against Liberation* (1994; pp. 31–3, 159–63). They are a pampered elite, the implications of which have nothing to do with other apes, monkeys nor the great unwashed of the brute kingdom which includes those destined to be killed for our tables or to contribute to scientific progress in experimental laboratories.)

PAINFUL PROBLEMS

Mary Warnock, a distinguished bioethicist (and Chair of a recent British Royal Commission on genetic engineering), takes Singer to task for unduly attenuating the understanding of what counts as being a person (and the greater weight of significant interests that goes with it) by neglecting the role of moral agency or responsibility integral to the term (1986, pp. 15–16). Singer simply selects rationality and self-consciousness 'as the core of the concept' (1979, p. 76). But he has self-interested reasons for doing so and Warnock is right to criticize. Infants and subnormals (the moral *patients* invariably compared with animals) may or may not attain, or even approach, a level of moral personality, depending upon their imma-turity or disability. But as and when they do (the judgement is often a hazardous one) they demonstrate a sense of give-and-take, of obli-gations and dues, and thus become liable for praise, censure and punishment. Yet no liberationist would dare to countenance this of brutes, even the Ameslan apes, since it would justify chastizing them for *wrongdoing* (rather than for training purposes), of which all are agreed that they can have no conception.

Yet despite the squabbles and alleged sleights of hand over the concept of a person, it is still possible for the animal enthusiast to fall back upon the less ambitious claims of mere sentience. Indeed in *Animal Liberation* Singer restricts himself to the contention, in support of Bentham, that animals can suffer *pain*, which he clearly thinks is enough to convince people that the treatment of animals in slaughterhouses, factory farms and experimental laboratories (his main targets) is deliberate exploitation and torture. Strategically this was the right medicine. Successful campaigns for the more humane treatment of animals have tended to rouse the general public if the rallying cry is one of maiming and cruelty.

The initial battles have long been won. The legal requirements to anaesthetize all possible research subjects, or pre-stun cattle for ritual slaughter, is not just to ensure that they remain quiescent but to prevent pain; nor ought anyone reading of children stretching rats over a candle flame to doubt their discomfort, given their squeals and writhing. The grounds for attributing sensation to animals and human beings are equally imperative. To be sceptical over the susceptibility of mammals to pain (allowing that the case weakens progressively for invertebrates) is to find oneself in the counter-intuitive position of implying that the screaming astronauts being incinerated in their defective capsule were just conceivably all play-acting. Such doubts are seventeenth-century legacies of Cartesianism. Similar strategies can be used to dispel indecision over brute consciousness; as opposed to *self*-consciousness which involves far more than the ape's merely responding to a mirror image by signing 'Me Washoe'. For *self*-awareness to be attributable in such a case we would need to be convinced that the ape was aware of recognizing herself *as herself*; a sophisticated transaction beyond even some language-users. Anthony Kenny puts this well: 'A dog may well think that his master is at the door: but unless a dog masters a language it is hard to see how he can think *that he is thinking that* his master is at the door' (1975, p. 5). Against Singer, dumb brutes cannot possibly be self-aware. In the absence of a developed language it doesn't even *make sense*.

Nonetheless it is almost universally agreed that animals and human beings share the attributes of sensuous consciousness and a proneness to pain. Yet again, however, the plot thickens since the implications for the two parties diverge, particularly on the critical issue of sentience (upon which I shall concentrate). There are two main difficulties. The first was alluded to above, in posing a query over invertebrates. The frenziedly bleating ewe with a crushed leg is uncontroversially in pain. But what of the wriggling earthworm mutilated by the garden spade or the fish on a hook (activists in the UK have recently begun disrupting fishermen)? All liberationists take the line, acknowledging the diminishing complexity of nervous systems and mammalian pain behaviour, that the presence of sensation in such lower life forms is an open question; 'it may be so, we don't know!' This recalls the sceptical Cartesianism dismissed above. Rollin, emboldened by reports of the discovery of pain-killing endorphins in worms, is more positive: 'the presence of these chemicals in invertebrates strongly suggests that these creatures do feel pain' (1981, p. 31). But this is a hazardous line to take. The mere presence of chemicals is inadequate grounds for attributing *pain* to creatures so anatomically and behaviourally distant from ourselves. Such arguments pushed to the limit cannot rule out the *conceivability* of sensation in *anything*, even viruses and plants. Clark is unwary enough to accept that 'some plants may feel' (1977, p. 171). But sensible observers *do* wish to rule out that plants feel and perhaps prefer not to have to be sceptical about every higher life form. The liberationist's error is a symptom of philosophical *dualism*; the assumption that pain is an ineradicably mental event, available only to private introspection, and for which no publicly specifiable criteria (whether neurological, organic or behavioural) is necessary. Wittgenstein, typical of the twentieth century, is pre-eminent in rejecting dualism. Private mental events, including the mind itself, are, in the absence of publicly observable criteria, corrosive myths bred of linguistic confusion. Thus pain typically involves sensation, which is private, but allied not only to behavioural or organic symptoms, but a lot else besides. The Wittgensteinian alternative is to deny therefore that it *even makes sense* to claim unequivocally that plants or worms just *might* feel pain. The concept has its primacy in its application to human beings and other mammals and is gradually watered down as it descends the spectrum of organic life until a point is reached, perhaps with worms and certainly with protozoans and plants, where it has been diluted beyond recognition and serves no useful purpose.

PAIN AND SUFFERING

Our own consciousness ranges widely. Language is the key which unlocks horizons light-years beyond those of animals. With it we make the thoughts of others our own, can share their hopes and contemplate our personal past and future. Stuart Hampshire in *Innocence and Experience* stresses the necessity of language for a developed sense of the past and makes much of our individual 'singularity' of awareness to which memory gives rise. It is this, he argues, which is the source of our psychical superiority and gives the lie to speciesism (1989, pp. 117–20). However, when it comes to suffering pain this superiority can work as an irritant and make us, some might say, far *more* wretched than an injured sheep. There are four distinctions to be made:

(1) An injured dog will lick the affected part, may whimper or shriek, or betray symptons that are the stock-in-trade of veterinarians. It tends to recover quickly. A beast's pain is surprisingly short-lived, in part because of the effects of thanatosis; a temporary paralysis, akin to hypnosis, brought about by the shock of confrontation (which also causes the phenomenon of some mammals and birds (e.g. pigeons) shamming dead or 'playing possum'; mistakenly attributed to deliberate cunning). But humans are far more discomforted by mere pain, however intense.

(2) Humans can of course suffer when there is no pain at all or very little. Unexpected lumps that do not hurt can nonetheless have catastrophic consequences and reduce people to the depths of despair. This is all beyond the wit of animals.

(3) Mary Midgely mentions, for instance, that 'social birds and mammals are upset by solitude, or by the removal of their young' (1983, p. 90). This would be termed 'mental' suffering in human beings. This surely is sentimental talk when used of animals, the language misleadingly specific in recalling the human paradigm, where what we are confronted with are mere prototypical survival strategies.

(4) Human beings can 'suffer in silence'. Are animals capable of it? Babies appear not to be. Mothers, almost intuitively, diagnose specific cries and whimpers as symptoms of needs of which the baby is unaware. But as infants mature they note the advantages of adopting a 'stiff upper lip' and so regulate their vocalizing on this or that occasion and for this or that *reason*. Even the most optimistic liberationists are wary of attributing this competence even to

chimpanzees. Wittgenstein questions a teasing variant of this in his *Philosophical Investigations* (1953, sect. 250):

> Why can't a dog simulate pain? Is he too honest? . . . Perhaps it is possible to teach him to howl on particular occasions as if he were in pain, even when he is not. But the surroundings which are necessary for this behaviour to be real simulation are missing.

So if we claim that the creature *can* inhibit pain we imply that it knows the reasons why it is doing so. This seems excessively anthropomorphic in the absence of language. But if we *deny* it then there are unpalatable implications of another sort. It then becomes difficult to sustain the tempting claim that creatures which have appalling injuries, but which are nonetheless quiescent and not betraying other tell-tale symptoms, *must be* in pain. But if they cannot suffer in silence then they cannot be in pain. This would make the alleged horror stories of the suffering of neglected beef cattle awaiting slaughter, for example, highly misleading. The atrocities so stressed by Linzey are put at risk. It would also undermine much of the catalogue of alleged atrocities in some US research laboratories compiled by Pacheco and Francione (1985, pp. 135–47). Similar careful thought might well show up the perennial violent protests in the UK over the export of live cattle as sentimental hot air, and prompt second thoughts over the assumption that veal calves in stalls *must* be in agony.

HOW ANIMALS SHOULD BE TREATED

It is normal and typical of our species to feel basic (perhaps instinctive) impulses to assist non-human creatures in distress, to admire their beauty and somatic skills and often to enjoy their close proximity. There are also reactive aversions. But despite these dispositions it does not follow that we know how to treat them. We may be in doubt whether to handle a trapped bird for fear of exacerbating its plight, or be uncertain if the bitch giving birth needs assistance. In such cases we consult the veterinarians. But there are, of course, cases which test our initial impulses. Is the peasant's donkey pulling a loaded cart, the sheep penned outside the abattoir, or the dilapidated parrot on a perch, being cruelly exploited? If we are inclined to intervene, should we do so? Here the expert's opinion will be less decisive.

How we answer these sorts of question will depend crucially upon what we think animals to be. Regan and Linzey argue for animal welfare on the same model as for human beings:

> It is no defense of consigning either human beings or animals to environments that ignore their biological, social or psychological interests . . . to claim that these individuals do not know what they are missing and so cannot be any worse off for not having it.
>
> (Regan, 1983, p. 117)

So the implication is that animals would be worse off. But how? Overt *suffering* might result, but Regan rules this out: such environments are detrimental to the interests of humans *or* animals 'whether they cause suffering or not' (1983, p. 117). The alternative is that a dog, like the child holding its lead, has the capability of becoming *aware* of the misery of its present existence although it may never in *fact* do so. Regan insists that animals enjoy a range of cognitive abilities *in the same sense in which we ascribe them to human beings* (1983, p. 116). I have argued that this is misleading nonsense.

AGAINST LIBERATION

My alternative to Regan's and Linzey's liberationist orthodoxy is that animals are *primitive beings*, far removed from our own species, despite behavioural and physiognomical prototypes to the contrary. Variations between brute species allow for degrees. Judging their welfare now becomes a much more straightforward matter since we can dispense with the intervention of cognitive excess baggage with which liberationists saddle beasts in the absence of speech. Our only legitimate guide must be their *perceived needs*, their simple appetitive wants wiped clean of the human complications of self-awareness. The needs of brutes, what *we* require to be 'in their interest', cannot be guided by their own views of themselves for they cannot have any. An animal does indeed strive instinctively to keep alive, much as it will migrate and forage (plants do also, in even more stereotypical and less mobile ways), but it is unduly anthropomorphic to praise its endeavour and describe it as 'desiring' to live to a ripe old age or 'missing' its babies, except perhaps to children. We can only look to the practices within which *we* treat animals, be it as pets, in field sports (hunting, shooting, fishing), as providers of meat and experimental subjects, or their preservation as endangered species or denizens of the wild. Our treatment will be tempered by the natural disinclination to abuse them or cause them *needless* suffering. This qualification is not imprecise nor pious hand-wringing. Our varying practices involving animals *dictate the criteria* for our judging what constitutes needless suffering. For a licence-holder to kill a buck with an approved weapon and in season, is no abuse. But were the creature a threatened species, in a protected area, and the assailant unauthorized, then it becomes a criminal offence. The *needless* suffering of racehorses, for example, is assessed differently from that of laboratory beagles or pigs in slaughterhouses. There are international variations as well. Similar arguments can be used to defuse the claim by liberationists like Harriet Schleifer that animals awaiting slaughter suffer from awareness of what approaches. They wait, she writes, 'close to a building that all of them must enter to die. They cannot remain unaware of their fate, and intense fear is the natural and inevitable result' (1985, p. 71). This is well-meaning but dangerous muddle-headedness. It is the rhetoric of the death camps but inappropriately applied. Schleifer is confusing the agitation or even prostration which occurs in badly run holding-yards as a result of heat, noise, overcrowding or lack of water, with the uniquely human fear of impending death.

CONCLUSION

There are both respectable and intellectually disreputable defences of vegetarianism. Some will merely dislike the taste of meat or the idea of consuming dressed-up dead things. The highly cautious valetudinarian will not risk even the outside chance of contracting BSE or BIV (an AIDS-type virus) and give up all meat, contrary to medical advice, despite enjoying it. But others will *take* the advice. It is equally justifiable to eat meat whilst being concerned about alleged current abuses in its production and slaughter, none of which, given time and application, is thought by liberationists like Midgely and respected bodies like the RSPCA, to be ineradicable. One can be equally ambivalent over Linzey's *bêtes noires* and the other alleged areas of exploitation. Pharmaceutical scientists are at pains to minimize the use of mammals in experiments because of their cost. I avoid field sports because I find fishing tiresome and the smell of horses repulsive.

But attempts to convince us that factory farming, animal experiments, zoos, pets, hunting and the eating of meat and fish are evil invasions of the inalienable rights of brutes and must cease forth-with, should be resisted as mischievous humbug. They can only succeed by attributing to animals opportunistic flights of fancy such as Regan's 'inherent value' or Linzey's *theos* rights, or by otherwise obscuring the differences between creatures like ourselves, who have the benefit of language and self-consciousness, and those that do not.

Abolitionists like Regan, Linzey and their extremist supporters who scorn the claims of human utility and wish a plague on *all* our houses, seeing it as a wholesale surrender to partiality, insensitivity and vested interests, are in a problematical situation. For a start they assume the burden of proof to convince their opponents (most of whom eat meat, keep pets, visit zoos, perceive the need for experi-ments *in vivo* and so on) that these practices are riddled with *unavoidable* cruelty and exploitation. In so doing they need to defuse the arguments in this chapter. Having done this to their own undoubted satisfaction they then find themselves ranged against politicians, legislators and (yes) vested interests who have powerful economic and financial clout, backed by weighty arguments (food, jobs, recreation, health) to maintain the *status quo*. Like so many moral reformers of the past, convinced that the tested laws and practices of their society would be much better supplanted by their own wishful thinking, the animal liberationists need to be marginalized.

15

LINZEY'S REPLY

Michael Leahy's response is impish and ungenerous: more importantly it is full of misrepresentations – not surprising since he concentrates so little on what I actually wrote and insists on reading me through the thought of fellow thinkers – some of whom I agree with, and some of whom I do not. The task of unravelling it is, as editorially constrained, beyond me: a mere thousand words cannot begin to show fully how misguided Leahy is.

Let me try rather – in an eirenical spirit – to push the debate on by indicating one point of agreement. Leahy writes:

> The grounds for attributing sensation to animals and human beings are equally imperative. To be sceptical over the susceptibility of mammals to pain (allowing that the case weakens progressively for invertebrates) is to find oneself in the counterintuitive position of implying that the screaming astronauts being incinerated in their defective capsule were just conceivably all play-acting. Such doubts are seventeenth-century legacies of Cartesianism.
>
> (p. 198)

I am glad that Leahy acknowledges sensation and pain in mammals. But, as his reference to Cartesianism indicates, such acknowledgement is not, and has not been, without controversy. It may be 'counterintuitive' but it is not (for that reason alone) insupportable. It remains philosophically possible to argue that mammals don't feel pain: indeed, philosophically, as Leahy will know, it is impossible in strict terms to *prove* the existence of pain outside of one's own experience of it. And if there can be doubt here, there can be doubt everywhere. It just *may be* that the astronauts are not screaming but laughing; it *may be* that contrary to our *intuitions*, they are having a heaven – rather than a – hell of a time.

ANDREW LINZEY

I state the obvious because the obvious is rather lost in Leahy's response. Yes, there are doubts and difficulties in ascribing sensation and pain – and suffering and self-consciousness and language – to mammals. No sensible liberationist wants to deny these things – indeed, some like myself, have spent years addressing many of these difficulties (the literature which Leahy does *not* address). No position is philosophically doubt – and difficulty – free. But are they *reasonable* doubts and, crucially, are they *morally relevant* doubts?

As to the first, Leahy's position is touchingly metaphysical (I won't say 'theological' since that would mean colluding with the common, but erroneous, denigration of that word). Leahy *knows* by counter-intuition that because animals don't possess human language and can't articulate precisely (to us) their interests, they can't have any. He *knows* that animals can't be self-aware or endure mental suffering. He *knows* all this with all the force of a fanatical liberationist or rather anti-liberationist. His knowing – in truth – is all *a priori*. Whatever empirical evidence there may to the contrary – and there is much of it – he doesn't even address.[1] It is not for nothing that one leader in this field, Donald R. Griffin, writes: 'The question of self-awareness is one of the very few areas of cognitive ethology where we have some concrete experimental evidence' (Griffin, 1984, p. 249). Leahy is welcome to his doubts. I am not (I hope) so closed-minded as to think that these things are incapable of even Wittgensteinian argument; but that his doubts are *reasonable* – as opposed to sheer speciesist prejudice – has yet to be shown.

Even if we accept for a moment the minimalist view which Leahy espouses, we have, first of all, the fact that animals feel pain and, accordingly, that humans have a prima facie duty to avoid their infliction of it. This is itself enough to advance a massive liberationist agenda. An attempt to seriously eliminate the amount of human-inflicted pain would eclipse almost every area of human interaction: painful sport hunting, painful farming, painful experimentation – to take only three examples. (Leahy is disingenuous in supposing that it is a legal requirement to anaesthetize all 'research subjects' – more than a majority of UK experiments are performed without anaes-thesia.)

But, second, are these differences, even if established as reason-able, also *morally relevant*? Well, some may be. If it could be shown, despite the evidence, that animals cannot suffer mentally, it would certainly be perverse to speak of the 'cruelty of confine-ment' for example. But, what Leahy fails to grasp is that most of the differences he identifies – language possession for example – even if lacking in mammals, may make the maltreatment of them harder rather than easier to justify. Leahy pleads the ways in which such characteristics make human suffering especially intolerable (pp. 200–2) but the converse is as, if not more, likely to be true. 'Animals and children who cannot fully vocalize or comprehend their misery, and who – in the case of animals at least – frequently suffer the deprivations of their natural instincts, are the victims of a greater cruelty' (Linzey, 1994 p. 38).

Such arguments invoke this response: 'It is a favourite strategy of liberationists to recycle, some would say hijack, our ethics of child-care such that animals enjoy equal protection on roughly similar grounds' (p. 191). Leahy here betrays his ignorance of the history of anti-cruelty work. Far from hijacking such ethics, liberationists have pioneered them. It was members of the RSPCA who founded and generously supported the emergence of the NSPCC in the UK. The founder of the ASPCA, Henry Bergh, brought the first prosecution for child cruelty in the US. The movement against child cruelty has constantly had to face Leahy-like arguments; thank God for the liberationists who saw the connection.

Lest the connection be utterly lost, let it be reiterated now: infants, like animals, are utterly in our power, defenceless, vulnerable and unprotected: moreover they are both morally innocent. Although we cannot precisely fathom out the nature of their inner life, we can be as reasonably sure as we are of anything that they both suffer *something* like us. Their relative weakness – far from being an argument for exploitation – should be at least one consideration that makes adult humans draw back from the exercise of power. Leahy's work would benefit from one or more 'intuitions' – not least of all concerning how morally 'primitive' we humans still are.

NOTES

1 See e.g. G.G. Gallup, Jr, 'Self-recognition in Primates. A Comparative Approach to the Biodirectional Properties of Consciousness', *American Psychology*, 32 (1977), 329–38, and 'Self-awareness and the Emergence of Mind in Primates', *American Journal of Primatology*, 2 (1982), 237–48; See Taylor Parker, Robert W. Mitchell and Maria Boccia (eds), *Self-awareness in Animals and Humans: Developmental Perspectives* (Cambridge: Cambridge University Press, 1994). (I am grateful to Paul Waldau for alerting me to this literature.)

BIBLIOGRAPHY

Aquinas, St Thomas (1918) *Summa Theologica*, ed. by the Fathers of the English Dominican Province, New York: Benzinger Bros.
—— (1945) *Summa Contra Gentiles*, in A. Pegis (ed.), *Basic Writings of Saint Thomas Aquinas*, vol. 2, New York: Random House.
Aristotle (1976) *Nicomachean Ethics*, trans. J.A. Thomson, Harmondsworth: Penguin Books.
Bentham, J. (1960) *An Introduction to the Principles of Morals and Legislation*, Oxford: Blackwell, first published in 1789.
Broome, A. (1824) 'Prospectus of the SPCA', 25 June 1824, *RSPCA Records*, vol 2.
Brown, L. (1988) *Cruelty to Animals: The Moral Debt*, London: Macmillan.
Carruthers, P. (1992) *The Animals Issue: Moral Theory in Practice*, Cambridge: Cambridge University Press.
Catechism of the Catholic Church (1994) London: Geoffrey Chapman.
Clark, S.R.L. (1977) *The Moral Status of Animals*, Oxford: Clarendon Press.
—— (1978) 'Animal Wrongs', *Analysis*, 38(3), 147–9.
—— (1994) *How to Think about the Earth: Philosophical and Theological Models for Ecology*, London: Mowbray.
Clarke, P. and Linzey, A. (eds) (1990) *Political Theory and Animal Rights*, London and Winchester, Mass.: Pluto Press.
Frey, R.G. (1979) 'What has sentiency to do with the possession of rights?', in R.D. Ryder and D.A. Paterson (eds), *Animals' Rights: A Symposium*, London: Centaur Press.
—— (1980) *Interests and Rights: The Case Against Animals*, Oxford: Clarendon Press.
—— (1983) *Rights, Killing, and Suffering*, Oxford: Blackwell.
Garner, R. (1993) *Animals, Politics and Morality: Issues in Environmental Politics*, Manchester: Manchester University Press.
Griffin, D.R. (1984) *Animal Thinking*, Cambridge, Mass.: Harvard University Press.
Hampshire, S. (1989) *Innocence and Experience*, Cambridge, Mass.: Harvard University Press and Harmondsworth: Penguin Books.
Harrison, R. (1964) *Animal Machines*, London: Vincent Stuart.
John Paul II, Pope (1987) *Sollicitudo Rei Socialis*, Encyclical letter, London: Catholic Truth Society.

BIBLIOGRAPHY

Kenny, A.J.P. (1975) *Will, Freedom and Power*, Oxford: Blackwell.
Leahy, M.P.T. (1994) *Against Liberation: Putting Animals in Perspective*, London and New York: Routledge.
Linzey, A. (1976) *Animal Rights: A Christian Assessment*, London: SCM Press.
—— (1987) *Christianity and the Rights of Animals*, London: SPCK and New York: Crossroad.
—— (1991) 'The theological basis of animal rights', *The Christian Century*, 108 (28) (9 October).
—— (1993) 'Created not invented: a theological critique of patenting animals', *Crucible*, April–June, pp. 60–9.
—— (1994) *Animal Theology*, London: SCM Press and Chicago: University of Illinois Press.
—— (1995) 'Animal Rights', 'Speciesism', and 'Cruelty', in Clarke, P. and Linzey, A. (eds), *Dictionary of Ethics, Theology and Society*, London and New York: Routledge.
Linzey, A. and Regan, T. (eds) (1989) *Animals and Christianity: A Book of Readings*, London: SPCK and New York: Crossroad.
Magel, C. (1989) *Keyguide to Information Sources in Animal Rights*, London and New York: Mansell Publishing.
Midgely, M. (1983) *Animals and Why They Matter*, Harmondsworth: Penguin Books.
Murray, R. (1992) *The Cosmic Covenant: Biblical Themes of Justice, Peace and the Integrity of Creation*, London: Sheed and Ward.
Newman, John Henry (1868) 'The Crucifixion', in *Parochial and Plain Sermons*, vol. vii, London, Oxford and Cambridge: Rivingtons.
Pacheco, A. and Francione, A. (1985) 'The Silver Spring Monkeys' in P. Singer (ed.), *In Defence of Animals*, Oxford: Blackwell.
Palazzini, P. (ed.) (1962) *Dictionary of Moral Theology*, London: Burns and Oates.
Primatt, H. (1776) *Dissertation on the Duty of Mercy and the Sin of Cruelty to Brute Animals*, Edinburgh: T. Constable.
Rachels, J. (1991) *Created from the Animals: The Moral Implications of Darwinism*, Oxford: Oxford University Press.
Rawls, J. (1972) *A Theory of Justice*, Oxford: Oxford University Press.
Regan, T. (1983) *The Case for Animal Rights*, Berkeley: University of California Press.
Rodd, R. (1990) *Biology, Ethics and Animals*, Oxford: Oxford University Press.
Rollin, B.E. (1981) *Animal Rights and Human Morality*, Buffalo, NY: Prometheus Books.
—— (1989) *The Unheeded Cry: Animal Consciousness, Animal Pain and Science*, Oxford: Oxford University Press.
Ryder, R.D. (1989) *Animal Revolution: Changing Attitudes Towards Speciesism*, Oxford: Blackwell.
Sapontzis, S.F. (1987) *Morals, Reason and Animals*, Philadelphia: Temple University Press.
Schleifer, H. (1985) 'Images of Death and Life: Food Animal Production and the Vegetarian Option', in P. Singer (ed.), *In Defence of Animals*, Oxford: Blackwell.

Singer, P. (1979) *Practical Ethics*, Cambridge: Cambridge University Press.
—— (1983) *Animal Liberation*, Wellingborough: Thorsons, first published in 1975.
—— (1987) Interview, in *The Animal's Agenda*, September, pp. 7–10.
Sorabji, R. (1993) *Animal Minds and Human Morals*, London: Duckworth.
Tester, K. (1991) *Animals and Society: The Humanity of Animal Rights*, London: Routledge.
Thomas, K. (1983) *Man and the Natural World: A History of the Modern Sensibility*, New York: Pantheon Books.
Turner, J. (1980) *Reckoning with the Beast: Animals, Pain and Humanity in the Victorian Mind*, Baltimore: Johns Hopkins University Press.
Warnock, M. (1986) *The Uses of Philosophy*, Oxford: Blackwell.
Wittgenstein, L. (1953) *Philosophical Investigations*, New York: Macmillan.
—— (1967) *Zettel*, ed. G.E.M. Anscombe and G.H. Von Wright, Oxford: Blackwell.

Part VI

LIBERATION
THEOLOGY

16

A NEW AGENDA
FOR SOCIETY

Dan Cohn-Sherbok

The evolution of liberation theology is arguably the most important theological development of the last few decades: beginning in South America, this movement has profoundly challenged traditional ways of doing theology. In 1968 a Latin American Bishops' Conference was held at Medellin, Colombia: this gathering was followed by a second conference in 1971 in Santiago, Chile, and a third at Publea, Mexico in 1979. At these meetings Christian participants focused on the injustice done to the poor in their own countries. Confronting modern forms of oppression and exploitation, they looked to the scriptural sources for a discernment of God's saving action in the world. Latin America thus became the breeding ground for this new movement which subsequently spread to other Third World countries and also had a major impact on thinkers in the First World. Because of its global significance liberation theology has undergone numerous manifestations, yet despite its diverse forms it has embraced a number of central themes in the proclamation of the message. Most importantly for the Jewish–Christian encounter, liberation theologians have gone back to their Jewish roots in the Hebrew Bible. Suddenly Jewish and Christian writers find themselves using the same vocabulary and motifs, and this bond paves the way for a mutual examination of commonly shared religious ideals.

What is of crucial significance for Jewish–Christian dialogue is the primary emphasis in liberation theology on understanding Jesus as a first-century Palestinian Jew. It is the flesh-and-blood Jesus of history who is of fundamental importance for liberation theologians; the concrete preaching and actions of Jesus himself provide the basis for the formulation of Christian theology. The historical context of the gospels is in this way reclaimed for Christians, and Jesus' teaching in the New Testament is related directly to God's design as recorded

213

in the Old Testament. In particular, Jesus is viewed as following in the footsteps of the great prophets of Ancient Israel. From a historical standpoint, then, the picture of Jesus that emerges from the gospel narratives is inextricably connected to his Jewish background. The consequence of this for Jews is profound, for it opens the way to a fresh vision of Jesus' mission. His criticism of the religious establishment, like that of the pre-exilic prophets, should not be understood as a rejection of Judaism itself, as it certainly was not, but as a call to the nation to return to the God of their fathers. Seen in its true light, Jesus' teaching stands in the tradition of the ethical prophets of Ancient Israel, and it is to the prophetic books of the Bible that we should turn to find the crucial links that relate Jesus to his Jewish past. In this context the Jew can recognize Jesus as following the prophetic tradition even though he cannot say with the Christian liberation theologian that Jesus is 'God of God, light of light, very God of very God, begotten not made, being of one substance with the Father' (Nicene Creed).

THE KINGDOM OF GOD

Liberation theologians insist that the kingdom of God as understood by Jesus is not the denial of history, but the elimination of its corruptibility. In the words of the Argentinian theologian José Miguez Bonino: 'God builds his Kingdom from within human history and its entirety; his action is a constant call and challenge to man. Man's response is realized in the concrete area of history with its economic, political and ideological options.'[1] The growth and ultimate fulfilment of the kingdom rests on a struggle against exploitation, alienation, oppression and persecution; it embraces all: the world, society and the individual. It is this totality which is to be transformed through the activity that God has initiated but not yet fully completed.

Within this unfolding of God's eschatological scheme, liberation theologians maintain that Christians have a crucial role. It is the responsibility of each person to engage in the quest for the liberation of the oppressed – this is a task which obliges all Christians to offer assistance not only in the religious and spiritual domain, but in the sphere of politics, economics and culture. According to P. Bigo, 'It is not enough to say that doing so is a condition of salvation; it is the very coming of the Kingdom in its temporal form'.[2] The way of the kingdom implies the building of a just society.

As Gutiérrez notes, a situation of injustice is incompatible with the kingdom: 'the building of a just society has worth in terms of the Kingdom, or in more current phraseology, to participate in the process of liberation is already in a certain sense, a salvific work.'[3] Entrance into the kingdom is open only to those who practice justice and distribute to the poor whatever they have over and above their real needs.

The heart of the gospel message is subversive; it embodies the Israelite hope for an end of the domination of man over man. The struggle for the establishment of God's kingdom involves the overthrow of established powers – political involvement is imperative. To know God is to be concerned for the creation of a new order regulated by the principle of love. In the words of M. Echegoyen:

> Our hope may refer to the Kingdom, to the second coming of Christ, but it begins here and now, in this society in which I happen to live and for whose transformation – humanization – I am inescapably responsible ... loving one's neighbour, which is the first commandment by definition, today means working to change the structures that can destroy my neighbour, the people, the poor.[4]

For liberation theologians such change involves the eradication of poverty which is incompatible with a kingdom of love and justice. Some theologians even go so far as to advocate the necessity of violent revolution as a means of altering the economic structures of society.[5]

In the writings of these theologians there is a common conviction that the rights of the poor must be upheld in a quest for the liberation of the oppressed. Peace, justice, love and freedom are dominating motifs in their understanding of the coming of God's kingdom. Breaking with traditional Christian theology, liberation theologians emphasize that these are not internal attitudes – they are social realities which need to be implemented in human history. Gutiérrez eloquently formulates this shift away from the values of the past: 'a poorly understood spiritualization', he writes, 'has often made us forget the human consequences of the eschatological promises and the power to transform unjust social structures which they imply. The elimination of misery and exploitation is a sign of the coming of the Kingdom'.[6] Thus the kingdom of God, contrary to what many Christians believe, does not signify something that is outside this world. It involves the effort of each individual to bring about a new order, a mission based on Jesus' actions and teachings as recorded in the gospels.

What is of central importance for the Jewish–Christian encounter is the liberationist's insistence that the coming of the kingdom involves individual participation in the creation of a new world. Though Judaism rejects the Christian claim that Jesus has ushered in the period of Messianic redemption, Jews have steadfastly adhered to the belief that God is a supreme ruler who calls all men to join him in bringing about the kingdom of God on earth. This understanding is an essential element of Psalmist theology, and it is a central theological motif of the Hebrew Bible. In later rabbinic literature, this vision of man's role in bringing about God's kingdom is elaborated further.

According to the rabbis, the kingdom of God takes place in this world; it is established by man's obedience to the divine will. The kingdom of God consists in a complete moral order on earth – the reign of trust, righteousness and holiness among all men and nations. The fulfilment of this conception ultimately rests with the coming of the Messiah; nevertheless, it is man's duty to participate in the creation of a better world in anticipation of the Messianic redemption. In the words of the rabbis: 'Man is a co-worker with God in the work of creation.'[7]

According to rabbinic theology, man is the centre of creation, for it is only he among all created beings who can through righteousness make the kingdom glorious.[8] In rabbinic *Midrash*, the view is expressed that God's kingship did not come into operation until man was created:

> When the Holy One, blessed be he, consulted the Torah as to the creation of the world, he answered, 'Master of the world, if there be no host, over whom will the King reign, and if there be no peoples praising him, where is the glory of the King?'[9]

It is only man then who can make the kingdom glorious; God wants to reign over free agents who can act as His co-partners in perfecting the world. What God requires is obedience to His ways of righteousness and justice: 'You are my lovers and friends.' 'You walk in my ways', God declares to Israel. 'As the Omnipotent is merciful and gracious, long-suffering and abundant in goodness so be ye ... feeding the hungry, giving drink to the thirsty, clothing the naked, ransoming the captives, and marrying the orphans.'[10] Throughout Biblical and rabbinic literature, Jews were encouraged to strive for the highest conception of life in which the rule of truth, righteousness and holiness would be established among mankind. Such a desire is the eternal hope of God's people – a longing for God's kingdom as expressed in the daily liturgy of the synagogue.

Here we can see the point of intersection between the Jewish faith and Christian liberation theology. For both Jews and liberation theologians the coming of the kingdom in which God's heavenly rule will be made manifest is a process in which all human beings have a role. It involves the struggle for the reign of justice and right-eousness on earth. The kingdom is not – as has been the case in traditional Christianity – an internalized, spiritualized, other-worldly conception. Rather it involves human *activity* in a historical context. Drawing on the Old and New Testaments, liberation theologians have attempted to demonstrate the tasks Christians must undertake in the building of the kingdom. Similarly, the rabbis elaborated the teaching of the Torah about man's partnership with God in bringing God's rule. For both faiths, the moral life is at the centre of the unfolding of God's plan for humanity. Such a shared vision should serve to unite Jews and Christians in a joint undertaking to trans-form our imperfect world in anticipation of the divine promise of the eschatological fulfilment at the end of time.

AREAS OF SOCIAL CONCERN

For liberation theologians the poor are the starting point of theo-logical reflection rather than abstract metaphysical theories; the view 'from below' is essential. Liberation theology claims that it is in the situation of the poor that God is to be found; as in Scripture, God is the saviour of the enslaved. What is required then is soli-darity as a protest against the poverty in which the poor are forced to live. As the major exponent of liberation theology, the Peruvian theologian Gustavo Gutiérrez, explains, it is a 'way of identifying oneself with the interests of the oppressed classes and challenging the exploitation that victimized them'.[11] Poverty is something to be fought against and destroyed; God's salvation is achieved in the process of liberation. The problems and struggles of the poor are our own – the vocation of every person is to opt for human love and compassion.

As God's long-suffering servants, the Jewish people should find this message of solidarity with the poor of paramount significance. In the Bible the prophets condemned every kind of abuse. Scripture speaks of positive action to prevent poverty from spreading – in *Leviticus* and *Deuteronomy* there is detailed legislation designed to prevent the amassing of wealth and consequent exploitation of the unfortunate. Jews should thus feel an obligation to eliminate poverty and suffering from contemporary society. In particular, they need to address the economic problems that affect various groups: the young who are frustrated by the lack of opportunity to obtain training and work, labourers who are frequently ill-paid and find difficulty in defending themselves, the unemployed who are discarded because of the harsh realities of economic life and the old who are often marginalized and disregarded. In all such cases, the Jewish people – who have consistently endured hardship – should feel drawn to the oppressed of modern society, sharing in their misery.

In pleading the case of the poor, liberation theologians – who are predominantly South American – have focused on the plight of the oppressed in the Third World. The underdevelopment of the poor countries, they point out, is the consequence of the development of other countries. In the words of Gutiérrez, 'the dynamics of the capitalist economy led to the establishment of a centre and a periphery, simultaneously generating progress and growing wealth for the few and social imbalances, political tensions, and poverty for the many.'[12] The countries of Latin America were born in this context; they emerged as dependent societies in consequence of economic exploitation. Such unequal structures dominate and determine the character of the particular cultures of these countries, and they necessitate a defence of the *status quo*. Even modernization and the introduction of a greater rationality into the economies of these societies is required by the vested interests of the dominant groups. Imperialism and colonization are the hallmarks of the past and present economic and cultural climate. From a cultural point of view as well such imbalance between 'developed' and 'underdeveloped' countries is acute – the underdeveloped areas are always far away from the cultural level of the industrialized centres.

The perception of the fact of this dependence and its consequences has made it possible to formulate a policy of reform. According to liberation theology, human freedom cannot be brought about by a developmentalist approach that maintains elitism. Instead liberationists grapple with the existing relationships based on injustice in a global frame. By analysing the mechanisms that are being used to keep the poor of the world under domination, liberation theologians assert that authentic development is possible only if the domination of the great capitalistic countries is eliminated. What is required is a transformation that will radically change the conditions in which the poor live. In this process, human beings are seen as assuming conscious responsibility for their own destiny. As Gutiérrez explains:

> this understanding provides a dynamic context and broadens the horizons of the desired social changes. In this perspective the unfolding of all of man's dimensions is demanded – a man who makes himself throughout his life and throughout history. The gradual attainment of true freedom leads to the creation of a new man and a qualitatively different society.[13]

These themes of liberation and emancipation have important resonances for the Jewish community. The Biblical narrative portrays the Ancient Israelites as an oppressed nation redeemed by God. Throughout history the Jewish people have been God's suffering servant – despised and rejected of men, smitten and afflicted. Through such suffering Jews are able to gain a sympathetic awareness of the situation of others. The lesson of the Passover is at the heart of Jewish aspirations for all humanity, as we read in the Passover liturgy:

> May He who broke Pharoah's yoke for ever shatter all fetters of oppression and hasten the day when swords shall, at last, be broken and wars ended. Soon may He cause the glad tidings of redemption to be heard in all lands, so that mankind – freed from violence and from wrong, and united in an eternal covenant of brotherhood – may celebrate the universal Passover in the name of our God of Freedom.[14]

In this spirit, it is possible for Jews to heed the plea of those who are downtrodden in the Third World; linked with liberationists, they can press for a restructuring of the economic sphere. By combatting exploitation and indifference, it is possible for both Jews and Christians to participate in the struggle to bring about a better way of life.

This preoccupation with the Third World does not preclude concern for the oppressed in First World countries. Liberation theologians stress that in the First World there are also grave inequalities between rich and poor. Despite the higher general standard of living in these countries, there nevertheless exist, for many, substandard conditions, poor health, concern about jobs and constant worry about money. Further, as the American theologian L. Cormie points out,

> the epidemic rates of alcoholism and other forms of drug abuse, of rape, wife-beating, child abuse, and other forms of violence,

of psychosomatic diseases like certain kinds of ulcers and heart disease, suggest the depths of anguish and alienation which many experience in our society.[15]

He goes on to argue that there are essentially two different segments in the labour market: primary sector jobs involving high wages, good working conditions, employment stability and job security, and secondary sector jobs involving low wages, poor working conditions, harsh and arbitrary discipline and little opportunity for advancement.[16]

Consumerism is a dominant ideology that contributes to such inequality – the most important questions are frequently concerned with how to save taxes and where to get the best prices for goods. As the German theologian Dorothee Sölle explains:

> this attempt to focus our interests and life priorities on hairspray, cat food, and travelling to the Virgin Islands represents an assault on the One in whose image I am created. It is an assault on human dignity. Consumerism means that my eyes are offended, my ears are obstructed, and my hands are robbed of their creativity.[17]

Exploitation in the First World is hence different from what is found in Third World countries. Inhabitants of the First World nations have become enmeshed in a cultural system that frequently perceives value in quantitative economic terms with an emphasis on having rather than being. Such hedonistic tendencies – generated by fiercely competitive economic interests – divide the affluent from the poor; nowhere is this more apparent than in the situation of the black community. In the United States, for example, as Cormie explains, slavery did not disappear with the disintegration of the plantation economy; in the period after the Civil War most blacks were relegated to work as sharecroppers. And even after the expansion of Northern industries, most blacks were channelled into the least desirable jobs and forced to live in the dilapidated city areas. Only a minority of blacks have been able to gain access to the privileges and status promised by the American dream.[18]

Having once laboured under the Egyptian yoke as slaves of the Pharaoh, Jews today are in a position to sympathize with the plight of such underprivileged sectors in the First World. In these countries, as in the Third World, the gap between the rich and the poor needs to be bridged, and facing such a challenge Jews are able to unite with their liberationist brothers and sisters. The attempt to build a more just society should propel Jews into the vanguard of those who attempt to restructure institutions along more egalitarian lines. By putting themselves in the shoes of the disadvantaged, Jews can envisage what life must be for the underprivileged. In this way Jews – along with liberationists – would be able to bring to the community policies of caring and sharing; this is theology 'from below', from the standpoint of those who are neglected and marginalized. By bringing their suffering to bear on these problems, the Jewish community can make a major contribution to the redemption of the poor.

In connection with this discussion of First World poverty, liberation theology has focused on life in the inner city. Here the distinction between the powerful and the powerless is most clearly evident. What is needed to remedy this situation is a new consciousness, an awareness of the calamities of inner-city deprivation. First World theologians influenced by liberation theology contend that the proper Christian response is to engage in urban mission. By ministering to those at the bottom of society, Christians affirm through their efforts that God is concerned with the plight of those facing adversity. Such activity constitutes an acted parable of the kingdom, bringing into focus the meaning of the gospel. Such a parable declares that the Christian cause is served best not in places of power and influence, but in situations of vulnerability and powerlessness. According to liberationists, Christ is incarnate in the inner city. In his own time be belonged to the lower end of society; in today's world he is to be found also among the lowly. Urban mission therefore aims to discover Jesus' message in the economic and cultural impoverishment of city life; from this vantage point, the Christian can strive to ameliorate the conditions of the downtrodden.

In pursuit of this goal, Jews too can enter into the life of the inner city and embark on a task of reconstruction and restoration. Remembering their sojourn in the land of Egypt, they are able to identify with the impoverished; by going into the city, Jews can work alongside and for the betterment of the poor. The facts of the inner city demand such commitment to change, and in this vocation liberationists should stand shoulder to shoulder with their Jewish brothers and sisters. Through the urban mission Jews and Christians can affirm that hope for the modern world lies in a sympathetic response and dedication to the weak. Beginning at the bottom, it is possible to work for the creation of a community in which all people are able to regain their sense of pride and self-fulfilment. By labouring together in the neediest areas, the two faiths can join forces to bring about God's kingdom on earth.

WOMEN'S EMANCIPATION

Liberation theology has also been concerned about the plight of women. Feminist theologians in particular have attempted to delineate the Biblical traditions encapsulating the liberating experiences and visions of the people of Israel so as to free women from oppressive sexist structures, institutions and internalized values. In the view of these writers, women have been and continue to be socialized into subservient roles – either they are forced into domestic labour or they hold badly-paid jobs. Only seldom do a few women manage to occupy jobs in male professions. According to the American theologian Rosemary Radford Ruether:

> Work segregation is still the fundamental pattern of society. Women's work universally is regarded as of low status and prestige, poorly paid, with little security, generally of a rote and menial character. The sexist structuring of society means the elimination of women from those activities that allow for and express enhancement and development of the self, its artistic, intellectual and leadership capacities.[19]

Throughout society, these theologians maintain, the full humanity of woman is distorted, diminished and denied.

To restore women's self-respect, liberationists concentrate on a number of Biblical themes – God's defence and vindication of the oppressed; the criticism of the dominant systems of power; the vision of a new age in which iniquity will be overcome; God's intended reign of peace. Feminist theology applies the message of the prophets to the situation of women; the critique of hierarchy thus becomes a critique of patriarchy. For these writers, images of God must include feminine roles and experiences, and language about God must be transformed from its masculine bias. For Christians, they believe, it is necessary to move beyond the typology of Christ and the Church as representing the dominant male and submissive female role. Within Church structures, women must be given full opportunities to participate at every level, including the ministry. In the civil sphere too women must be granted full equality before the law – a stance which calls for the repeal of all discriminatory legislation. There must be equal pay for equal work and full access to the professions. Many liberationists also insist on women's rights to reproduction, self-protection, birth-control and abortion as well as protection against sexual harassment, wife-beating, rape and pornography.

In the Jewish community there has similarly been a growing awareness of discrimination against women. Over the last two decades a significant number of Jewish feminists have attempted to restructure the position given to women in traditional Judaism. In the past Jewish women were not directly involved with most Jewish religious activity. Today, however, Jewish women are trying to find ways to live as full Jews. In their attempt to reconcile Judaism and feminism these women are rediscovering various aspects of Jewish life: some study the place of women in Jewish history; others examine religious texts for clues to women's influence on Jewish life; others redefine and feminize certain features of the Jewish tradition.

In seeking equal access with men, these feminists stress that women should be allowed to participate in the areas from which they have previously been excluded, namely, serving as witnesses in a religious court, initiating divorce proceedings, acting as part of a quorum for prayer, receiving rabbinic training and ordination as well as qualifying as cantors.

For these Jewish feminists, all formal distinctions between men and women in the religious as well as the secular sphere should be abolished. As the American Jewish feminist Susan Schneider explains: 'We have been trying to take charge of events in our own lives and in every area of what we call Jewish life: religion, the community, the family, and all our interpersonal relations.'[20] Given this impetus to liberate women from the restrictions of patriarchal structures, there is every reason for Jewish and Christian feminists to share their common concerns and objectives.

ECOLOGY

Not only do liberation theologians advocate a programme of liberation for all human beings, they also draw attention to human responsibility for the environment: ecological liberation is an important element in their policy of emancipation. Ever since the scientific revolution, nature has been secularized; no corner of the natural world has been immune from human control. Yet in this expansion of material productivity, the earth has been exploited to such a degree that pollution, famine and poverty threaten humanity's very existence. In this light, liberationists assert that human beings must accept responsibility for the environment. In the words of Radford Ruether,

> the privilege of intelligence ... is not a privilege to alienate and dominate the world without concern for the welfare of all other forms of life. On the contrary, it is the responsibility to become the caretaker and cultivator of the whole ecological community upon which our existence depends. ... We need to remake the earth in a way that converts our minds to nature's logic of ecological harmony. This will necessarily be a new synthesis, a new creation in which human nature and non-human nature become friends in the creating of a liveable and sustainable cosmos.[21]

Such reform calls for changed attitudes to the natural world; liberationists argue that human beings must accept that balance in nature is an essential characteristic of the earth's ecosystem. Human intervention inevitably upsets such a natural balance; thus steps must continually be taken to restore equilibrium to the earth. In particular, environmentalists point out that care must be taken about the use of pesticides. Habitations previously available to many living creatures have been destroyed; for agricultural purposes, people should attempt to maintain diversity within nature and this requires a careful monitoring of the use of chemical substances. Pollution too has been regarded as a major problem in the modern world; industry, urban waste and motor transport have all adversely affected the environment, and conservationists maintain that adequate control must be exercised over the use of pollutants which infect air and water resources. Furthermore, environmentalists contend that human beings must take steps to preserve endangered species and avoid inflicting cruelty on wild and domestic animals. In all these endeavours there is a role for the Jewish community; the recognition that humanity is part of the ecological whole is fundamental to Jewish thought. According to the Jewish faith, human beings have been given authority over nature, and such responsibility ought to curb the crude exploitation of the earth for commercial purposes. Such a divine fiat should foster a sympathetic understanding of the whole ecological situation engendering for Jews as for Christians an attitude of caring concern for all of God's creation.

These then are some of the areas in which Jews are able to unite with Christian liberation theologians to bring about God's kingdom. In pursuit of a common goal of freedom from oppression, committed Jews and Christians can become a saving remnant in the modern world, embodying the liberating message of Scripture. Like Abraham they can hope against hope in labouring to build a more just and humane world. In the words of the theologian Helda Camara, they can become an Abrahamic minority, attentive to the cry of oppression:

> We are told that Abraham and other patriarchs heard the voice of God. Can we also hear the Lord's call? We live in a world where millions of our fellow men live in inhuman conditions, practically in slavery. If we are not deaf we hear the cries of the oppressed. Their cries are the voice of God.
>
> We who live in rich countries where there are always pockets of underdevelopment and wretchedness, hear if we want to hear, the unvoiced demands of those who have no voice and no hope. The pleas of those who have no voice and no hope are the voice of God.[22]

CONCLUSION

In contemporary society, where those in the First World are often comfortable and affluent, the prophetic message of liberation can too easily be forgotten. Liberation theology, however – with its focus on the desperate situation of those at the bottom of society – should act as a clarion call. The Jewish tradition points to God's kingdom as the goal and hope of mankind – a world in which all people shall turn away from iniquity and injustice. This is not the hope of bliss in a future life, but the building up of the divine kingdom of truth and peace among all peoples in the here and now. As Isaiah declared: 'Keep not back: bring my sons from far, and my daughters from the ends of the earth' (*Isaiah* 43: 6). In this mission all those drawn to a liberationist perspective are able to join ranks; championing the cause of the oppressed, afflicted and persecuted, they can unite in common cause and fellowship to create a better world.

NOTES

1 J.M. Bonino, *Doing Theology in a Revolutionary Situation* (Philadelphia: Fortress Press, 1975), p. 138.
2 Bigo, 1977, p. 131.
3 Gutiérrez, 1973, p. 72.
4 Echegoyen, 1971, p. 464ff.
5 Davies, 1976.
6 Gutiérrez, 1973.
7 Babylonian Talmud, Shabb, 119b.
8 Agadoth Shir Hashirim, pp. 18, 61.
9 Pirke Rabbi Eliezer, ch. 3.
10 Agadoth Shir Hashirim, pp. 18, 61.
11 G. Gutiérrez, 'Liberation Praxis and Christian Faith', in Gibellini, 1980, p. 14.
12 Gutiérrez, 1973, p. 84.
13 Ibid., pp. 36–7.
14 *The Union Haggadah* (USA: Union of American Congregations, 1923), p. 78.
15 L. Cormie, 'Liberation and Salvation', in Richesin and Mahan, 1981, p. 29.
16 Ibid., p. 33.
17 D. Sölle, 'Liberation in a Consumerist Society', in Richesin and Mahan, 1981, p. 9.
18 Cormie, in Richesin and Mahan, 1981, p. 33.
19 Ruether, 1983, p. 178.
20 Schneider, 1984, p. 19.
21 Ruether, 1983, pp. 87–92.
22 Camara, 1974, p. 16.

17

SOME PROCEDURAL PROBLEMS

John Wilson

I read 'A New Agenda for Society' with great interest and a good deal of sympathy: sympathy, certainly, for the aims and motivation which inhere in it. Who, after all, would not want (to pick out some phrases more or less at random) 'to bring about God's kingdom on earth', or 'to unite in common cause and fellowship to create a better world' or 'to be concerned for the creation of a new order regulated by the principle of love'? Is anyone *against* 'the building of a just society'?

None of this, I hope, is in dispute. It might be possible to dispute whether these are the only, or even the chief, aims in the Judeo–Christian tradition or the theology of that tradition. People who do not want to be too much bullied by the term 'liberation' (again, who does not want to be liberated?) might claim that there are other aims, more concerned with the individual soul and its salvation, and having little or nothing to do with 'politics, economics and culture': and they might argue that these other aims are equally, perhaps more, important. We are only too familiar, however, with that sort of dispute: a dispute between 'traditionalists' and 'progressives', or 'conservatives' and 'radicals'. Each party will claim its own scriptural or other authority, and press its own ideological stance on the other. In some quarters one side will be at least temporarily victorious, in others the other side: or some more or less uneasy compromise will be arranged (as currently within the Church of England on many, perhaps most, practical issues).

That sort of dispute seems to me largely a waste of time, the mere clashing of ideological dinosaurs, more interesting for its psychological pathology than for its intellectual content. Much more important is a question, or a series of questions, that lies behind such disputes: questions like 'How, in principle, can such disputes be reasonably settled?', 'What, in principle, should theologians be trying to do?', 'What sort of discipline and expertise are they supposed to wield?' and perhaps particularly 'How far should these questions themselves be settled on the basis of the Judeo–Christian tradition (or any other tradition), particularly since they seem to be about what the future of that tradition is to be?' These are, ultimately, philosophical questions, and I hope I can persuade the reader to take a firm step backwards from his or her own ideological commitments, in order to see whether pure reason can shed any light on them.

I think many people find it difficult to take this step backwards. They find themselves saddled with, or at least a (more or less willing) part of, some religious or cultural tradition; and they also find themselves saddled with certain fairly strong feelings – of sympathy with the underdog, or the strong desire to preserve what is good in the past, perhaps a *depositum fidei*, or whatever. Then they may either simply (1) act these out, doggedly defending past tradition or fervently trying to change it or at least put it in a new light; or else (2) reflect, in a calm hour, on how such feelings (and the tradition itself) may most reasonably be handled. In much the same way a child or adolescent brought up in a certain tradition of parental authority may simply (1) cling on to it and identify with it, or else rebel against it and feel a desire to be 'liberated' from it, and act out these feelings; or, with luck (2) actually think about how to live, using both the tradition and his or her own feelings as subject-matter and not regarding either as authoritative.

AUTHORITY

One way of approaching these procedural questions – that is, again, questions about how to settle such issues – is via the notion of authority. By chance this morning's newspaper offers quite a good example (*Oxford Times*, 3 February 1995):

> A service at New College, Oxford ... outraged some members of the congregation by including an attack on homosexuals. A passage read from the Old Testament condemning 'unlawful' sexual relations was slammed as grossly insensitive. ... The New College chaplain ... said he deeply regretted that offence had been caused by the reading from Leviticus. He recognised that a terrible mistake had been made. ... 'If I had checked beforehand what was to be read that afternoon I would have had those verses omitted.'

So we have here a case of a religious (Christian) foundation apologizing for offending people by readings from the Bible.

Well, of course, an apology may be in order: just as, if we go by the criterion of what gives offence, we may want to apologize to rich members of a congregation for reading Biblical passages in which Jesus speaks (fairly strongly) about the difficulties and dangers of being rich. But if we do this – and perhaps we should, I do not want to take sides – clearly our locus of authority has changed. It is not now the scriptures that are authoritative, but the feelings of the congregation. In the same sort of way women might well (no doubt do) object strongly to some of the things St Paul says about women (let alone St Jerome a more extreme case). The rules of the game have now changed.

The Judeo–Christian tradition is sufficiently rich and multifarious to accommodate quite a wide variety of different feelings and ideologies, so that we can get away with fairly substantial changes in ideology whilst still claiming to remain faithful to that tradition. That process has its limits: at a certain point we may begin to wonder whether it is just that we have changed our emphasis on certain features of the religion, or rather that we have begun to change the religion itself. (Two ladies of my acquaintance jumped different ways on this: one took the view that Christianity was essentially patriarchal, and therefore abandoned it altogether: the other thought that it could be feminized (so to speak), that its essence remained intact if we talked of a maternal God, wrote off St Paul and others as just not sufficiently 'liberated' from their cultural background, and so forth – and she became a priest.) But even if it is just a matter of emphasis or interpretation, rather than of substantive revision, the same question still arises: that is, by what criterion do we decide to jump one way or the other?

It is clear that the criterion cannot inhere in the existing authority itself (the Bible, the Talmud, the early Fathers of the Church, the rabbinical tradition or whatever), for it is precisely this that is being evaluated or challenged. Driven by our own ideologies (which we may choose to call 'insights'), and perhaps always able to claim that what we want is in accordance with the 'spirit' of the tradition, we may of course put more or less any kind of pressure we want on it. We shall select those passages from scripture which support our feelings and disregard or play down those that go against them. But that, of course, is a form of cheating: it does not even face the question of what criterion we should use. Yet we shall not, in a calm and non-ideological hour, be wholly at ease with the idea that our feelings are themselves authoritative.

That is perhaps an obvious point, but commonly disregarded. It is parallel to the question, again commonly not even faced, of what language or behaviour is really or genuinely 'offensive', offensive to any reasonable person, as against simply being found or thought 'offensive'. Perhaps the presence of blacks in Alabama restaurants is offensive to whites, perhaps some men may find it offensive if women are not kept behind veils: but that does not (I hope) tempt us to say that these things are really offensive. When pressed, few of us relapse into extreme relativism on these matters. Or if we do, we shall have to say that one set of feelings, a desire to 'liberate', is no better and no worse than any other set (a desire to conserve and keep people 'in their proper place'); that all we can do is either fight, or work out some kind of consensus; that reason has no grip on such matters. But then there would not be much point in discussing or arguing about them (in this book or elsewhere).

THE INTUITIONAL APPROACH

I have to say – or at least, I don't *have* to say, but it would be disingenuous not to – that Dan Cohn-Sherbok seems to me not to have faced these (rather obvious) points at all. What he has done, as indeed most people do, is to start with certain political, moral or ideological intuitions which lead him, with the help of selective quotation, to suggest a particular 'agenda for society'. Cohn-Sherbok is obviously a nice chap, and these intuitions are predictable: he is tender-minded, 'caring', egalitarian, pro-feminist, in favour of dignity and self-respect, against violence, in general politically correct. And I might frame a reply to his article (if I happened to catch myself in the right ideological mood) in terms of a different 'agenda': one which stressed responsibilities and duties as much as rights, emphasized the need for conserving tradition, suggested that people's need for security in a rapidly-changing world was at least as important as their need for 'liberation' and so forth. That sort of thing, fairly easy to churn out, might be thought of as an appropriate 'answer' to his piece: the two pieces could be put alongside each other, and different readers would give either of them a warm or chilly reception according to temperament.

Alas, that is not what I am saying at all. What I am saying is different, and perhaps nastier. I am saying that this whole way of proceeding – of acting out one's preferred intuitions and values, and trying to give these some kind of spurious traditional or scriptural authority – is feeble-minded and disgraceful. We all feel the temptation to do it, but we all have the duty to resist it and turn our attention to the key question of what *criterion* we are using (if any), of how we know we are getting things *right* rather than just sounding off. But Cohn-Sherbok writes as if he did not even understand that there was such a question: or at least as if he did not wish to become involved with it (perhaps because that would then inhibit him from following his intuitions).

IDEOLOGICAL ASSUMPTIONS

The question of what criterion, what authority, to use relates to (perhaps is ultimately the same as) the question of how we identify ourselves when trying to answer it, of what ideological lumber (so to speak) we bring with us. I mean this: I may face a certain question about what is true or valuable, and say to myself 'Can I accept (believe, practise) this as a Jew/Christian/white/black/woman/man/North Oxford academic/Anglo-Saxon?' (and so on, the list is endless). People identify themselves in various ways: they have very strong pre-existing attachments: and, understandably enough, they want to know whether they can retain those attachments and at the same time do or believe X or Y or Z. In much the same way a man might ask himself 'Can I behave like this and still be "a real man"?', or a woman might say 'I want to see myself as a "nice girl": do "nice girls" do this sort of thing?' People want to be faithful to their ego-ideals, or commitments, whilst at the same time wanting (if they reflect at all) to do what is right and believe what is true.

But clearly in the present case our attachments are, to speak boldly, strictly irrelevant. If, as Cohn-Sherbok contends, we really ought to 'liberate' the oppressed, stand shoulder to shoulder with the poor, feel guilty about not trying our best to remedy injustice and so on, then the reasons for this cannot be simply that we are Jewish, or Christian, or whatever. The point is not just that the Jewish and Christian traditions are, so to speak, controversial and elastic enough to accommodate various viewpoints – though that in itself, as I have said, requires some external criterion to adjudicate these viewpoints. It is rather that, if there actually are good reasons for (say) remedying injustice, as of course there are, such reasons (if they really are good) will apply to *anyone*.

Again, we have to distinguish between our reason and our feelings. Thus we may ask whether we ought to forgive our enemies; and if we conclude that we ought, that will (as it were, incidentally) apply to the case of forgiving Nazis for the holocaust. Of course it will be, psychologically, more difficult to do this if we are Jewish (or, come to that, gypsies and lots of other people). If I ask 'Can I, as a Jew, forgive the Nazis?' I am struggling with my own feelings and cultural background: and such struggles of course deserve our sympathy. The question is close to 'Can I be expected to . . .?' But the question 'Ought I, as a Jew, to forgive . . .?' really makes no sense in the light of reason. For reason – that is what reason is – operates on general principles, e.g. that of forgiving enemies, to which in reasoning we subject ourselves.

The parable of the Good Samaritan makes this point effectively enough. The point is that how we should behave towards other people (or whom we should count as 'our neighbour', and what would count as 'loving' our neighbour) is governed by criteria of reason that have nothing to do with particular religious or ideological attachments. The relevant criteria have to do with notions like justice, need and benevolence: they are to do with being human and recognizing other people as equally human, not with traditional, sectarian or other attachments.

SETTLING ISSUES

I am claiming then that these questions can only be answered by putting firmly on one side both our particular traditions and our particular cultural or psychological attachments: because, obviously enough, it is just these which we have to evaluate. We need to generate some notion of authority, distinct from our preferred ideologies, which will enable us to settle these issues – to work out, for instance, how far (if at all) the churches or congregations of institutions with which we are concerned should engage 'not only in the religious and spiritual domain, but in the sphere of politics, economics and culture' (p. 214). Cohn-Sherbok clearly thinks that they should.

It is important to be clear about just what the dispute is here. It is not (I hope) about whether some agency – perhaps all of us, working in various fields – should do things like help the poor, remedy injustice, 'liberate' the oppressed and so on. As I said right at the beginning, nobody is going to deny this. Even those who, following at least one interpretation of the Beatitudes, think that it is somehow advantageous or 'blessed' to be poor, oppressed and so forth, will probably not object to a diminution of poverty and oppression: they will rather think, perhaps, that specifically religious (rather than purely secular or social) organizations should not make this their prime aim. So the question is not whether this should be done, but rather whether religious organizations (if I may use this rather cumbrous phrase) have a specific part to play in doing it.

Whether they have such a part, and what that part is to be, must turn (yet again) on the question of authority. And now that will not mean 'Can they find something, at least, in their traditions which will support such aims?', for of course they can – though it will still be a question whether they should attend primarily to those elements of the traditions rather than others (to Christ healing the sick rather than to the Beatitudes, for instance, or to his feeding the hungry rather than to his kingdom being 'not of this world'). The crux will be this: if, as a Jew or Christian (or anything else), I am going to go in for 'politics, economics and culture', and operate 'not only in the religious and spiritual domain', then what right, authority or expertise do I have which justifies this? (It may be worth adding here that the distinction which Cohn-Sherbok thus makes between these domains will turn out already to have given most of the game away: once one acknowledges that politics and economics are different from the 'spiritual domain' – just as mathematics and medicine and agriculture are different from it – then one can perhaps see in advance how the argument is likely to go.)

THE NEED FOR EXPERTISE

We have to address, then, the problem of expertise. It is essentially a Platonic one, and it is raised in a general form in the first two books of the *Republic*. There Plato distinguishes between the art (*techne*) of medicine on the one hand, and the art of making money on the other. Of any practitioners of any art, it can be asked what specific or *sui generis* expertise they possess which is not possessed by others, what specific goal they seek and what specific work they do. The idea connects with the importance Plato puts on each person doing his proper job (*to ta heautou prattein*), which for Plato is a necessity for justice. We do not want cobblers ruling, or doctors being generals; or at least, we do not want to confuse the various arts of cobbling, ruling, medicine and generalship. We must distinguish between various enterprises in order to see what each is and how it can best be done.

This is basically a simple thought, but very strongly resisted. It is especially likely to be resisted when the question of expertise is posed in terms of *authority* in a society which is distrustful of or antipathetic to authority in general. For psychological reasons which need not to be discussed here, professional agents – teachers, doctors, priests and others such as Cohn-Sherbok – in liberal societies such as Britain are currently resistant to the idea of authority, and extremely anxious not to appear in authoritarian postures. Their style is egalitarian, often bordering on the relativistic. Assumption of *any* expertise is construed as an assumption of authority (with which of course it is logically connected), and hence the expertise is apt to be denied along with the authority which it should command. It is quite unsurprising that these professions should recently have become – to use political terms – much more left-wing than they were even a few decades ago, at least in Britain and some other liberal societies.

Nevertheless the question has to be faced. We have (or could have; the point is a logical one) expert social workers, psychiatrists, doctors, economists, sociologists, moral philosophers and others: now, what does Cohn-Sherbok do or know that they do not? But perhaps even this form of the question is not stringent enough: for one possible answer is 'nothing'. This answer is actually given, more or less explicitly, by various religious groups (the Quakers might be a fair example). But such an answer might deny the need for anybody playing a special *role* without denying the existence of special *expertise*, so that our basic question will still be unanswered. I mean this: one might believe that (for instance) there was a special expertise, or at least a set of particular qualities and capacities, which enabled people to do well at making friends or choosing marriage partners, and yet not believe that any individual or group should be called upon to play a particular social role in relation to these enterprises – that there ought to be official and paid-up marriage brokers or friendship arrangers. One might believe that (for one reason or another) individuals best look after these enterprises in their own case for themselves – that they do not need any outside expertise.

THE RELEVANCE OF RELIGION

For anyone who takes religion to be more than a hobby, the basic question remains. Perhaps we have been premature in using the term 'expertise'; – perhaps the qualities of rabbis or ministers of the Church, or of the Church as a whole or of individual believers, are not well described by 'expertise'. We could use some even more down-to-earth and wider phrase, and ask what they have on the ball that others do not have; and to this there must surely be some answer, because otherwise their faith or religious affiliation would have no point. It must bring certain *advantages*. Nor is it plausible to say that these advantages are entirely motivational (as if the only point to having a religion was to gain more incentive to be and behave in ways which we were quite clear about already). Some of the advantages must surely be in terms of knowledge or understanding or skill: which brings us back to some such idea as 'expertise'.

Nevertheless it would be odd if some reasonable categorization of the enterprise of religion did not have some pragmatic weight. Cohn-Sherbok might possibly say, for instance (I have heard it said), that there can be no serious place or time for religion, for preaching the gospel, to people who are starving or politically oppressed or in some other way severely disadvantaged. But I do not know of any religion that regards itself as (so to speak) a social luxury in this sort of way; on the contrary, most religions (certainly Judaism and Christianity) incorporate very clearly the idea of the special importance of religion – of *religion*, as against some kind of social or political work – to the disadvantaged. Even if individual believers have to act as doctors, or teachers or politicians, they will do so in the understanding that they subordinate themselves to medical, or educational or political expertise. A minister of the Church may be obliged to grow corn in a famine, but is then only a farmer *faute de mieux*.

Expertise is a concept parasitic on the concept of knowledge. There must be a body of knowledge which religion (or particular religions) claims to deploy, and which is, as it were, more thoroughly mastered, understood or communicated by paid-up religious experts – the clergy – than by others. Just what is this knowledge? Obviously enough the answer will lie, in the first place, in the realm of theology: though I am not sure if 'theology' is today a sufficiently unequivocal term to make the point, since it is commonly invaded by matters which might rather be classified under the headings of 'morality', 'psychology' or even 'politics'. It is, indeed, just here that our main difficulty lies, which I will now try to confront explicitly.

JOHN WILSON

TECHNICAL REQUIREMENTS

The difficulty is that few religious believers would seriously claim expertise in arts or sciences that are now well-established: I mean, such *technai* as physics, medicine, agriculture and so forth. But they do claim, or seem to claim, expertise in those enterprises in which judgements of value, or ideals or morality, are of central importance: morality, psychiatry, politics and the like. Now suppose they were asked to justify this: suppose we said something like, 'Look here, there are people who have devoted their entire energies to these enterprises – professional psychiatrists, philosophers, economists, statesmen and so forth. No doubt there is more room for disagreement in these fields than in (say) medicine or agriculture: but by what right do you claim expertise *qua* religious believers?' Cohn-Sherbok's reply would be along the lines of, 'But the ideals which inform, and inevitably inform, these enterprises must flow from some conception of the world, life, the human condition: and we claim expertise in *that*. We know, or think we know, that there is a God who is not only a very important *fact* in the universe – powerful, creative, forgiving, saving, and so on – but who also demands certain *values* from us. He is essentially a moral – if you like, also a political – God who backs and instantiates certain specific values (love, chastity, mercy and so forth) and is against other values (greed, cruelty, etc.). That just *is the nature* of the god we worship: and how could that not be relevant to such enterprises as morality and politics?'

Before replying to this it is worth noticing that religions could – some actually do – set up a god whose nature is far more demanding, demanding in far more detail, than this. Such a god could require, for instance, dietary and medical behaviour which contravened the accepted findings of science and medicine; or personal behaviour which, according to psychiatric consensus, led to neurosis and psychosis; or economic behaviour which led to bankruptcy or starvation. One might then say – I imagine most modern Jews and Christians would in fact say – 'Well, but you should not set up or worship that kind of god – that is, a god who (as it were) goes against established expertises: no god worth his salt, no god worth worshipping, would make such demands. That is not the sort of job a god is supposed to do – that really is not the province of *religion*.'

We have either to say something like that, or else to cede to any religion and set of believers the right, in terms of what is reason-

236

able, to believe in a god who could, as it were, totally nullify and contravene all well-established enterprises and expertises and *technai*: a god who operated *against all reason*. But nobody (in their senses) would make this move: we think that the choice of what god we are going to worship should not be just random, or dictated by irrational feeling, but based upon *good grounds*. And amongst those grounds must figure the notion that, whatever sort of god we have, he should not contradict common sense and the rationality of established enterprises (if indeed they are properly established: of course this can always be questioned).

THE NEED FOR RATIONALITY

But now if we are unwilling to say this, we are admitting – quite rightly – that the whole constellation of concepts, represented by religion/god/divine authority/what is worshipful, is not absolute and unbounded, but must be regulated by existing rational expertises. Whatever the proper connection between a god and (say) science, medicine, economics, education, politics, art and so forth, it will not be a connection of *authority*. We are not, in effect, to allow ourselves to say, 'medical/scientific/economic, etc. experts say such-and-such, but we know better because we know what God wants here'. And now that conclusion will stand, whether the expertises are in areas which most modern Christians are happy to relinquish (like the physical sciences), or in areas which they are not (like politics).

One can see various Christian authors (and perhaps Cohn-Sherbok also) struggling with this in relation to particular items which are on the borderline between the two types of enterprise. C.S. Lewis, for instance, wished at one point to defend the traditional Christian view that usury was a sin, but admitted that the economic invention of the joint-stock company may have rendered this view obsolete, and there are few believers today who would, either in practice or in theory, eschew all cases of receiving interest on money. Similar contortions are found in discussions about gambling; and even traditional sexual morality is called into question by a shift of opinion which has been much influenced by the social sciences and psychology (consider the questions now raised about homosexuality and polygamy).

Such shifts of opinion convey the impression of an ongoing *retreat*. We give up a belief in *Genesis* as a scientific document because of the established enterprise of science; the dietary laws of *Leviticus* because of established medicine; the exorcism of devils because of psychiatry. Now we may withdraw claims to expertise in economics and sexual behaviour in a similar way: that is – and this is the crucial point – *we define what God wants, or what sort of god we worship, by our (secular) understanding of these fields, rather than insisting that our secular views in these fields are governed by a predetermined and inflexible picture of what God wants.* (This of course alarms, very understandably, people of a traditional cast of mind who feel that permanent security in religious belief is being eroded, and who thence predictably return to some puritanical or fundamentalist position. In such a position the traditional god is pre-eminent, at the cost of throwing over established expertises; 'Creation science' is a fair example.)

THE ROLE OF RELIGION

We can avoid this impression of permanent retreat only by taking our stand on what is *sui generis* to religion. That must (to put it briefly) lie somewhere in the area of what is worshipful *independently* of the progress of any human expertise. There can be no such ground to stand on for people who either (1) are prepared to fly in the face of such expertise, maintaining a god who carried detailed authority only at the price of abolishing science, medicine, economics and any and every other enterprise, or (2) worship a god who is little more than a cover or sponsor for their own values in morality, politics or other enterprises. Those of type (1), the 'fundamentalists' or 'traditionalists', cannot succeed because (when we are sensible) we know quite well that some enterprises are well-established, and cannot be gainsaid. Those of type (2), the 'modernists', cannot succeed because they reduce God to the role of some sort of ideal Social Worker, who (with his priests and congregation) has not much more to do than to set society straight, ensure justice, make the appropriate economic and social arrangements and so forth. (Both (1) and (2) are of course parodies: I caricature the positions to make the point clear.)

We thus need to explore (further than I attempt here) the kind of god, or those aspects of our own God, that stand above and beyond the sublunary world of human enterprises – including the most fashionable one today, namely politics. The prime function and *sui generis* task of religion, the ground from which it cannot logically be driven, must be to communicate those features of life and the human condition which are permanent and important, whatever the condition of secular life. To put it in one way, the kingdom of heaven, or the notion of salvation, must not be defined by this or that kind of morality, social order, economic arrangements or political system: it has to be defined, and communicated, in a way which will bring understanding and comfort and grace to people living under any set of conditions. That does not of course imply that believers should rest content with such conditions, but their improvement rests with the established enterprises (and, a very important task, with putting some enterprises which we are now unclear about on a sounder footing: this has happened with medicine and science, and needs to happen with morality and politics). To put this another way: the notion of Jewish or Christian politics or economics makes no more sense than the notion of Jewish or Christian mathematics or agriculture. But – and this may be a consoling thought to some – it also makes no less sense: Jews and Christians, who believe in a god who wants the best for his world, have an added incentive to become (or at least to understand) good economists and politicians, just as they have to become and understand good mathematicians and agriculturalists. The heart of their belief, however, does not lie in these enterprises, important though they are: it lies in the more strictly theological picture which transcends any sublunary conditions, and is painted in terms of creation, grace, salvation, sin, forgiveness and a kingdom which is not of this world.

CONCLUSION

My claim then against Dan Cohn-Sherbok is that the expertise and authority of religion lies (unsurprisingly) in its own sphere, and not in other spheres already demarcated (science, medicine, politics, etc.). That does not answer the question of the nature of this expertise and authority. I am saying, more or less, that religious expertise consists in showing us what sort of god we should worship, and in the light of this addressing certain very basic features of the human condition which remain in place under any social or other circumstances. I have tried to show that this is not just a personal preference for some 'traditional' view of religion, but logically entailed by even a comparatively brief reflection on the notion of authority and expertise itself. But the question remains of how religious believers are to deploy their expertise (in the purely 'spiritual domain', if you like) *well*: how they are to *get things right*.

I have written at some length elsewhere on this and do not want to repeat it here. But it is worth adding, perhaps, that if (as I think) the proper deployment of such expertise depends largely on the education of the emotions – roughly, on whether we have enough mental health and insight to worship proper objects rather than improper ones (like Hitler or Baal, perhaps), then that sort of education is itself likely to affect our views on 'liberation' and many other things. If we manage to develop enough understanding of our own (and other people's) feelings, we shall then – only then – adopt appropriate attitudes to (for instance) women, the poor, the oppressed and so on. That will be hard enough; but at least we shall be tackling the issues the right way round. Instead of simply using elements in a tradition to support our own ideologies, or even to alter our pictures of what our god is like, we shall get some grasp of how a sane person would view such matters. And that will affect our whole thinking on practical issues. How such thinking would in practice turn out seems to me a premature question: for instance, it will be only when we are clearer about what women are really like – something on any reasonable account clearly controversial – that we can know what it is to do them justice, and how to modify our religious tradition (perhaps even our image of God) in the light of this. Without the benefit of prolonged and honest analysis of our emotions – and, I think, also some philosophical analysis – we shall do no more than act out our own feelings, perhaps encouraged by prevailing fashion.

18

COHN-SHERBOK'S
REPLY

John Wilson asks what kind of expertise theologians have. 'We have', he writes, 'expert social workers, psychiatrists, doctors, economists, sociologists, moral philosophers and others: now, what does Cohn-Sherbok do or know that they do not?' (p. 234). In response, he suggests: 'a possible answer is "nothing!"' Is this fair? I think not. Theologians do not simply give vent to their feelings – as Wilson seems to suggest – and then attempt to find some justification for their prejudices in authoritative sources. On the contrary, they begin from religious presuppositions, and then attempt to draw out the implications of these beliefs. Wilson himself at certain points appears to acknowledge this type of procedure – but he is at pains throughout his essay to emphasize the theologian's lack of expertise in anything.

Arguably, however, theologians are as skilled in their own professions as nurses, doctors and lawyers are in theirs. The skill is not as obvious, but it is gained through years of training and reflection. As far as Jewish theologians are concerned, they must be able to read Hebrew and Aramaic, and translate and understand religious texts (such as the Hebrew Scriptures, the *Mishnah*, the *Midrash*, the *Talmud* and the *Code of Jewish Law*). Further, they should ideally be familiar with the history of Jewish philosophy and theology. In a word, they should be experts in their own faith-traditions, able to interpret the Jewish heritage in a way which is relevant to the modern world. Much the same could be said, of course, of Christian, Muslim, Hindu and Buddhist theologians; they should equally be at home in their traditions.

The task of the theologian is to quarry from these sources insights which are of significance for men and women living in contemporary society. This is not simply an academic endeavour like philosophy or sociology: it is a sacred trust. Wilson would no doubt object to such a notion, yet it is the cornerstone of the theological enterprise. As Anselm remarked, theology should be understood pre-eminently as *fides quaerens intellectum* (faith seeking understanding). It is in this spirit that I have proposed a new agenda for the liberation of society based on religious principles.

Wilson maintains that my argument begins from a set of political, moral and ideological intuitions, and then proceeds through selective quotation to argue for a new vision of the modern world. But this is a distortion. Rather, I begin from a set of religious assumptions about the nature of God and the world as reflected in Scripture itself. The Hebrew Scriptures with their depiction of a God who acts on behalf of his oppressed people is the starting point of the argument. The God of the *Exodus* narrative, rather than a conglomeration of intuitions, serves as the framework for what follows. The prophetic tradition – informed by the *Exodus* experience – drives the argument forward. And, all this is directly linked to rabbinic teaching about the nature and activity of God.

These theological foundations then, rather than my subjective feelings, operate as the basis for the discussion. There are of course moral, political and sociological implications of these beliefs, and I have attempted to sketch out in brief what they are. But at the heart of this enterprise is the quest to ascertain and do God's will. Thus, Wilson's critique of my position fails to recognize the seriousness of the theologian's task in formulating a programme of liberation for those of us who live in the First World.

Furthermore, and more seriously, Wilson does not point to some of the real difficulties with the position I have outlined. First, he could have said much more about the religious basis of my argument. Certainly there are many today who would distance themselves from the religious assumptions of the Judeo–Christian understanding of God's nature and activity. In a post-Holocaust world, is it still possible to believe in a God who acts? Where was God when six million died? These are the serious questions that should be placed alongside a theology of liberation which presupposes the existence of a deity who is concerned with the plight of those who are oppressed. Moreover, Wilson could have been far more critical of my use of scriptural and rabbinic material. He does emphasize the dangers of arbitrary and selective use of religious sources; but he dismisses such potential criticisms as a waste of time. Yet they are not trivial matters! Certainly, theologians themselves who have been opposed to the theology of liberation have been anxious to illustrate the arbitrary nature of the liberationist's handling of religious literature. Arguably, a case could have been made against my exposition on such grounds. This, it seems to me, would provide a much more telling criticism than what Wilson offers instead.

BIBLIOGRAPHY

Bigo, Pierre (1977) *The Church and Third World Revolution*, trans. Jeanne Marie Lyons, Maryknoll, NY: Orbis Books.

Boff, Leonardo (1978) *Jesus Christ Liberator*, trans. Patrick Hughes, Maryknoll, NY: Orbis Books.

—— (1980) 'Christ's Liberation via Oppression', in Rosino Gibellini (ed.), *Frontiers of Theology in Latin America*, trans. John Drury, London: SCM Press.

Brown, Robert M. (1978) *Theology in a New Key: Responding to Liberation Themes*, Philadelphia: Westminster.

Camara, Dom Helder (1974) *The Desert Is Fertile*, Maryknoll, NY: Orbis Books.

Cohn-Sherbok, D. (ed.) (1992) *World Religions and Human Liberation*, Maryknoll, NY: Orbis Books.

Cormie, L. (1981a) 'The Challenge of Liberation Theology', in L. Dale Richesin and Brian Mahan (eds), *The Challenge of Liberation Theology: A First World Response*, Maryknoll, NY: Orbis Books.

—— (1981b) 'Liberation and Salvation', in L. Dale Richesin and Brian Mahan (eds), *The Challenge of Liberation Theology: A First World Response*, Maryknoll, NY: Orbis Books.

Croatto, J. Severino (1981) *Exodus*, Maryknoll, NY: Orbis Books.

Davies, J.G. (1976) *Christians, Politics and Violent Revolution*, Maryknoll, NY: Orbis Books.

Dussel, Enrique (1976) *History and the Theology of Liberation*, Maryknoll, NY: Orbis Books.

Echegoyen, M. (1971) 'Priests and Socialism in Chile', *New Blackfriars*, 52, 464ff.

Ellacuria, Ignacio (1976) *Freedom Made Flesh*, trans. John Drury, Maryknoll, NY: Orbis Books.

Gibellini, Rosino (ed.) (1980) *Frontiers of Theology in Latin America*, trans. John Drury, London: SCM Press.

Gutiérrez, Gustavo (1973) *A Theology of Liberation*, trans. Sr Caridad Inda and John Eagleson, Maryknoll, NY: Orbis Books.

—— (1975) 'Liberation Praxis and Christian Faith', in Rosino Gibellini (ed.), (1980) *Frontiers of Theology in Latin America*, trans. John Drury, London: SCM Press.

—— (1983) *The Power of the Poor in History*, trans. Robert Barr, Maryknoll, NY: Orbis Books.

Miguez Bonino, José (1975) *Doing Theology in a Revolutionary Situation*, Philadelphia: Fortress.

Miranda, José (1974) *Marx and the Bible*, Maryknoll, NY: Orbis Books.

—— (1983) *Communism in the Bible*, London: SCM Press.

Pérez-Esclarin, Antonio (1978) *Atheism and Liberation*, trans. John Drury, Maryknoll, NY: Orbis Books.

Pixley, George V. (1981) *God's Kingdom: A Guide for Biblical Study*, trans. Donald E. Walsh, Maryknoll, NY: Orbis Books.

Richesin, L. Dale and Brian Mahan (eds) (1981) *The Challenge of Liberation Theology: A First World Response*, Maryknoll, NY: Orbis Books.

Ruether, Rosemary R. (1983) *Sexism and God-Talk*, Boston: Beacon Press and London: SCM Press.

Schneider, Susan (1984) *Jewish and Female*, New York: Simon & Schuster.

Segundo, Juan L. (1976) *The Liberation of Theology*, trans. John Drury, Maryknoll, NY: Orbis Books.

Sobrino, Jon (1978) *Christology at the Crossroads*, trans. John Drury, Maryknoll, NY: Orbis Books.

Sölle, Dorothee (1981a) *Choosing Life*, London: SCM Press.

—— (1981b) 'Liberation in a Consumerist Society', in L. Dale Richesin and Brian Mahan (eds), *The Challenge of Liberation Theology: A First World Response*, Maryknoll, NY: Orbis Books.

—— (1981c) 'Thou Shalt Have No Jeans Before Me', in L. Dale Richesin and Brian Mahan (eds), *The Challenge of Liberation Theology: A First World Response*, Maryknoll, NY: Orbis Books.

Topel, John (1979) *The Way to Peace: Liberation through the Bible*, Maryknoll, NY: Orbis Books.

Vincent, John J. (1982) *Into the City*, London: Epworth Press.

19

AFTERWORD

Michael Leahy

PREAMBLE

Readers will excuse a personal note at the outset. Editing this collection has been invigorating work, if only because of the forbearance and good humour with which our distinguished contributors acceded to (and sometimes resisted) our outrageous demands. Their inquisitorial interest, right from our first enquiries, encouraged us to believe that the enterprise was a worthy one. The 'our' and 'us' is a reminder that the editorship is a joint one, which has eased some difficult decisions. Not least is the possible conflict of interest when both editors are also contributors. There is nothing odd or disgraceful about this; indeed it is normal practice in academic circles. But in an editorial Afterword of the type upon which you are about to embark some brief explanation is called for. The Introduction to the book, it was decided, would be the responsibility of one editor (Cohn-Sherbok), leaving the other (Leahy) to put together the Afterword. This latter is a reflection upon common themes which tend to point up similarities between the various topics. It is also, in the polemical spirit with which contributors have faced their opponents, not always a model of immaculate impartiality.

Certainly there *are* lessons to be elaborated from such a closely-knit clutch of issues. Our Introduction made passing mention of an obvious one – the conceptual duality of the book's title. Martha Nussbaum, in the course of some initial skirmishing, put it amusingly in a letter:

> As for my question about 'liberation', the problem is that this is such an antiquated term that it makes the book seem weirdly dated before it begins. My daughter, who's 20, says that she

246

has never heard that term except in historical discussions of the 60's. I would say 'women's rights', if I were you.

There is a point here; but not one to outdate the book. The use of 'liberation' to label a cause is more emphatically emotive than the somewhat legalistic and pedantic talk of 'rights'. When gay or anti-racist activists are on the march the banners of 'liberation' far outnumber those of 'rights' (for the simple reason that the marchers know full well that they *have* innumerable rights). But there is a profound, even atavistic, reason for liberation's emotive force. It speaks of a people in chains, as it were; physically and mentally oppressed by despotic forces. Thus in the context of this book it is most apposite to use the term of animals, who (even with the authority of *Genesis*) exist with the tacit consent of human beings, and of those mainly Third World masses who make up the congregation for liberation theologians. There is also a case, albeit a less peremptory one, to include the claims of children (argued by Purdy and Harris) in terms of liberation since they are in the legal care of their parents. But the other groups, viz. women, blacks and gays, are different. Disgruntled they may be, and with justification, but they are all consenting adults with minds of their own, able to plan and advance their causes as citizens of, in general, civilized nations. For them the banner of 'liberation' is an exercise in rhetoric, the power of which is incendiarism enough to provide hot air for 'rights' as well. But these three latter groups are not in need of *genuine* liberation nor, I suggest, were two of them (women and gays, unlike blacks) *ever* in need of it. So Nussbaum's espousal of *rights* is, in a precise and limited sense, fair enough in the women's arena and that of gays: yet, even in those, 'liberation' has a public relations role to play.

Reminders of the turmoil of civil rights in the 1960s are timely for other persistent themes with fresh (well, not quite!) flags to wave; those of 'sexism', 'racism', 'homophobia' and 'speciesism' (there are others, like 'ageism', which await other books). Each of these concepts labels specific yet different areas of discrimination although, as the bulk of our book demonstrates, the arguments justifying the name-calling are remarkably similar. To refuse goods or services or otherwise annoy any being exclusively on the grounds of their being a woman, black, gay, a child, old, disabled, Catholic or an animal or brute, is invidious and might well incur legal sanction. Perhaps the most well-known paradigm is Peter Singer's *Animal Liberation*, which gave currency to the sin of 'speciesism', although the term itself had been coined by another liberationist, Richard Ryder. Singer quite explicitly (and shrewdly) published the book in 1975 in the spirit of the rights movement of the preceding decade from which it gained vicarious momentum and considerable success.

It is now time to share the stage with our contributors.

WOMEN: PROFESSORS JEAN HAMPTON AND ANTONY FLEW

Is it instructive that Jean Hampton's main essay is couched in terms of *feminism*, remembering Nussbaum's preference for 'women's rights'? That a man or woman has an interest in making jobs or educational opportunities, traditionally enjoyed by men, available to women, is surely not to qualify either of them as a feminist. For many, including my wife, the term is provoking. Antony Flew's barely suppressed irritation in his response suggests that he too takes this view. So what is feminism? Stressing that it comes in all shapes and sizes, Hampton settles upon a unifying feature (a negative one) which is 'the rejection of a normative thesis maintaining that women, by virtue of their nature, ought to be subordinated ... to men' (pp. 3–4). But is it not difficult to imagine any civilized person, for example, who reads academic books, genuinely *agreeing* with such a view? On Hampton's criteria J.S. Mill would be an arch-feminist but of a moderate, classically liberal type (much like our exemplars above with an interest in opportunities for women). Flew too would qualify; as he puts it in the opening of his response: 'We are all feminists now' (p. 25). This appears to include Hampton herself. In both essays she strives to be conciliatory. But she seems to overreach herself, with damage to her argument, in describing feminists in academia.

She writes, in her reply to Flew: 'Despite their many differences, all feminists working in the academy today reject the subordination of men' (p. 41). Perhaps it was a slip; such a rank generalization must be wrong. There are fanatics and bigots everywhere and to believe that feminist academics are an exempt species is at best wishful thinking. But there is a more serious difficulty with which Hampton's first essay opens, which creates an unnecessary opportunity for Flew to strike. The menu of specifically *feminist* theorizing, particularly in the natural sciences but also in practically every other arena of intellectual and artistic endeavour, is not so much optimistic as fatally confused. The claim is not on behalf of the achievements of brilliant women physicists, biologists, psychologists, artists and the rest. These are acknowledged and documented. The critiques at issue are motivated by *feminist* concerns. And if we ask what precisely these are, we find ourselves returning to the rejection of the 'subordination of men', which hardly clarifies the nature of the 'creative theorizing', whilst Flew has sport with the sublimities of 'Jewish physics' and 'feminist epistemology' (p. 38). Had Hampton limited her palette of feminist prowess to those art forms and political and ethical theories which might further the cause of women's rights and, as she puts it, 'commitment to the equal dignity of both men and women, in the face of a history that has tried to deny women that dignity' (p. 23), then her argument would be clearer but its content more properly modest. Consistency might also incline her to drop the charge that Flew is mistaking ghosts for New Wave feminists. First of all, Hampton allows that there are 'all sorts of feminists generating (sometimes opposing) theories in all sorts of areas' (p. 3). So who knows what lurks in the closet? Second, it might well be that other contributors to the volume produce some qualifiers. Laura Purdy, countering children's liberation, discusses the educational theories of two radical practitioners, Shulamith Firestone and Philippe Ariès, who would probably welcome the description.

A typical theme that will surface in most of the debates in the book questions the strategy, much favoured by reformers, of calling upon the machinery of state, for example by legislation or financial aid, to put right the perceived wrongs. (Hence frequent references to 'equal opportunities' and 'rights'.) *Berkman v. City of New York*, disagreed upon by Hampton and Flew, is a specific case in point. Relevant also are the feminist proposals for laws to outlaw pornography, on the grounds that it motivates the sexual abuse of women, and of course children. Hampton appears to take a courageous line in agreeing with Flew that the resultant restrictions of speech and liberty might rebound counterproductively upon women's progress. She urges liberal reformers 'to have faith in the power of their reform movements to change the structure of society . . . without the help of government' (p. 21). But her conviction wavers in the face of the feminist objections that 'the liberal state has helped to reinforce the "affirmative action" favouring men' (p. 22). It is this tension that she boldly attempts to resolve in her conclusion, 'The Liberation of Feminism'.

MICHAEL LEAHY

BLACKS: PROFESSORS BERNARD BOXILL
AND MICHAEL LEVIN

Boxill, a distinguished author in the field, is certainly not averse to talking of the need for black *liberation*. To hark back to our 'Preamble', the necessary element of radical oppression in this instance is that of pervasive racial discrimination, particularly in the USA. But Boxill, in his main essay, although stressing the need for all strata of black society to unify to counteract the threat, gives hardly any account as to how it is that discrimination is the cause of their lagging both economically and academically. Both Boxill and Levin agree that it is not a matter of poor education since this begs the questions 'of why blacks remain poorly educated' (i.e. through their school life and throughout the system from nursery to university). Levin argues that discrimination is an irrelevance in this context, and his contentious diagnosis is that 'blacks are less mentally able than whites, and [it is] possible in turn that a black deficit in ability is due to adventitious environmental factors, or genetic factors ... rather than obstacles imposed by whites' (p. 69). Levin argues for this in formidable detail but, particularly on the claims of IQ and genetic factors, his statistics require careful scrutiny. Boxill is not at all amused by this and his reply to Levin, quite at odds with 'Black Liberation – Yes!', is abrasive and contemptuous.

Boxill is in favour of the 'colour-blind society', a worthy and very liberal ideal, 'where a person's skin colour is no more noticed ... than his eye colour is' (p. 63). One might well believe that some feminists and gays would cling to similar ideals. A well-known serious objection to such a society (at which I will just hint) is that it would militate against fruitful diversity. Only madly vain people cherish the blue of their eyes, but to be Jewish, a woman, a New Englander, gay and (yes) black, is frequently a source of self-esteem. Valuing such contrasts is at variance with the colour-blind society, in which the loyalties which now give rise to black and white solidarity and the consequent racism of both, would have dissipated. That is the point of Boxill's proposal. But he immediately undermines it: 'Colour-blind policies that take no notice of racial difference ... would probably be ineffective because they are likely to leave inequalities ... that would make race seem significant' (p. 63), and he promptly returns to the need for 'affirmative action'. If the whole point of the colour-blind society is to submerge such differences then how is it that inequalities remain? Is it that they are irremediable after all?

250

In all of the areas of liberation under discussion in the book, where claims are made on behalf of (or by) allegedly disadvantaged groups, the crunch comes with the division of the spoils, be it jobs, cash or legal redress. But the criteria we apply will vary. Are we buying off, or being generous, or punishing (by giving nothing), or helping short-term or most likely, giving what is just or deserved? Much of the debate between Boxill and Levin involves the logic of these criteria. Boxill scorns the claim that affirmative action for blacks *by whites*, for example establishing the NAACP or enacting laws prohibiting discrimination, is generous, because it is their just deserts, whereas being generous implies doing *more* than justice demands. Fair point, but he then judges harshly: 'Since Levin thinks the white majority was generous . . . I can only conclude that he thinks that it would not be unjust to discriminate against blacks.' (This needs explanation. Levin thinks the whites are being generous beyond the calls of strict justice – the laws of the land – whereas Boxill, in like vein, is claiming that what blacks *deserve* transcends the same strict justice of law. But Boxill objects to many laws, understandably given his brief, that in his view discriminate against blacks – because they 'deserve' better.) However sympathetic to Boxill's argument one might be, it is difficult to deny that it is partisan and persuasive. In particular it trades upon the ambiguities in the concept of 'discrimination'. Many will claim, surely confusedly, that to execute a black, whatever their crime and circumstances, is discrimination. Levin would regard this, with justification, as woolly-minded liberalism.

Discrimination as a concept is, like murder, morally 'loaded' by definition. As murder means wrongful killing, so discrimination carries with it moral guilt. But such behaviour need not necessarily be *illegal*; for example discrimination in the UK against gays and some religious groups. So Levin could claim that it is *morally* wrong to discriminate against blacks, and, in addition, generous because it had legal standing (in that moral imperative and positive law each promote the other).

Nonetheless, the question of *what* is *deserved*, in this case moral status, legal status or both, remains open. Boxill plays fast and loose with similar concepts again on the next page in discussing job-hiring; and again is too quick to castigate Levin. Rationality is not a touchstone of moral rectitude. Some hirings and firings will be *wrong*, on grounds other than the rational (e.g. to get rid of a black) and be discriminatory – as some killings are murder; and others will be *right*, on grounds other than the rational, and *not* be discriminatory – as legal executions are not murder.

Boxill is equally tough, and far more justifiably, in dismissing Levin's qualifications as an expert witness in genetics; although I doubt that Levin would claim such expertise and would probably refer sceptics to his bibliography for authority. Furthermore, to conclude, Boxill is far too impulsive in dismissing correlations that 'do not establish causation'. The concept of causation is an informal one; it has no scientific standing. Research into such behaviour is assessed in terms of probabilities, which is another name for correlations (p. 104).

GAYS: PROFESSORS MARTHA NUSSBAUM AND ROGER SCRUTON

Both contributions are models of their kind, rich in style and original in content. Although gay liberation raises issues common to the other areas, it is also quite unique in certain fundamental respects which emerge from Nussbaum's lucid opening section in which she tackles the complex task of 'identifying the people'. Her interest is definitional: who is a gay? Are lesbians and bisexuals included? What need they get up to for qualification? Is sodomy necessary? Or is mere 'orientation' enough? And so on. These are more than just revelatory quibbles. As she makes clear, discrimination and jail sentences are at issue. (Given the well-publicized antics of some British members of parliament it is salutary to learn that the maximum penalty for consensual sodomy in Georgia is twenty years.) But the uniqueness of the issue takes another form. Women, blacks, dogs and chickens, and children are, in general, easily identifiable as such. But *anyone* might be homosexual, or a fellow-traveller, and escape recognition unless (as Nussbaum points out in her reply to Scruton) one knows the telltale signs and gestures. Rarely is one confronted by a Wildean lookalike with green carnation; and even then mistakes are possible. This anonymity is a two-edged sword. For sympathizers, like Nussbaum, who paints a lurid picture of rampant policemen and gangs of 'gay-bashers' roaming the campus and shopping mall, it is a welcome protection of their privacy (and all the better for that – particularly if Comstock's statistics are correctly glossed). But for the sceptic, like Scruton perhaps, and many other 'straight' fathers, worried at the prospect of a malign influence (as they see it) enveloping their children through ever more hysterically 'liberal' influences, the menace is exacerbated simply because the enemy is at best hypothetical and otherwise invisible.

Both writers squabble over the other's reading of J.S. Mill. Rightly so! His and Jeremy Bentham's influences are rarely absent from books such as this one. Nussbaum, in her reply, mentions Mill's *The Subjection of Women* with only time to throw an obscure brickbat at Scruton as she passes on. But she has not only this (splendid if over-long) text in mind, but also *On Liberty*, in objecting to Scruton's criticism of Mill as 'hasty and unfair'. Again, she has no time to elaborate; but it might well be his description of Mill's famous *harm principle* as 'a hostage to fortune', implying that it is damagingly equivocal. To parody Mill: he argues that adults may do as they please without censure as long as their behaviour brings no harm upon others. Commentators have chattered ever since over Mill's alleged failure precisely to define 'harm'. I think he saw the futility of this and would adapt Nussbaum's description of Mill's 'pleasure' to argue that he has 'a rich conception of qualitative distinctions' of *harm* as well (p. 126).

Scruton would probably agree at least with the spirit of this but Nussbaum, wanting something more specific, would wish to wait and see. Her argument seems to be a copy of our parody of Mill but with no lack of certainty over the presence or absence of harm – backed up by her roll-calls of statistics and legal judgments. Talking of sodomy she is adamant: 'adult consensual activity does no harm' (p. 97); and equally so where she should qualify: 'Even in the sensitive area of education, there is no evidence to show that the presence of gay and lesbian teachers harms children and adolescents' (p. 98). Nussbaum fails to justify this, yet hers is the burden of proof since it can be assumed that teachers will do what they are trained to do, even unintentionally, which is to influence those in their care. This is in line with her view of the UK Local Government Act (the so-called 'Clause 28') of 1986, which bans the promotion of homosexuality in schools, which she argues is 'morally repugnant' (p. 99). Mill would be more cautious, allowing as he does that such goings-on might set bad examples to young people which constitute a harm. Furthermore, he allows that where a law is not in breach, it is properly available for society to express its repugnance as it thinks fit. Of course, Nussbaum can reply through her ally, Judge Posner, that such laws (where they do exist, for example banning sodomy in several US states like Georgia) or informal antipathy 'express an irrational fear and loathing of a group that has been subjected to discrimination' (p. 97).

To reply to this we must turn to Scruton's serious and imaginative response to Nussbaum. Sex is not to be modelled on a form of personal sensation-seeking and subsequent gratification. It can only be understood in the cultural and legal contexts of the traditional family unit within which most of us were born, brought up and will die. This dramatically shapes our identity, our inmost fears and aspirations. To meddle with it on a serious scale is both personally disruptive and might spell trouble for others. Scruton would reply to Posner, I think, that a distaste for, say, proselytizing (or just practising) homosexuals is *not* irrational. Against an omnipresent background of AIDS, drugs, discrimination and above all, in certain cases, the possible eventual breakdown of the family, it is an arena to avoid. Upon those who disagree with us and insist that such fears *must* be irrational, even morally repugnant, we should turn our backs.

CHILDREN: PROFESSORS JOHN HARRIS AND LAURA PURDY

The liberation movements on behalf of women, blacks and gays are taken with deadly seriousness. The first two have long histories of struggle and sacrifice which add to their distinction. When it is a question of the inevitable priorities, certain subgroups will be targeted, notably the jobless and, with educational needs in mind, children. But the idea of a liberation movement specifically for children, apart from Plato's *Republic*, Rousseau's *Emile* and scattered remarks by Mill and other Victorians, dates back little further than the early 1970s. A tidy literature has developed since then (Harris' 'avalanche of interest' is perhaps optimistic) but it is difficult to take it very seriously or imagine its challenging the supremacy of the leaders for many decades. Where it has been genuinely fertile is not so much in grabbing a vast portfolio of rights for the oppressed child, but, as we shall see, its influence for good in sociological and psychological research into topics such as child abuse, innovative infant upbringing and experimental education.

Harris provides the bare bones of the argument in favour, which fits together well but carries little flesh to chew on by way of examples. Purdy remedies this illuminatingly, to which we shall return. Harris begins dangerously: 'Children's rights can only be coherently defended as a dimension of human rights' (p. 136). Scruton, it will be recalled, makes the same point about Nussbaum's claims but, given the American context, it is a question of *constitutional* rights, having the same peremptory status as human rights, natural rights, Paine's 'Rights of Man'. But Harris' claim is less fruitful if one is trawling for specific rights to remedy ills. Unlike the USA, which has a Supreme Court which makes precise judgments upon the Constitution, the UK can only appeal to the International Court at the Hague which has no sanctions and only issues judgments after lifetimes of bureaucratic delay. Perhaps this is not surprising if, as Harris continues, no one knows where such rights come from. It would surely have been more helpful to agitate for *legal* rights, the ones with teeth and of which we know the source (see Nussbaum for examples). The provenance of *human* rights is not, as Harris surely knows, that mysterious. God and the UN Declaration of 1948 are frequently cited as sources, but the most sensible suggestion is Bentham's in his *Anarchical Fallacies* of 1795 in which they are depicted as emerging from wishful thinking awaiting legal status.

Harris models the children's case upon that of women (as Peter Singer with that of animals):

> Both imply that children have in most cases the same moral and political status as most adults. . . . They are entitled not only to the same concern, respect and protection as is accorded to any other member of the community, no more and no less, but also are entitled to the same freedoms and self-determination.
>
> (p. 137)

Everything pro and con is encapsulated here. Would feminists acknowledge the close analogy? They might well focus on the equivocal nature of 'protection', which was used historically, even by Mill, to patronize women as chattels and thus restrict their rights. (See Hampton on Aristotle's view of women as 'permanent children'.) Modern feminists would rightly reject this contemptuously. They would now claim only the protections of any other group of *adults*. Most women would accept the traditional view that children, depending upon their age and competence, require special care and discipline. Of course, some radical feminists (would Flew call them 'New Wave'?), such as Firestone and Ariès with strong views on education, would deny the reservations, and grant children the autonomy and self-determination of adults which Harris claims (see Purdy, p. 156ff).

Harris rejects the widely-held view that children (he never distinguishes a 5- from a 15-year-old) lack full autonomy and, for their own good, are subject to various forms of benevolent 'protective custody'. His argument is that many *adults* (the feckless, addicted, ill-educated, one assumes) also lack mature competence to make choices; thus, 'if we really care about protecting the incompetent we would have to take many adults into protective custody' (p. 139). One cannot help smiling at this. Of *course* there are adults who are unable to control their lives. Society has niches for them; the criminal in jail, others in menial jobs, the unemployed and so on. But the various age barriers that children cross into adulthood (to drink, have sexual relations, to drive, to vote) are not a lottery. They have a history of regular debate in which experts, the general public, the media and finally the politicians have their say. Purdy's counterexamples to the view that children are capable of full autonomy and self-determination are clear and compelling. Children's liberation is a blueprint for disaster. A nation that was misguided enough to put it into practice would, in a generation or so, be inhabited by morons. Harris is very cursory about Purdy's case-studies in his reply.

ANIMALS: PROFESSOR ANDREW LINZEY AND DR MICHAEL LEAHY

The first paragraph of Linzey's reply is par for the course. It is normal in academic wrangling, particularly when the stakes are high (as they are for all of our contributors), to claim that one has been totally misrepresented. Hampton, Boxill and Cohn-Sherbok complain similarly. In contesting Linzey's case, I (Leahy) have discussed Peter Singer's views of sentience theory. Tom Regan's are probably a better example, which are more convincingly elaborated than in Linzey's account. I acknowledge this in my reply and emphasize Singer's rather crude utilitarianism, for example on using human imbeciles for research purposes, of which Linzey (with his talk of 'innocents') would obviously disapprove.

The proposed eirenicon, a conciliatory gesture, is generous but Linzey self-destructs by falling into the Cartesian trap himself. The third paragraph of his reply is a dramatic demonstration of the weakness of his case – and, indeed, that of Singer's and Regan's as well: 'It remains philosophically possible to argue that mammals don't feel pain: indeed, philosophically, as Leahy will know, it is impossible in strict terms to *prove* the existence of pain outside of one's own experience of it' (p. 205). Leahy, alas, does *not* know this, nor do

Ryle, Davidson, even Marx, Heidegger, Althusser and, in particular, Wittgenstein and his followers, together with most of the remaining twentieth-century pantheon. Readers should dwell upon Linzey's almost maniacal comment about the incinerating astronauts. If Cartesian scepticism allows *seriously* that the poor devils might be 'laughing' and enjoying themselves, then so much the worse for philosophy. But it is a strictly minority philosophy. This corrosive scepticism is, as Linzey cheerfully allows, fatal to his own protective impulses towards animals. There is a sizable minority of insensitive butchers in research laboratories the world over who use such arguments with effect against their critics.

We now move to Linzey's charge of *a priorism*: that Leahy knows this, that and the other, without *observing* it. Of course, as he points out, there is a mountain of empirical evidence, but, it is what it (or its lack) *establishes* that is at issue. One does not need to examine the (lack of) responses of, for example, a stone, or even to break it in pieces, to be *certain* that it cannot use language, nor has awareness of any sort. The higher animals provide more complex evidence that they can move, sustain themselves, have sensuous awareness, but, lacking any similarity to human speech, do *not* provide necessary conditions of *self*-consciousness. Yet ethologists and veterinarians quite properly refer to 'mental stress' in animals (which even *a priori* philosophers can observe and note) when abnormal behaviour patterns obtrude. Linzey taunts me with the unspecified researches of a few minor scientific figures gambling upon my being unaware of what they have to 'prove' (Linzey's term). I am, unfortunately, well aware of the work of Gallup and Griffin, and what they have to prove is *nothing* – beyond merely the behavioural data they adduce. Had Linzey merely glanced at my book, *Against Liberation* (pp. 145–6 on Gallup, and 35–6, 60, 140–2, 145–7, and 159–61 on Griffin) he might have cause to regret his bluff. The limitations upon the lengths of the essays precluded my entangling the reader in such esoteric detail. But it is on record. (See pp. 195–6, above.)

Linzey then moves to the claim that the propensity of animals to feel pain, with which I and any sensible person must agree, is 'itself enough to advance a massive liberationist agenda' to eliminate all instances of alleged animal exploitation, for example hunting, farming and experimentation. But Linzey's abolitionist ardour, akin to that of Regan, trades upon the knee-jerk reaction by which the average person identifies the pain and suffering of animals with that of human beings. This is the fallacy of anthropomorphism, which figures prominently in my response and upon which I shall dwell only a little further. Humans, unlike animals, are apt to dwell upon past pain and view a prognosis with horror. Brutes lack this cognitive awareness and, as any competent vet will confirm, the behavioural evidence (screeching, writhing and so on) shows that their pain dissipates quickly and usually without stress. Thus it is routine to see badly mutilated cattle or fighting dogs frisking around as if nothing were wrong. These conclusions can provide a justification for equestrian sports and even fox hunting and, without doubt, for laboratory experiments in worthy human causes. (I take Linzey's parenthetical criticism about anaesthetics but it looks like a *non sequitur*. It is a legal requirement in the UK under the Animals (Scientific Procedures) Act of 1986 that subjects must be made comatose when *necessary*, but the majority of regulated procedures are largely observational in character and quite *un*necessary. This hardly deserves Linzey's charge of disingenuousness.)

THEOLOGIANS: RABBI DAN COHN-SHERBOK AND DR JOHN WILSON

What is liberation theology? And why does it figure in the book? The latter question will be more pertinent for the typical reader. Liberation theology *is* relevant. Stripped of its theological trappings it is an amalgam of allegedly revolutionary concern for the suffering of blacks not only since the American Civil War (for whom, one assumes, little can be assuaged in retrospect), but also for their present indignities in the urban slums. There is much talk also of women's rights 'to reproduction, self-protection, birth control and abortion as well as protection against sexual harassment, wife-beating, rape and pornography' (p. 223). Cohn-Sherbok, on behalf of liberation theology, allies himself with Linzey, a fellow cleric, insisting that 'human beings must take steps to preserve endangered species and avoid inflicting cruelty on wild and domestic animals' (p. 224). Liberation theology goes even further in advocating *ecological* liberation: 'We need to remake the earth in a way that converts our minds to nature's logic of ecological harmony' (p. 224). How does one set about 'liberating' a tree or the ozone layer? (No matter! We know what's meant.) Indeed, Wilson (p. 227), taking a leaf out of Flew's espousal of classical feminism, is incredulous that anyone would refuse to applaud such worthy ideals: 'Is anyone *against* "the building of a just society"? . . . None of this, I hope, is in dispute.'

Readers will surely agree (or will they?). Non-theologians, however, will need to be patient in demythologizing much of Cohn-Sherbok's heady terminology, particularly that of his citations from the Third World, despite their arcane elegance. It should remind us that liberation theology is, above all, motivated by religious commitment; a progressive breakaway frowned upon by many traditionalists. *God* plays a role, not just conceptually, but as a star. This is both a strength, as religious sentiment can be a power for good, but also a potentially fatal drawback. One may bustle about convinced that 'Christ is incarnate in the inner city' but to spread the good news will hardly have the black and hispanic youngsters, gripped with AIDS or heroin addiction, jumping for joy in the streets of Buffalo or Detroit. This, I take it, the hopelessness of seeming to marry the demands of a dynamic world, requiring action and expertise, to an ineffable one, is the thrust of Wilson's brilliantly lucid reply. Cohn-Sherbok's 'New Agenda for Society' (in all fairness it is by no means his alone) would make the 'colour-blind society' a mere matter of boiling an egg by comparison; yet Boxill and activists sympathetic to the notion worldwide haven't the faintest idea what the colour-blind society entails nor what might bring it about. The litany of rights involving blacks, women, animals and ecology, listed above, is more than enough to begin with. Two centuries of feverish activity, as several have argued in this book, may have dented many of the abuses but certainly not cracked them. But liberation theology seems to be impatient for all this and lots more: 'The overthrow of established powers' on a global scale involving 'the necessity of violent revolution as a means of altering the economic structures of society' (p. 215). It is when sabre-rattling of this sort emerges (as reminders for example of the explosive tactics of the Animal Liberation Front in the UK) that some might well waver in their previously blanket approval of liberation theology's ideals because it confirms what we all know, but often find it convenient to forget, that the most impeccable intentions can have a seedy side. Does Cohn-Sherbok, rabbi and decent fellow that he is, *approve* of violent revolution on a global scale? It seems so. He doesn't condemn it. Nor does he give any practical comfort to those believers in liberation theology keen to further its cause and certainly not to a pagan public waiting to be convinced. In the absence of all this one might be tempted to accuse him and his fellow-travellers of wishful thinking.

Wilson would probably agree with this criticism but his overall response is more subtle and genuinely philosophical. He is concerned with the role of theologians *as such*, their encouraging congregations of ignorant and needy masses to believe that a millenium of milk and honey awaits them around the corner. This might be practical if optimistic for affluent international aid agencies, with planeloads of VSOs, linguists, social workers and similar professionals in tow, but in the absence of these what can a relatively few clerics, lacking any relevant expertise, actually *do*? Should they *pray* for the New Agenda? Yet prayers are notoriously not answered. As Cohn-Sherbok asks in his reply, 'Where was God when six million died?' So what should the clerics do *now*? Cohn-Sherbok takes refuge in being able to read Aramaic and debate Jewish history. But, seriously, that is of no avail given the proposed agenda, and he knows it. Wilson is challenging theology to redefine its very nature in a highly original way. It will be for the worse if its adherents take no notice.

INDEX

261